Spiritual Journey of
A Third-Worlder

Spiritual Journey of A Third-Worlder

A Story of Self-Determination - Endurance - Extravagant Love And The Power of Prayer

Stephen N Rosemond

Copyright © 2024 by Stephen N Rosemond

All rights reserved. No part of this book may be reproduced or used in any manner without written permission of the copyright owner except for the use of quotations in a book review.

For more information, contact:
snrosemond@sluauthor.com

First paperback edition 2024

978-1-80541-441-4 (paperback)
978-1-80541-442-1 (ebook)

Contents

ACKNOWLEDGEMENT 1

A NOTE TO READERS 3

FOREWORD 5

PREFACE 7

CHAPTER ONE 13
    My Animated Birthplace 13
    A Welcome Change 17
    My Position Served Me Well 22
    Mama and The Saints 23
    Why I Broke with Traditional Courtesy 26
    Silvie Got the Beating 28
    Our Daily Chores 30
    Punctured Hearts 34
    Breadfruit—Always on The Menu 38
    The Far-kar-we Tribe 42
    We Sold Racoona and More 45
    My Bosom Friend 51
    My Stimulating Psalm 52

CHAPTER TWO 55
    A Legitimate Candidate 55
    Too Young, Then Too Old 57
    Doom and Gloom 59
    Stench of Evil 62
    More Stumbling Blocks 67

CHAPTER THREE 69
- Sons of Our Father 69
- A Harsh Reality 72
- My Seven Elements of Prayers 73
- The Chance to Prove Myself 75
- How I Kept Hitting My Targets 77
- Charlo, a true Mentor 80

CHAPTER FOUR 83
- Blessings and Rewards 83
- Popo's Policy 85
- My Baby Had No Nose 90
- Jealousy Breeds Obeah 93
- Mama's First Plane Ride 96
- Maam's Crab and Callaloo 98
- Where Was Mama 101
- Breaking with Tradition 105
- A Quickie Marriage in the Making 107

CHAPTER FIVE 111
- Responsibilities, Expectations, and Adversity ... 111
- Kindness or Foolishness 113
- Stout and Ganja – A Lethal Combination 115
- The World of Obeah? 118
- God Always Prevails 122
- Our Shocking Discovery 123
- Down but Standing 129
- My Half Loaf 133
- Quitting Was Not Easy 134
- An Optimist, a Realist 136
- Pig Farming? Not for Me 138
- Test of Endurance 141
- The Power of Evil 142

    My Leap of Faith 147
CHAPTER SIX 151
    Welcome to the First World 151
    Meeting the Family... 152
    Regena Popped the Question 155
    No Time to Ponder.. 157
    Time Would be My Saviour 159
    I Quit 160
    My Quickest Pay Rise Ever 162
    Breaking out of the Bubble of Insecurity 165
CHAPTER SEVEN 169
    Leave it to God! 169
    Trust No One 171
    I Needed No Sympathy 174
    My Commanding Tone in Prayer...................... 175
    My Lucky Dip... 179
    My Indispensable Lesson................................. 180
    Caught in the Act... 182
    My Blessing In Disguise 185
CHAPTER EIGHT... 187
    Family Start-up.. 187
    An Obsolete Tradition 189
    It was Evolution 191
    Joe's Frenzy and Profanity 192
    The Business of Putting Together 197
    My Role Was Big Brother's Spotlight.................200
    A Hard-up Family 202
    Mutton Dressed as Beef Steak..........................204
CHAPTER NINE 209
    Climbing the Ladder...209

Strength, Courage and Cash 210
I'd be Damned Not to Know 212
My Dying Lawyer 215
My Desperate Moment 216
Hilbert's Callous Remarks 218
Papa's Welcome Respite 220
The Manifestation of My Father's Blessing 222
Floop 224
Echoes of Mr Isaac 226
Fire Hazard in the Neighbourhood 230
Killing Myself to Develop New Skills 231
A No-cooking Day 233
The Flintstones' Turkey and the Caterpillar 234

CHAPTER TEN 239

Does Success Breed Jealousy? 239
No Goodwill for Family 242
My Guiding Principles 244
Nothing Short of Betrayal 246
Our Five Gallon Bucket 250
Mama's Desperate Moment 253

CHAPTER ELEVEN 257

Mama's Testing Times 257
Time to Say Goodbye 261
How to Accomplish My Goal 264
IBM – That's all I knew 266
This Man is Never Free 269
The Caribbean Man's Major Pitfalls 272
My 20P Win Yankee 276
The Joke We Could Not Share 278
Vodka and Vodkanese 281
Safeguarding Myself 282

CHAPTER TWELVE 283

- Reaching My Ultimate Goal 283
- A Promising Future 285
- Hunger for Knowledge 286
- A Win-Win Proposal 288
- Building Our Capital 290
- Beelzebub Proved Me Right 291
- The Brother Who Shared My Goal 293
- Building the Pillar Upon My Corner Stone 297
- Yes Means No 299
- Phil's Acidic Pill 302
- The Intelligence Deficiency Syndrome 304

CHAPTER THIRTEEN 307

- His Statement Was No Bluster 307
- The Power to Make Things Happen 312
- The Need for Reflection 313
- My Reunion With Jenny 314
- One Five-letter Word on My Mind 316
- An Absurd Policy 317
- Rejecting the Picket Line 318
- Blatant Injustice 321
- Testing My Capacity 325
- Challenges and Opportunities 326
- My Sigh of Relief 328
- Judgement Day 330
- Insubordination 333
- I Turned the Tables 336
- Contempt for Colour 339
- How Could I Disagree? 345
- Symptoms of Matrimonial Exhaustion 349
- Uncomfortable Listening 352
- Rose's Declaration 354

CHAPTER FOURTEEN 357
    Corridor of Insanity 357
    Safeguarding Our Bond 359
    The Passing of George 360
    It became a Reality 362
    Our First Bumper Christmas 370
    A Test of Fortitude 372
    Rose's Memorabilia 373
    All in the Name of Love 376
    An Invalid Claim 379
    My Total Anguish 382
    The Good Bastard 384
    God is Good 386
MY SPECIAL PRAYER 389

ACKNOWLEDGEMENT

My gratitude goes out to my few enduring friends and family in my circle who inspired me with their request to tell my story. To those who supported me in compiling the record of my existence thus far, I thank you. I have used pseudonyms for certain people mentioned in my writing to protect their identity and privacy.

Reminiscing with the remaining neighbours from the older generation was hilarious: Miss Babes, Say-say, Mariella, T-marwe, Hugh, Hozney, Alfred, Earnest and more. Thank you all for your contributions. I remain grateful to those who have placed their trust and confidence in me since my journey began. To my teachers: Lauren, Greg, James, and Daniel; Parish Priests, Father Bertrand and Father Parker; and my mentors, Chalmer, Clint, and Hunter, your influence in my life stood me in good stead; I am forever thankful.

I pay tribute to my parents, Mama and Papa Ray, for your unrelenting love and support until the end; I thank you in prayer for all your blessings that contributed to defining my life. May your spirits live on.

A NOTE TO READERS

A hilltop view of a neighbouring village

Masked by its natural physical beauty were the tentacles of malignancy in the soul of the Eastern Caribbean Island that, from the colonial days, became known as the Helen of the West Indies—this was where my journey began.

At noon one Sunday in September of 1956, I became a new member of the east coastal farming community in Micoud village, one of ten districts of the picturesque 238-square-mile island of Saint Lucia. My parents were small-scale farmers. However, my dad's primary occupation was tailoring. My best description of my father would be that he was calm, soft-spoken, and never failed to provide for his family. My mum was a seamstress by profession; she stood more like the head of the household. Etiquette at home was in abundance, but finance was scant.

I started my schooling in 1960 and completed it in 1974. We were a devout Catholic family, and nothing would keep us from attending Sunday Mass. Though my circumstances were testing, it was from such challenges that many of my blessings derived. During my journey, I recognised the need to develop traits critical to producing positive outcomes.

There were instances when my curiosity drove me to make some courageous choices. In 1979, my decision to liberate myself from my perceived sanctuary of third-world conditions forever changed my perspective. I knew the journey ahead would not be plain sailing, but I remained steadfast. My permanent return to Saint Lucia in 2002, far sooner than I had anticipated, was precipitated by moments of utter despair. This situation would have given rise to an unrecoverable slump, yet by the power of the Almighty God through prayer, I stumbled but kept my footing.

FOREWORD

In the captivating journey that unfolds within these pages, we are invited to witness the indomitable spirit of Stephen, a man whose life has been a tapestry woven with threads of faith, resilience, and an unwavering belief in the divine. Born on the enchanting Caribbean Island of St Lucia, Stephen's early years were marked by a collision of the sacred and the profane—a struggle that would define his existence.

From the very foundations of his faith, Stephen found solace in prayer, an anchor that steadied him amidst the tumultuous waves of life. His departure for England in 1979, seemingly an escape from the supernatural shadows cast over his homeland, unfolded a new chapter laden with challenges, the most formidable being the spectre of racism. Undeterred, Stephen's commitment to his convictions and the recitation of sacred psalms became his armour, allowing him to surmount the obstacles that threatened to engulf his aspirations.

A hierarchical legacy, handed down through generations, guided Stephen as he navigated the intricate web of familial expectations and societal dynamics. In a dance with progress and tradition, he stood at the intersection, a testament to the evolving spirit within.

The pivotal moment of Stephen's life arrived with his union with Rose, a union that not only altered the trajectory of his personal narrative but also demanded an adaptation to an unfamiliar cultural landscape. The challenges he faced were not only external but internal, shaping a man who sought to harmonise the contrasts of his identity.

A poignant return to St Lucia in 2002 marked a juncture of introspection, where moments of despair spurred Stephen to draw upon the deepest wells of his faith and unyielding determination. In the face of seemingly insurmountable obstacles, he found the strength to conquer, echoing the resounding theme that threads through the fabric of his life—the power of the Creator and an unwavering resolve to triumph.

As we embark on this odyssey through the pages of Stephen's life, we are reminded that within the crucible of adversity, the human spirit has the capacity to transcend, evolve, and emerge victorious. This is a story that resonates with the universal themes of struggle, triumph, and the enduring power of faith—a narrative that invites reflection, empathy, and a celebration of the human spirit's capacity to soar against all odds.

Publishing Push - January 2024

PREFACE

To folks who doubt the existence of sorcery, I say to you, spare a moment—the encounter is terrifying; it is bewildering. I have heard those who say, "I know that voodoo exists, but I don't believe in it." Yes, I respect your opinion. You do not need to accept it, but if you know it exists, I suggest you consider protecting yourself against dark forces. You begin by building and maintaining total devotion to the power of your creator.

There were benefits to growing up on the tiny Eastern Caribbean Island of Saint Lucia, with a population of no more than one hundred and eighty thousand. There was a degree of trust and mutual respect. Raising children back then was a community task. However, those days were far from perfect. The travesty was glaring. Nepotism was the order of the day to counter hardship. The practice of voodoo was prevalent. These were the extremities of the malice in the island's soul where I started my journey.

From the age of nine, I would wake up on mornings, sporadically, with deep scratches over my body. Mama would apply a home remedy to soothe the burning sensations from my inflicted wounds. The straight, needle-like cuts to my skin were always parallel and varied in length, between two and four inches. Even though Mama seemed to suggest I caused the marks while I slept when she asked: "What have you done to yourself?" I was sure Mama knew this was associated with black magic but did not share her thoughts for fear of causing panic among my siblings. While maintaining total confidence in the power of God through prayer, it never escaped my mind that Satan remains a powerful force in our midst. Mama's chosen weapon to ward off adversity was the Holy Bible, from which we solicited God's guidance and protection when the family gathered nightly for prayers.

As professional clothing makers, my parents struggled to support the family. They also cultivated various crops for our upkeep in their one-acre vegetable garden deep in the forest, approximately five miles from the village.

The coveted Windrush movement gave us a way out of poverty, and in 1960, our eldest sister, Mary-Anne, journeyed to England. Between 1961 and 67, our eldest brother Hilbert, followed by Papa Ray and older brothers Joe and John, made the journey to the UK. Silvie our youngest sister, I, and our last-born brother, Phil, were left in Saint Lucia in the sole care of tenacious Mama Ray. At that point, I became Mama's eleven-year-old salesperson, selling her homemade confectionery product on a tray throughout the village.

From childhood, I understood the difference between people born with a silver spoon in their mouths and those who used their bare fingers to scrape the crumbs out of bowls made from the dried-out shell of a calabash. Dare I say I was fortunate to have identified with the latter. The fundamental lessons I gained from my family struggles were the guiding principles that shaped my life. Through my humble upbringing and petitions to the Almighty using the proper psalms, The Lord bestowed on me the understanding, appreciation, and ability to safeguard the essential qualities I needed to detach myself from the *calabash class*. Though my circumstances were testing, I welcomed this grounding as a leading source of inspiration. The threatening third-world environment compelled me to navigate beyond the shores of Saint Lucia in search of a more meaningful life.

My eventual voyage to England in 1979 enabled me to recognise the need to develop traits critical to producing positive outcomes, triggering a shift in my attitude. This change necessitated adapting to my unfamiliar environment as the way forward. My marriage to a former schoolmate, Rose, was a turning point within months of my arrival in the UK. Life in England was anything but easy. My wife and I needed to make hard sacrifices to achieve our goals; however the births of our two children were precious gifts which gave us hope.

I viewed every obstacle I encountered as an opportunity, a circumstance that would, in one way or another, help decide my fate. Still, enduring egregious racism in my profession was harrowing. Yet, my abiding faith in the divine power ensured my overcoming every hurdle.

My repatriation to Saint Lucia in 2002 to join my wife, who had returned to the island permanently two years earlier, came abruptly and was all in the name of saving love.

The quote, "Turn the other cheek", referenced in the King James Version Bible, Matthew 5:39, was pertinent; I lived it. My experience of staring through the corridor of insanity was punishing. It was humbling too. The Supreme Being granted my appeal for intervention while I maintained my willpower to preserve my stability.

Indeed, with such firmness of purpose, I was further able to assess my ability by assembling the content of this work. Time was never on my side throughout my writing process, and the discipline needed to achieve this milestone needed to be steadfast. I chose to present my life experiences with extreme care and accuracy in this format, as I believe the book will inspire the readers. I feel confident that the material will motivate those concerned about life's uninterrupted adversities. I have revealed the events in my writing as a third-world citizen with utmost humility; thus, I have not attempted to dramatize any of the information included. Endurance, resilience, perseverance, ambition, self-motivation and resoluteness are other attributes I developed throughout my life experiences. These are the qualities that empowered me to produce this book.

CHAPTER ONE

My Animated Birthplace

Among the nine of my parents' offspring, the first and third died in infancy; I was the only other who narrowly escaped the same fate. As a fragile infant, I was often ill, to the extent of requiring several admissions to the hospital. Based on Mama Ray's account, my chances of survival during my last hospitalisation had diminished gravely. Thankfully, by the power of the Almighty God, I would survive.

For me, growing up was too slow a process. I was the six-year-old *little man* who always brought cheer and laughter to the people around me; I was the family comedian. Shaking and boogieing to the slightest sound, even if it came from the banging noise of an old tin bucket, was what I enjoyed most. I entertained the adults when I joined other kids and danced to the sound of Cock-Shat's music. Cock-Shat, his Creole nickname, was the special village drummer who never parted with his 3ft high Tumba drum, which he carried on his back. The base of the oversized drum hung only a couple of inches from the ground, and the top rested on his neck as he walked in a motion that pointed to the varied lengths of his legs. Every weekend, he played at Back Street. Spectators throughout the village came to view Cock-Shat's theatre of drum beating, where the kids' dancing competition took place. Often, the spectators voted me the winner.

Back Street, in the village of Micoud, was my animated birthplace. It was *the* place to be. It was where after school, kids in the community gathered to pitch marbles, spin their homemade wooden tops, and push their homemade carboway (carts), all in the spirit of competition. We played until sunset. Also, many strangers who moved to Micoud would end up renting a spare room. It was a popular location for *Jn-Vee-nee* (Newcomers). It was the place where Mr King's cinema, the only one in the district, was located. There were shows no less than twice weekly, drawing large crowds from nearby communities.

Down Back Street, neighbours would hear the penetrating sound of players slamming dominoes on tables. With each slam of a domino came a loud, emphatic shout of triumph, defeat or humour, all laced with expletives. The afternoon gambling sessions would often continue until nightfall. Gambling didn't only pertain to domino games though. There was also cockfighting on Sundays, and this drew even larger crowds.

Present day Back Street

One of our strangest neighbours, Mr Isaac, lived here, too. He was a guy we all thought was hiding a 30-litre oak beer barrel under his shirt, so large was his belly. Without fail, the guy sat in the same position on his front doorstep every God-given day from about 2 p.m. until nightfall. He often fell asleep on the stairs. His wife, Ma Isaac, sold vegetables at her front door. Mr Isaac's posture gave the impression that he was cemented to the concrete steps; he never attempted to chase away the goats that roamed the neighbourhood and ate his wife's vegetables.

"Isaac!" Ma Isaac would shout, "You mean to tell me you're sitting there. You did nothing to stop the goats from eating my food!"

Mr Isaac would give the strangest response, "I did not tell the goats to eat your food."

Who would have expected him to instruct the goats, I wondered.

While playing football on the street, our ball would often accidentally hit Mr Isaac's head. "Oops! Sorry, Mr Isaac." But why did I bother apologising? Well, I had to; it was the right thing to do. The man never budged, blinked, complained or acknowledged. I assumed he had no sensation in his head either, because he never reacted.

Our next-door neighbours, Miss Babes Shoshon and Soonoot, were the co-stars of the main event, *roe-roe* (spectacle). They craved to find something to squabble over, often turning trivial issues into X-rated roe-roe. Neither of them conceded unless someone called their attention to some other matter. The most amusing thing was that Miss Babes would routinely begin the show after setting up her dinner, a large black pot of breadfruit on firewood. Occasionally she would be so engrossed in the squabble that she forgot her cooking until someone would shout: "Babes, pan manjayou car bwelay!" (Babes, your pot of food is burning!) The heavy smell of cacklen (burned food that sticks to the bottom of the dried-up pot) from her pot of breadfruit permeated the neighbourhood. Miss Babes would run to her house, shouting: "Oh shate! Shordier bwapen moi car bwelay!" (My pot of breadfruit is burning!). The show would stop, allowing Soonoot and onlookers to ridicule her. Television was unheard of in our community during the sixties and early seventies, so this late afternoon show spiced up the entertainment for me and the other children in the neighbourhood.

Mama never disguised her annoyance whenever the roe-roe started. She occasionally sought to intervene and shouted: "Why don't you two women show some respect? So many children are on the road, and you keep using this foul language. Why do you have to be cursing like this?" Both ladies would ignore Mama, who would call me out with an irritating tone if I was among the playing kids: "Stephen! Come inside. Go to your books." Mama set up a challenge for herself when she tried to shield me from the obscenities. Even if I could object to Mama's challenge, I did not have to. Every word uttered echoed through our wooden house.

A Welcome Change

I remember when, in 1960, my eldest sister, Mary-Anne, travelled to England. I was about three, moving on to four years old. Sitting with the family in a sombre mood, with an air of silence indistinguishable from the passing of a loved one, I made my feelings known. "Mary-Anne make me sorry so much my belly hurt me." These were the words I murmured as a toddler. My parents and older siblings recognised my deep sense of reason and understanding. I had developed a special bond with my sister, whom I looked to as a second mum. It was clear in my mind that my eldest sister, who carried me wherever she went and to whom I was much attached, would be away for a long time; I would miss her dearly.

Mary-Anne was the first in our household to travel abroad, a journey that became possible during the sought-after Windrush initiative of the late 1940s to the early 70s. Furthermore, the trip would not be possible without my parents' appeal for financial support from good family friends who had already made the voyage and with whom Mary-Anne would reside in England. Although this post-war British Nationality Act presented potential benefits for my family, it was bittersweet. It was bitter because Mary-Anne left home at the tender age of sixteen to travel this long distance to a country only known to us as the home of our colonial masters. In addition, the sea voyage from Saint Lucia to the UK took at least fifteen days, and for my parents, it was an agonising wait to find out if our loved one had safely arrived at her destination. It was sweet because we accepted this opportunity as a blessing—an escape route to ease the family's financial struggle, the hope of one step towards a better life.

My family intended to follow the survival strategy of most immigrants from the Caribbean Islands who travelled to the UK during that period. The plan's basis was the first family member bravely emigrating to the UK, borrowing money from associates and relatives who had made the journey and settling in England. In other instances, they would obtain the fares from people of influence: businesses, lawyers, and government officials. It was common for those who borrowed from influential people to use their immovable property as bonds. Once the first borrower repaid the cash, it would be loaned again to repeat the process for the second, third, or however many would be willing to make that journey. This method would sometimes continue until the entire family travelled—my parents continued to strive towards that goal; Hilbert was the next to follow one year later, in 1961.

In the meantime, Mama and Papa Ray continued farming alongside their tailoring profession. Infrequently, their return from their forest garden was as late as 8 p.m.; there was no street lighting then, so they used kerosene lamps made from bottles as flashlights. Even though we knew our parents would pray throughout their journey, my siblings and I would become anxious once darkness fell if Mama and Papa had not arrived home. Unsurprisingly, Mama's first question upon her late arrival was: "Have you all said your prayers?" The bundles of food they carried included farine and bread made through a long process from the cassava roots for home use and sale in the village. My parents' late returns from the bush got me thinking, *oh, how I wished I could make life easier for Papa and Mama.*

Cassava bread in the cooking process of about twenty minutes

I had only known Papa Ray for five going on six years before he embarked upon his journey to England in 1962; he would be residing with Mary-Anne. Undoubtedly, our dad's departure brought incredible sadness because Mama was left to cope as a single parent to young children for a considerable period. However, even before Papa left for England, our mum had consistently proven her ability to manage because she had never limited her function to just being a mum. I remember my mum taking the lead in organising the home. While I never doubted Papa's capability, Mama was proactive. She devised various ideas to ensure the family's well-being, from holding the purse strings to disciplining. Furthermore, her faith in God's power through daily prayers was undeniable; therefore, we were confident that her talent would continue to shine. She was a true matriarch.

The decrease in our family size was a change we embraced. We understood the need for considerable sacrifices to achieve our parents' goal of reuniting the family in England. Once Papa had settled in London, earning a regular income and finding suitable accommodation, he would pave the way to welcome his wife and remaining children. In the interim, my dad continued his absolute dedication to providing much-needed financial support to us in Saint Lucia. In his letters to Mama, he never failed to express his sadness for leaving us behind.

My Position Served Me Well

Papa ensured his wife and five remaining children in Saint Lucia managed well while he continued his efforts in England. He demonstrated devotion to us when he invariably posted a monthly allowance of £10.00. During the 1960s and 70s, the British pound fluctuated between EC$4.80 and EC$5 to the Eastern Caribbean Dollar. I hear you ask, "How did you survive on such a pittance?" Well, it sure took us a long way. Today, this £10.00 allowance would be equal to approximately £200.00, in the region of $600.00 Eastern Caribbean Dollars, which was a very sizable sum. Back then, Papa could not afford the luxury of express mail options or money transfer services. Instead, for security, he used registered mail that took approximately three weeks to reach us. I cannot recall Mama ever not receiving her allowance on time, and rather than spending it all, she saved a large part.

My four siblings and I remained excited about our father's move because we hoped our turn to travel would come soon. I knew my turn was far behind because my position was near the bottom of the family tree. Joe was third in line, followed by John, Silvie, me, and Phil.

In those days, the parents managed their home affairs on a seniority basis. They all used the system of the eldest sibling taking charge whenever the parents were away from home. If there was undisciplined behaviour, and Mama was dissatisfied with our explanation for the disorder, she would start to whack the person in charge. Beginning with Joe, she would work her way down. When Mama got to me, her emotions would kick in, and I would sense a feeling of compassion coming from her. Mama would spare me and Phil the punishment. How merciful. Therefore, from my standpoint, my position of being one before the last served me well.

Mama and The Saints

My strict upbringing did not stop me from being a normal kid; it did not transform me into a saint. However, I could have easily qualified as one, compared to my older brother John, who had a rebellious streak.

Mama had baked approximately thirty delicious cakes made from dried-out cassava starch mixed with various spices and sugar. We called them starch cakes, but they looked more like candy in multiple shapes with a starchy but flavoury taste. The weekend was approaching to celebrate Phil's First Holy Communion on Sunday. Mama had invited close friends and family to feast with us because of the event's significance in our religious calendar. With great enthusiasm, Mama went to get the cakes on Saturday, the day before the commemoration, from where she had secured them in the dining room cabinet, only to discover that approximately ten were missing. Mama was furious. She assembled my three older siblings and me—eight years old at the time, in the kitchen, and with an unforgiving look, she asked:

"Which of you took the cakes from the cupboard?" Our response was synchronous:

"Not me, Mama."

"How could any of you not have taken from the cakes? So why are so many missing?" Mama asserted. My three siblings and I protested our innocence while Phil was bound to remain in his room until the morning of his First Communion in compliance with the church's rules.

"Okay, I'll know who did it, and when I do find out, whoever is guilty will be sorry," Mama warned.

Even though I knew I was innocent, I still worried Mama would spank us all. I expected her to grab her belt; instead, she reached for a ten-fluid-ounce transparent glass half-filled with water and placed it on the kitchen table. She took a white piece of cotton thread about six inches long after doubling up. Mama tied her wedding ring in the middle of the string, with the ring hanging six inches on the cotton thread. She forewarned us that she would discover the truth by invoking two Saints; thus, she allowed us one last chance to speak up or face the consequences. We all sat nervously at the table, staring at each other's worried looks while Mama meditated for a minute with eyes closed, head bowed, and hands joined. She began the ritual.

In complete silence, Mama held the end of the strand, gently lowering the ring into the glass of water with only half submerged. My siblings and I gazed with our eyes glued to the glass. Our mum was trying to connect with the Saints in the Creole dialect, starting with the first question:

"Par-Sen Pierre Par-Sen Paul, avoir moi la vérité, keyless sé ma-mai la key pwens bon-bon-ar?" (St Pierre, St Paul, tell me the truth, which one of my children took the cakes?). Nothing happened. Mama then asked a leading question four times, referencing one child's name per question. Again, the ring stood still inside the glass. I wondered, "What if the Saints do not respond? What if they get it wrong?" Mama attempted once more:

"Par-Sen Pierre Par-Sen Paul, arvoir moi la vérité, eski sé John key pwens bon-bon-ar?" (St Pierre, St Paul, tell me the truth, is it John who took the cakes?) The pinging sound rang out rapidly, knocking the glass from side to side. Mama held the string for about forty-five seconds with a steady hand and focused on John—he admitted his guilt. This incident was the one I witnessed bringing out Mama's worst fury. Even though I was sympathetic to John, I would never have traded places with him. Thankfully, I never allowed Mama to resort to calling up the Saints if I misbehaved. Mama's traditional form of discipline was harsh, but it worked. However, I was once unfortunate to be on the receiving end of what I considered senseless and unreasonable punishment.

Why I Broke with Traditional Courtesy

One afternoon during my primary school days, I joined my classmates in the playground before going home. The parish was refurbishing our Catholic church, so the contractors had removed four giant bells from the belfry and placed them in a secure space in the schoolyard. While running about, we played around the bells and attempted to climb on top of them—the frolicsome things ten-year-old boys would typically do.

One of our neighbours, Alfraziar, who lived just two doors away from us, reported to Mama how improperly I behaved in the playground. She told

Mama I was lifting one of the church bells. What? All the bells must have weighed a ton, so how was that possible? My mum never gave it a second thought.

The modernised Catholic Church with the old school to the left

"Mama, I did not lift the bell." I pleaded. Nothing I said to defend my innocence was sufficient to quell the situation—Mama's leather strap was always within reach; she landed it three times on my back.

My mother knew I wasn't guilty of the accusation that Alfraziar had levelled at me. I did not, I could not, and would never be capable of lifting an object weighing tons, yet she punished me on account of this ridiculous story. Later, when the atmosphere calmed down, Mama gave me the real reason for the punishment: getting home late from school. Mama's subsequent explanation was no consolation to me.

My way of getting back at Alfraziar was to consider her unworthy of my greetings. I broke with the traditional courtesy, and I never greeted her again. I was lucky; Mama never knew I stopped saying hello to the woman who caused my unjust punishment. Had she known about it, the result would have been a second penalty of three lashings. It was our culture that the community considered anybody who did not greet an elder disrespectful; it was an unacceptable behaviour that parents did not tolerate.

Silvie Got the Beating

My brothers and I thought our sister Silvie was disadvantaged because Mama had little tolerance toward her—and she was not sufficiently brave to defend herself. Joe, John, Silvie, Phil and I attended an open-air music event on the grounds of our community centre. The Royal Saint Lucia Police Band staged this social activity annually in various communities around the island. Mama's rule was that we were leaving for the show as a group; therefore, she expected us to return the same way. She insisted that we look out for each other. Joe and John, being the eldest, were responsible for me, Silvie and Phil. While we understood our mum's concerns and would do our best to comply, we agreed that her strict rules wouldn't hinder our entertainment.

There was a large audience at the event. We all mingled in the crowds, but Joe and John must have forgotten about their three younger siblings for whom they were responsible. Deluta, a woman with a mental health condition known to turn violent whenever someone provoked her, was at the gathering. Despite her reputation, Joe and John joined in with those troubling her. Deluta lunged at the provocative crowd and grabbed hold of Joe's khaki shirt, which Mama had recently made. Joe's reflexes were not quick enough to avoid Deluta's *claw*. He tried to escape, but she stuck to him like a lion sticking to its prey. Poor old Joe! No one would have imagined a quiet, *well-behaved* guy like Joe would end up as Deluta's victim.

Joe's new khaki shirt was in shreds. It looked like Deluta had used scissors to cut through the shirt. The poor chap never stood a chance. Joe was lucky that the skin on his back remained intact. It was pretty embarrassing watching my brother make his escape and head home. Predictably, he became a laughingstock for the crowd, but Mama never saw the funny side of it.

We had broken the rule, and it compounded the problem. Phil and I stayed together and returned ahead of Silvie and John. Mama was incensed when we were all reunited at home. She quarrelled and blamed all of us except Joe for what had happened to Joe. Sadly, no one else but Silvie ended up being penalised. But why was Silvie punished for Joe's mistake and misbehaviour? Mama was in charge; she did what she thought was best, and that's how it stayed. In Micoud, girls were more restricted and protected. Routinely, the parents had a brother go with his sister whenever she attended social events; the parents would discipline that sister if she stepped out of line. In contrast, the boys received more lenient treatment. They were more likely to get away with bad behaviour. Joe remained in charge during Mama's absence even though he had shown his inability to protect himself against Deluta.

Our Daily Chores

Since being in charge was based on the order of seniority, I knew that the practice would not apply to me because Phil was the only one who would have been my subordinate. It was Joe's turn to take charge whenever Mama was absent. While Mama applied the *carrot or cakes and stick or leather strap* method, Joe enjoyed ruling with only the leather strap. We all despised his regimental approach, but only John was brave enough never to conceal his displeasure. Inevitably, Joe's approach did not earn him any popularity. John was defiant and was seldom bothered about the consequences of his wayward behaviour toward Joe.

We were all allocated our daily chores. Apart from Joe's role as the boss in Mama's absence, a position he cherished, he cleaned the house and cooked. Joe doing the cooking? Can you imagine eating a bowl of soup with okra and white dumplings? Dumplings can be slippery, and okra is slimy too. If you have no teeth, no problem; you could make this your favourite meal. It will find its way into your stomach and spare you the chewing energy. We wondered if Joe was playing cruel games with us; these meals were slippery enough to cause us to bite our tongues.

John's tasks included caring for the pigs Mama reared on a plot about four hundred yards from our home. On weekends and school holidays, he accompanied Mama to her forest garden in Capweece, approximately 5 miles or 8km from the village. He also fetched water from the Tromassee (pronounced *True-Mar-Say*) River. The Tromassee River is less than one mile away from Back Street. This stream was the village's primary water source for daily chores and drinking. It remained so until the government gradually introduced its pipe-borne water programme, starting with public standpipes in the 1960s. Whenever Joe asked John to fetch water from the river, he dragged his feet to display his disinclination. John would also bang the tin bucket repeatedly on a stone near our gate. Unsurprisingly, it was not long before we relegated that container to carrying garbage instead of water.

I filled in for John whenever I was required to do so. Stepping in to make the water trips to the river was one I never objected to. This task was my opportunity for river bath fun with friends.

Tromassee River flowing down into the sea

I recall Joe asked me one late Saturday afternoon to go for water. I was familiar with the river, but unlike my friends, I avoided the deeper parts because swimming was my weakness. As

I looked at the other boys plunging off the rocks as much as 9 ft high into the deep end, I was reluctant to join in as two friends egged me on. "Come on, Stephen, you can do it," they repeated. The other boys in the group of six teased me: "No! He can't; he can't swim." I focused more on the negative chants to prove the three wrong, climbed from the water and onto the rocks and nervously took my position as the boys chanted below: "Go. Go. Go. Go."

I had mistakenly moved some inches away from the usual dive spot before taking the plunge; I didn't resurface within seconds of hitting the water as the boys expected. Realising something was wrong, the boys came to my rescue and helped me out of the river. I had hit a rock below, resulting in a severe headache, a weird feeling of dizziness and an unconcealable gash on my forehead. I knew I had some explaining to do. Still, first, I needed one of my friends, Garth, to carry my bucket of water as I couldn't bear it on my very sore head. Uncharacteristically of Joe, the scolding I got from him quickly turned to empathy, while Mama's reaction, upon her return, was outright compassion. She washed my wound with antiseptic liquid and rubbed it using a soft candle. "I hope you behave yourself next time you go to the river," she said. I was blessed to have escaped bringing a tragedy to my family.

My primary task was caring for the sheep, and I took pride in it. Each morning I picked up their poop from the yard and then shepherded them away to graze on the nearby field before going to school. In the evenings, I took them back home from the grazing area. We needed to keep our animals closer to home at nighttime for fear of thieves carrying them away or wild dogs feasting on them. Rearing animals for our consumption and selling an extra pig or sheep, particularly at Christmas, was another of Mama's strategies to benefit the family financially.

One of Silvie's chores was to care for the chickens. Silvie loved her birds to the extent that she cried and refused to eat the meat whenever Mama slaughtered one for dinner. Well, thankfully for us, Silvie's loss was our gain. She received some sympathy, but we still enjoyed the poultry on our plates. The good thing about it was that we ate fast to avoid prolonging Silvie's sorrow.

Phil was the baby at home, and he had no unique role. However, he would occasionally join me in taking care of the sheep.

Punctured Hearts

In one of Papa's monthly letters to Mama, he advised her to prepare Joe for the journey, and in

1965, Joe was heading for London to join our dad. John, Silvie, Phil and I bid Joe farewell joyously because although we would be missing him, we were relieved from his domineering manner. John's turn to be in charge had arrived, but it was a position that he held only in principle.

Unlike Joe, John was not overly concerned about me, Silvie or Phil. We had a great relationship, and there was never any cause for disquiet. We all started the countdown as we lamented the inevitability of our last big brother's move to England. John's departure would leave Silvie, me, and Phil in a state of loneliness even though we had each other.

I remember that early morning at 4 a.m. in 1967, Mama, Silvie, Phil and I travelled by bus to the capital. With the bus's wooden enclosure and seats also made of wood and packed with as many as thirty people squeezed in, we were in for a one-and-a-half-hour, very uncomfortable ride along precipices, steep hills and winding roads peppered with potholes. John had started his long journey to England. We were all inconsolable as we bid our brother farewell in the crowded lobby before he boarded the ship at the Castries harbour. We waved goodbye as we watched him walk through the gates towards the vessel carrying his small brown canvas suitcase. Our brother's departure was reminiscent of Mary-Anne's leaving. We remained tearful until the next day, as our best brother was over the horizon sailing to join our dad and the older siblings.

Mary-Anne, Hilbert and Papa Ray had been in England for five to seven years, yet strangely, I never considered our situation akin to a split family until Joe and John left us. I was more conscious of my relationship with Joe and John, so, based on emotions, I considered Joe and John's absence more significantly. I missed them tremendously. The seniority system disappeared, and Silvie, Phil and I were of equal status. We continued our responsibilities but remained hopeful that it would soon be our turn to join the others in the UK and become a complete family again.

Once my two siblings and I had settled after John's departure and a year had passed, our anticipated relocation to England became the focus of our conversations. It was Silvie's task to check for mail twice weekly from the post office, and we always waited anxiously for Papa's letters. Whenever Silvie brought a letter, I thought, *ahh, that's the one!*

It was just another day, and Silvie walked in with a letter from the post. *Is this going to be the one with the good news?* I thought. My two siblings and I sat quietly at the kitchen table with high expectations as Mama opened the letter. Mama started reading aloud but suddenly paused after she read the line beginning with "I am sorry to tell you". That was it; immediately, we were deflated. I read the remaining words from Mama's looks. My heart sank. Mama consoled me and my two siblings as we suffered the pain from our punctured hearts Papa had brought about unintentionally. The dinner Mama had prepared that day was served for lunch the next day as our appetites vanished.

Papa declared that the remaining family member's move to England would not happen. We understood our father's reason for his decision, but it did not ease our disappointment. He explained that maintaining himself in England while sustaining us in Saint Lucia was demanding, restricting his ability to purchase a home in England. He, Joe, and John were residing with his daughter Mary-Anne, who by then had married. Furthermore, the family in England agreed it was not practical or wise for their dad to bring his wife and three young children to join him at his daughter's property—I was twelve years old, Silvie was fourteen, and Phil was ten.

In time, I gained better insight into this scenario and understood it more clearly. Papa did not seek independent advice about completing his family's relocation to England. Had our dad succeeded with his plan, his position would have advanced significantly. Papa would have obtained rented accommodation for his family until he could buy his own. Not only would he be free from the psychological impact of being separated from his wife and three young children, but he would also have avoided the additional cost of maintaining us in Saint Lucia. Moreover, Mama would have had a steady income in England; the job opportunities in that era were plentiful.

We had to come to terms with being left behind. We grew into a strong-knit family as Silvie, Phil and I strengthened our bond and performed our roles without intervention from Mama. Our mum continued managing her work skilfully without having to care for the animals, as she did not replenish her stock.

Breadfruit—Always on The Menu

Now that Mama had only the three of us to care for, life for her became more manageable. She continued with her gardening and made the trek to Capwece three times weekly because it was crucial for our upkeep. She produced a mixture of fruits and vegetables on her farm, including yams, potatoes and coconuts.

From age eleven, I took over John's previous task of accompanying Mama to Capwece on Saturdays and school holidays. Going along with Mama to her garden was the task I most disliked.

We started the journey by walking along the high road for the first two miles, occasionally getting a lift, which was okay. We trekked the remaining three miles through dense vegetation, narrow paths and a deep, fast-flowing river we crossed at three different points. This river flows down into the Tromassee area of Micoud, hence the Tromassee River. I held tightly onto Mama's clothes as we battled the strong currents gushing between the slimy rocks as we made our river crossings. Finding our footing between the slippery stones in the murky water was daunting. Often, Mama would have me remove my shorts and place them in her basket to avoid getting them soaked—I was a big boy at eleven years old; how embarrassing just wearing my underwear.

"Hold tight, ish-mwe." (Hold tight, my child) Mama kept repeating until we got to the other side. Of course, it never escaped my mind that we would have to repeat the process, which was riskier on our return journey because Mama would be carrying a large basket of food on her head while I would have a bunch of firewood or sometimes dried coconuts. Worst of all, we dreaded the typical heavy rainfall in the forest, which would cause the river to overflow—to avoid being trapped, Mama shortened our stay whenever the rain persisted.

I scorned all functions that would cause me to walk in the bushes. The thought of coming into contact with slimy creatures in the wild freaked me out. The way I dealt with this situation whenever I arrived at Capwece was simple. I sat in Mama's straw basket, which I placed under a mango tree; it became my refuge. I only grudgingly got out of the basket when Mama prompted me.

Hanging breadfruits can be seen from a breadfruit tree

Our mum often climbed tall breadfruit trees, pulling a fifteen-foot bamboo pole in her hand as she ascended through the branches. She used that specially designed pole to pick the fruits that would drop to the ground and roll through the undergrowth many feet away. Mama would yell from the top of the tree, "Stephen! Why are you such a coward? Come on, hurry up, get out of that basket, and gather the breadfruits so we can start packing up to go home." I would reluctantly leave my secure position to gather the fruits.

There was no getting away from that task. The green, round starchy fruits would be cooked and served for supper with stewed chicken backs, boiled fish, or dry roasted sprats soaked in coconut oil mixed with cucumbers and tomato salad. Often, there would be leftovers for the next day. Nothing went to waste. Any surplus would be roasted and served for breakfast with a cup of bush tea that we made with leaves from various fruit trees and herbs. There was sour orange, lime, citronella, ginger, cinnamon, soursop, and more. We reserved the canned powdered chocolate and the green or black tea and evaporated milk for Sundays. We seldom had lunch or dinner without breadfruit on the menu, but Mama included the other produce from her garden, such as green bananas, a variety of green peas, and avocados whenever she harvested them.

To me, Silvie and Phil, repeatedly eating breadfruit was torture. To this day, Silvie cringes at the mere mention of the word. When partially ripe, these fruits are delicious and have a sweet flavour instead of the typical starchy, dry, and bland taste when green. The downside to eating that fruit was that it produced tremendous discomfort from intestinal gas. For Mama, such uneasiness was longer lasting when she lay in bed. She was the head of the family, so she relieved her flatulence throughout the night. We hurriedly covered our heads with pillows when she indifferently blasted her thunderous and stinky gunpowder.

The Far-kar-we Tribe

As practising Catholics, we always looked forward to Sundays, our day of rest. However, another good reason for the excitement was our special Sabbath diet of tasty meals. After attending church service, we had the best breakfast, lunch, and later supper. Thank heavens, breadfruit was off our Sunday menu. Our favourite meal included cowheel soup mixed with spaghetti, dumplings, herbs, pumpkin, and other vegetables. It was also the only day we got the opportunity to wear our *Sunday best*. These outfits were often the much-appreciated, oversized used clothes we received from the family in

England. Mama's skill as a seamstress was handy because she made all the necessary adjustments that ensured we had an excellent fit. Of course, in addition to Mama's organisational skills, she was mindful in whatever she did, so no one knew or even noticed our altered clothing; well, even if they did, it wouldn't have mattered.

As for the oversized shoes, we stuffed them with cotton wool to make them sufficiently comfortable, though, in Phil's case, he couldn't conceal he was walking in someone else's shoes. Silvie and I couldn't resist giggling when Mama nudged Phil as we walked to church. "Come on, Phil, what's wrong with you? Walk properly." Our baby brother could hardly keep up with us as he walked in his big shoes, like a penguin, his arms firmly at his side and his ten fingers open. I thanked God for the platform shoes, or *brogues,* as we called them. Phil and I looked much taller when we wore them. Born two years apart, Silvie, Phil and I were the shortest at under five feet among our siblings. Mama measured in the mid-range of five feet, while Papa, well-proportioned, was nearer six feet.

Like me, my close friend, Keith, was twelve going on thirteen years but was much taller and bigger than me. Keith once quipped, "Hey Stephen, are you a descendant of the Far-kar-we tribe?"

I had no idea of the reason for this question. "How am I supposed to know? I've never heard of this tribe," I replied.

Keith explained, "If you lived in the countryside, people would have thought you came from the Far-kar-we tribe."

"Why?" I asked.

Keith stated, "The Far-kar-we tribe are the short people who live deep in the woods. They often got lost in highly overgrown vegetation which surpassed their height. They found their way through the overgrowth by using breaststroke swimming action. Working through the tall bushes, they repeatedly ask, "Where the F**k *are* we? "Where the F**k *are* we?"

Ha-ha-ha! I pretended to be amused because even though I thought my friend was inventive with his imaginary tribe, I did not see the funny side of his joke.

"Fantastic joke!" I jested.

But why did I play along? Well, had I not, the story would have stuck and become a playground tease simply because I wasn't fond of that gag. This case was typical of how schoolyard bullying started back then, so I played the game by falsely accepting Keith's taunt, which soon became an obsolete joke. My decision to play along was, in effect, my conflict management strategy, to which the alternative, resisting, would probably lead to a schoolyard fight. But would I have won this fight? I don't think so. There was no firebrand streak in my family's DNA. Papa was even-tempered, and Mama was emphatic and was never involved in altercations.

We Sold Racoona and More

Mama never entirely depended on her husband's monthly remittance from England for our upkeep. Some wives from our village were also blessed to receive an allowance from their husbands who had made the same journey as Papa. While Mama was prudent in managing her subsidy, the other spouses used their income on foodstuff, small basins of freshly caught fish, fresh beef, and weekend entertainment at the local bars; it was all free-spending. In Mama's case, she applied hers progressively. She gave priority to home improvement to enhance our overall standard of living.

Just as the government had introduced pipe-borne water to the people of Saint Lucia in the 1960s, electricity was one more amenity provided in various communities for street lighting and home supply. Those utilities did not come free of charge. Mama's exemplary home economics and management skills enabled her to achieve her goal—her electricity and water supply applications were successful. Thankfully, we ditched the river buckets and the kerosene lamps. Our mum's additional income for our day-to-day maintenance came from selling surplus vegetables and other crops she cultivated from her garden. Mama cleverly brought her ideas to life to make ends meet; she was highly creative.

Our mum drew lots of criticism from the neighbours and relatives when she used Papa's cash to refurbish our family home. Most of all, the disapproval intensified when she used her creative skills to cook and sell a confectionery called racoona. One racoona is the size of a cupcake but rectangular-shaped. The recipe, all mixed and cooked in a large pan, includes grated dry coconuts, brown sugar, cinnamon, flavouring essences and other spices. The brown, sweet, sticky finished product was so delicious that kids and adults found it irresistible. My job was to walk about with a tray of racoona for sale after school. Having to walk around the village to sell trays of racoona was no laughing matter. Mama also prepared Phil's trays while she and Silvie cooked the confectionery. She insisted that Phil and I walk through the village shouting, "Racoona for sale...!

Racoona for sale! Racoona for sale!.... People, get your racoona!"

While I was impressed by my mum's innovative ideas, I was not enthusiastic about applying her sales technique. There again, she was the boss. She just knew how things worked.

Modern-day Micoud Village

As a twelve-year-old, I would not have volunteered to become a racoona salesperson, let alone shout about it. I thought Mama was funny when she made the advertising suggestion. Whether I liked it or not, my duty, and Phil's, was to rake in the sales. We would hit the sales jackpot on Sundays because of the day's sporting events. Our product became so popular that customers started looking out for us; this boosted us tremendously.

As we became more relaxed in our role, Phil and I arranged sales competitions to prove who was better at selling the most. It was hardly surprising when one villager, Ma Ralph, began to copy our idea. She changed her product by chopping the coconuts into small pieces rather than grating them, and called it raccoon-coona. I suppose she too, was creative. She never hesitated to shout, "Raccoon-coona for sale!" and hearing her squeaky voice was amusing. Nevertheless, Mama was always one step ahead of the competition. Not only did we manage to sustain and boost our sales, but we also expanded our product lines to include other dessert-like confectionery such as coconut cakes and the cornmeal cakes traditionally called peń-me (try pronouncing "Pen" with a silent "N" and add "me").

Mama's products were tasty and well-presented, and our customers loved them. I admired and loved my mum for her resourcefulness and ability to brush off the criticism her talent attracted. The community members viewed our mum's ambition from two angles.

Firstly, they perceived anyone who walked about in the village trying to sell confectionery or other goods from a tray as disadvantaged—the sellers were considered to belong at the bottom of the economic ladder. In my mum's case, they viewed her as being selfish. Some people thought she had the means to get by without selling racoona and depriving those in need.

Secondly, others interpreted her efforts as having low self-esteem. How strange, we thought. Mama's sister-in-law, Miss May, never hesitated to express her views directly to Mama:

"Ma Ray, what are you doing with your husband's money? You mean to tell me things are so bad with you that you have reduced your children to selling racoona on the streets?"

I saw nothing wrong with our mother trying to earn an honest living. Contrary to the critics' opinion, I believe they exposed their profound lack of wisdom and inability to bring about a sustainable improvement in their living standards.

From the villagers' standpoint, our mother was comfortable simply because her husband and four children lived in England. Handling such gossip was no headache for our matriarch; she ignored those who denounced her. Mama did what she thought was best for her and her family without stepping on anyone's toes. Furthermore, her philosophy was never to cast aside the pedestal upon which our compatriots had placed us. Instead, let it symbolise the staying power in our quest for accomplishment. Always be proud and confident, knowing we have done our best, no matter our circumstances. Let whoever believes you are flourishing keep their belief.

In our mum's opinion, such attitudes toward anyone command respect. How true. If we were to acquire wealth based on compliments towards our family, we would have been in the bourgeois echelon. Mama selling racoona did not diminish residents from the wider district's admiration for the family. The more astute members recognised her as independent-minded and resourceful. They acknowledged that she was fearless and a great asset to her husband and family. Irrespective of public opinion, our mum continued with her brilliant ideas. Her entrepreneurial skills paid off. The returns from our confectionery sales brought much-needed subsidies. Prioritising between foodstuff and other household expenses became more manageable. Silvie, Phil and I started to earn pocket money from our sales. In addition, we grew into a joyful team that was never short of good conversation. We had lots of fun and laughter about various events, including our new *business ventures*.

Mama continued to groom us and explain the importance of self-esteem. Despite her efforts, I was timid about my role; I had not developed my mother's disposition to ignore the critics. Nonetheless, I realised how vital my function was in Mama's undertaking.

Apart from the immediate family, no one knew the level of our finances. However, people from the outer district believed that the respectable class was where we firmly belonged. Our clean appearances and firm discipline obscured our financial status of being able to manage without a penny to spare.

My Bosom Friend

The bond between me and Phil was exceptional. We were not just brothers; we looked like twins, and many in the community thought we were. I was highly protective of him. Wherever I went, Phil followed closely behind. I shared my clothes, friends, knowledge, and whatever my name was attached to.

Are you wondering how and why I did all this? It was easy for me. I did it on the principle that he was my bosom friend. I had his back, and he valued my attention. I never doubted that our understanding and love for each other were mutual. Playing my part as the big brother was a position I treasured and envisaged continuing long into the future. I felt confident that our nightly family prayers for peace, love and harmony, led by our mum, contributed to our closeness.

My Stimulating Psalm

Mama was unwavering in her faith. She never failed to remind us of the importance of prayers. To this day, my favourite short daily worship, which I fervently recite immediately upon leaving my bed in the mornings, usually before sunrise, is:

"I thank you, Heavenly Father, for the blessings you have bestowed upon me. Thank you for allowing me to see the beginning of this new day and equip me for whatever it brings. Thank you, Lord, for appointing your Guardian Angel to keep watch over me, for keeping me safe and free from harm. I beg of you, Lord, for your forgiveness for the sins I have committed through my thoughts, words, and deeds. This, I pray, Dear Lord, in the name of Jesus, Amen."

I then recite the Lord's Prayer and read Psalm 4 three times to attain blessings. After each reading, I state my unique appeal, which I attach to this psalm. I read one of the petitions before the actual reading of the psalm and the other at the end. I liken Psalm 4 to a daily dose of spiritual, physical and mental tonic, without which I would crumble; my stimulating psalm induces the feeling of being connected to my creator throughout the day.

I believe praying with confidence and devotion yields positive outcomes, but these are only part of a formula for success. While my faith has remained absolute, I knew trust alone is insufficient to produce the desired results. Therefore, combining conviction with other inherent elements is vitally important—actualising these components can sometimes be a real challenge.

CHAPTER TWO

A Legitimate Candidate

How strong is our willpower? Do we have what it takes to face a barrage of challenges plaguing our lives? Out of our human instincts, our response would undoubtedly be, "Of course, we have what it takes." But how can we be sure if we don't know the how, what, when, where and why scenarios? The only way we could respond confidently would be through individual lived experiences. We would not be entirely convincing without an illustrative case. All will depend on our expressive ability to tap into our inherent qualities, the building blocks of our creation.

Whenever people asked me the question that most children were asked, *"What would you like to be when you grow up?"* my response was always the same, "I want to be a fisherman." As I write, I admit that I had no other reason for this career choice besides my desire to provide my family with a daily supply of freshly caught fish. The luxury of fresh fish was one Mama struggled to afford. However, I often wondered how I would have achieved such a wish, when, surprisingly, I was not a swimmer, despite being born and raised on an island with many rivers and beautiful beaches. I often prayed for strength and courage, but somehow, I didn't dare to face the deep-flowing waters. Instead, I turned to my local Catholic Church for direction.

I was devoted to my role in the church and was on an earnest pathway to becoming a priest. Yes, I ditched the idea of wanting to become a fisherman for wanting to be a clergyman. My entire family was excited about having one of their own, a "Father Rosemond," in their midst. In the community's eyes, but specifically the congregation, I was the altar server from the group who came across as fitting the aspirational goal perfectly. I was honoured to have the confidence of my community, which they often expressed through words of encouragement.

There were no priests of colour. Caucasians were sent to our island for many years to serve as parish priests. Those ministers commanded considerable respect, and community members looked up to them as true redeemers. It was not until my teenage years that I first saw an Afro-Caribbean cleric. Therefore, I sometimes wondered whether my community leaned toward a colourist bias which caused them to see me as a more legitimate candidate; this was based largely on my mulatto looks, with an unmistakably fair and freckled face. My journey toward the priesthood would not be easy or without prejudice. My long and difficult struggle was beginning.

Too Young, Then Too Old

The support of the parishioners and the wider community would not be sufficient to curtail or even remove the many obstacles ahead. During my primary school education, I would never have imagined encountering such hurdles at such a young age. The overall passing grade required to advance to higher education was unattainable, regardless of my performance. I needed more than a pass mark to have obtained the "privilege" of secondary education. My father needed to be a banana farmer, and my family needed to be politically affiliated or strongly associated with affluent individuals with name recognition. In short, I needed a "godfather" to advance my cause.

Mama and I were thrilled when in 1968, at the age of twelve, my primary school principal, Mr Antonne, invited us to a personal meeting. We expected him to confirm the good news we had already learned from unofficial sources: I had passed my exams for entrance to the Vieux-Fort Senior Secondary School. We anticipated he would share in our excitement and deliver words of encouragement, beginning with, "Congratulations…"

Instead, with a blank expression, Mr Antonne said, "Thanks for coming, Mrs Ray. Stephen has passed his exams for entrance to the Vieux-Fort Senior Secondary School, but unfortunately, he is too young to be admitted." The delivery of such news instantly deflated us; it wiped out the smiles on our faces. With raised eyebrows and dejected looks, Mama stared at me as I gazed back at her.

Looking confused, Mama replied, "I don't understand. You selected Stephen to sit the exam, so what do you mean? How is this possible? Are all the other children not of the same age group? How can he be too young?"

Whatever points my mum raised failed to change the principal's mind. Equally, nothing he said pacified us or altered our opinions; we saw preferential treatment of others at my expense.

Sadly, I had no sponsor in my corner, so the system denied me the opportunity for higher education. I had to wait until the following year to redo the exams. Vieux-Fort Senior Secondary School, located in the south of the island, was one of the three most prestigious educational facilities. St Mary's College, an all-boys institution, and St Joseph's Convent, exclusively girls, were the other two in the north.

I continued with my studies to ensure my eligibility the following year. I realised perseverance had to be one of the indispensable elements in my quest for success. My determination paid off, and in 1969, I passed again. More than before, and although we had no reason to expect any more disappointment, Mama and I waited anxiously for our meeting with the principal.

Sitting impassively before us at the session, Mr Antonne declared, "I don't know how to explain to you, Mrs Ray, but unfortunately, Stephen is too old. We cannot admit him to the Vieux-Fort Senior Secondary School."

"What! Why? How can that be?" Mama asked in an aggrieved tone.

We were bewildered as we were facing a hopeless situation. Of course, Mama had always been the spokesperson in the family. She was a good negotiator too. Unfortunately, this predicament left her with no room to manoeuvre. She was visibly peeved, and rightly so.

I was speechless as I looked on; oh boy, here we go again! Mama is not making this any easier for me. My mum left Mr Antonne with no uncertainty about her displeasure with the corrupt system before we walked out of his office.

Doom and Gloom

I was anchored to the primary school while the other students who passed the entrance exam moved to higher education. My family and I did not doubt that the immoral practice of nepotism had a hand in my fate, and we were powerless to do anything about it. It looked like I was doomed to end my education at the basic primary school level, just as my older siblings did. I had no choice but to regroup; I remained resolute in my quest for progress while hoping for another break.

Our government was in the process of providing further opportunities for universal secondary education. The junior secondary school building programme in selected districts had begun in collaboration with the Canadian government. The new schools would serve as a stepping stone from primary education to the senior secondary level. In the meantime, I pressed on with my mission for the priesthood. I attended seminars and other functions to prepare and assist us towards that vocation.

Through a scheme initiated by the Diocese, the Bishop gave all aspiring seminarians one chance to complete the St Mary's College entrance selection process. They granted us this opportunity to secure a pathway towards our goal. I was among the few students who passed the exam. On this occasion, my family and I chose not to celebrate before our admission date. Nevertheless, the successful students, including myself, started the countdown toward the event's special announcement.

As we waited expectantly, our parish priest declared the results—it was official. The college's intake of students had reached total capacity. We would not be admitted. Once again, in my case, it was time to digest one more report that smothered my aspiration; it was simply dispiriting. This latest dashed expectation was a smack in our faces. Father Bertrand, who conveyed the bad news, was equally disappointed. For a third time, the system denied me access to further education. Did I give up? I was not entirely surprised, but I kept pushing forward despite feeling discouraged.

I did not express my feelings to Mama or our local parish priest because they had no power to do anything more. Naturally, they encouraged me to press on. While remaining at primary school, I continued my service in the church but was saddled with the thought that someone was snatching my future away.

To lighten the mood after the recent disappointment, I asked Mama jokingly during a family chat, "But Mama, why did you call me Stephen? Was I named after the Saint?"

I knew that in the past, Catholic parents customarily named their children after a saint or a prominent religious figure usually linked to their child's date of birth. Yet, I was curious to discover exactly how my name came about.

"Why do you ask?" She replied.

"Well, I was thinking of Saint Stephen because I know he was the first Christian Martyr?"

With a smile, she replied, "Yes, he was the first Martyr, stoned to death because of his faith, so why do you ask again if you already knew?"

Continuing with the pester, I responded, "Ahh, well, I like the name, but I don't fancy being a martyr." But frankly, I was beginning to think that my name was synonymous with misfortune.

It was not my family's imagination of some abnormality in our home when the spirit of doom and gloom was hovering around us. We sensed that the Angel of Death was lurking beneath us; a foul smell that seemed to be emerging from under the house was slowly intoxicating our space. But what was it, we wondered; we were deeply concerned.

Stench of Evil

Our mum never failed to pay close attention to events around the home. She always remained vigilant. Our mother would be the first to notice whether it was a strange object on our property, our physical appearance, or even funny smells around the house. She spotted a gradual change in my physique. She observed that I was losing my appetite and that her cheerful, fun-loving son was slowly becoming a skeleton. Why was I allowing my disappointments to affect me so severely? The fact was, I was not allowing it! It was just happening.

Strangely, Mama was also losing her appetite. Anxiety was taking over her usual optimism. It appeared that all the events related to failed attempts at my progress took their toll on Mama and me. We shared a close relationship, and we communicated freely and openly with each other. My mum understood that I was doing my best to manage my situation. She became troubled about me while the rest of the family worried about her.

Even though we were all sad about my case, no one expected me to be so depressed. We knew my setbacks were not the end of the world, and we had to continue. We tried to keep our spirits up, but our physical appearances suggested otherwise. Yes, we were disappointed, but certainly not to the extent of inflicting harm upon ourselves.

We continued seeking spiritual guidance to overcome the hurdles that plagued us. Mama was addicted to praying. She always prayed with absolute belief and complete passion. However, it was never far from our minds that the powers of a third force existed. It was common knowledge that there was a widespread practice of sorcery in Saint Lucia. We remained committed to our Christian faith and tried to overcome our plight once we discovered the likely source of our transformation.

Some would wonder how it was possible to experience so much strife while remaining steadfast in our belief in the Supreme Being. In the King James Version of the Bible, 1 Peter 5:8 hints about Satan's nature. He does not take a break, and no one is immune from his mischief. The devil is always on the prowl, and he is mighty, too. Satan uses the strategies of provocation in his desperate effort to lure us into his web.

I was about 13 years old when Silvie, Phil, Mama and I became conscious of this smell gliding through our modest home. The strange odour had existed for two days and worsened as time passed. Initially, we ignored the whiff because foul-smelling surroundings, though not common, were sometimes caused by dead rodents nearby. However, the revolting scent of decaying flesh was beginning to overcome our home. From our experience, we no longer believed it was a dead rat, because of the toxic smell. This weird situation became scary. We began the search for what I subsequently named the *stench of evil*. Our pet dog, Dandy, led us to the concealed, almost untraceable answer.

Dandy's bark under our house was loud and persistent. It was hard to imagine the reason for his continuous howling until we investigated. There was minimal space between the floorboards and the ground under the house. Mama covered her nose and mouth with a headscarf. She slid between the floorboards and the soil to follow Dandy. She noticed that Dandy was focusing on a tiny gap directly between the floorboard and the wooden pillar upon which the floorboard rested. As Mama moved closer to Dandy's location, the stench became overpowering. She saw that Dandy had discovered the mystery; it was horrifying! That was where the nauseating smell emanated. It was not our imagination, nor a bad dream.

There was a small package strategically placed in an inconspicuous location. Someone or something had carefully wrapped the item in the newspaper. Mama bravely and cautiously removed the wrapped-up bundle with a stick and examined the contents. It was a sickening parcel of damp, rotting flesh. Our mum realised that this was no ordinary rotting flesh. It was like tiny fragments of human or animal gut. Without any hesitation, we disposed of the package.

Frighteningly, we wondered, how long we would have to go on fighting the forces of evil. Mama cleaned the area using a combination of disinfectants and soapy water. The days went by, and life was returning to a semblance of normality, but questions remained. Was this package carried to this location by a rat or other animal? But why was the wrapping so intact? Would a normal creature take its time to wrap up its catch? Or, if the creature found a meal, would it have managed it with such care, tied it up, and secured it for later?

How bizarre! This pernicious act, irrespective of how it occurred, was troubling. Should we believe that Mama and I would slowly disintegrate while that flesh rotted away? At least, this is what Madam Celistin, a clairvoyant from a neighbouring district, led us to believe—the psychic confirmed Mama's suspicions that the package had contained human flesh. According to Madam Celistin, had Mama brought the item to her, she would have disposed of it appropriately, which would have led to the discovery of the guilty party within three days of its disposal. Whatever curse was wished upon us, she said, would have been returned to its source.

I firmly believe our family's nightly devotion, which included the recital of Psalm 30, ensured our protection from evil occurrences. Now that a worrisome distraction was no more, it was time for me to refocus and prepare to enter the newly constructed Micoud Junior Secondary School. In 1970, I was part of the first group of students admitted at the opening ceremony. The education department did not require us to take an entrance examination for this facility as it was the beginning of what was to become free, universal secondary education.

More Stumbling Blocks

I continued my studies at the Junior Secondary School from 1970 to 1972. In September 1972, I received the final opportunity to attend the Vieux-Fort Senior Secondary School. Thankfully, I eventually succeeded in admission to that facility. It was a much-needed breakthrough that would finally allow me to get down to the business of further studies. I had, at last, achieved what had eluded me previously.

My time at the Vieux-Fort Senior Secondary School was an enjoyable experience. There was a good mix of students from the island's east to the west coast. I was a happy pupil without any concerns or fears. Since I had overcome many hurdles, I was eager to settle into a positive frame of mind. Surely, there could be no more stumbling blocks! Nothing more would stop me from moving forward; these were my thoughts.

CHAPTER THREE

Sons of Our Father

I continued my education at the Vieux-Fort Senior Secondary School, while my youngest brother Phil was at the Micoud Junior Secondary. Soon, it would be his turn to move to a higher level. In 1973, Phil passed his entrance exams, thereby securing a place at the prestigious Vocational Morne Technical College in Castries to begin in September of the same year. We were thrilled at the prospect of Phil being a student at Morne Technical College while I attended school in Vieux-Fort. We saw these results as a testament to Mama's effort in our upbringing and Phil's determination to advance. We believed that this was a reward for keeping our faith. I consistently prepared myself spiritually daily by reading the three verses of Psalm 134. Our parish priest taught me that the daily recital of those three short Bible verses was vital for all students wishing to progress in their studies.

Mama was immensely proud because her two last children had gained success strictly on merit and not favour. However, there was one big hurdle to overcome. The school fees and all other expenses associated with the privilege of attending higher education away from home would be challenging. Of course, Mama also used our dad's contributions towards my education. But now that Phil was in the equation, the financial challenge doubled.

To ease the burden on Papa and find a solution to our dilemma, Mama applied for a bursary from the education authorities. Seeking such help was not unusual for families facing financial hardship. While we stayed hopeful, the response from the authorities suddenly ended our expectations. It was a devastating blow when they rejected our plea based on their premise that our dad and three older siblings were able to support us. They declared: "Having examined your request for support towards your sons' education, we regret that your circumstances do not qualify you for such assistance." Phil and I wished to shield our dad from the added pressure by contemplating giving up on our dream of pursuing further education together.

Supporting himself in England while maintaining his family in Saint Lucia was no easy task for Papa. He resorted to seeking help from the older siblings but received a disappointing response, which he thought was disrespectful. Papa was lamenting over his perceived failure to fulfil his obligation when the older siblings retorted:

"Stephen and Phil are your sons, their educational needs are your responsibility. You cannot expect us to educate your children."

Even though those siblings understood our difficulties, they could not lessen the liability. This predicament indeed highlighted the truth about our situation. We needed no reminder that Phil and I were the sons of our father, but we also thought we had a solid and united family who would follow tradition and support each other.

During that era, it was customary that the older employed siblings would prop up their families to cushion the financial hardship. The question was, *where did we go from here?* We brainstormed, but sadly, we found no easy solution. The money Mama earned from her fruit and vegetable sales was not enough to cover the cost of our education. So, should Mama be making more racoona to sell on the streets? The only alternative was that either Phil or I would need to give up our education. It was one of the most challenging decisions we ever made as a family. In the end, I chose to become the sacrificial lamb; I allowed my youngest brother to achieve his goal of becoming a certified electrician.

A Harsh Reality

In April 1974, I submitted my termination letter to Mr Greg Wallis, my school principal. Mr Wallis tried to persuade Mama and me to reconsider. While he was sympathetic to our cause, he understood our predicament. Nevertheless, he was unable to offer any solutions. Father Parker also tried to put a salvage plan together, to no avail. My situation was heartbreaking. With my education ending abruptly, my aspirations of becoming a priest also halted. Focusing on the church became difficult; my exit was gradual but inevitable, a bitter pill to swallow.

My consolation came from the realisation of making a huge sacrifice for my brother. Mama cried, and so did the rest of us. The atmosphere was parallel to a tragedy in the family. My sudden departure from secondary school was a big deal as I was the first in the family to achieve this level of education despite the many obstacles.

My relationship with my mum was an inspiring one. I gained much confidence through our extensive communication. Most importantly, she taught me explicitly how to apply faith in the power of prayers. My mum supported me throughout my ordeal and never ceased encouraging me to do well in whatever path I chose as I turned my attention to finding suitable employment.

My Seven Elements of Prayers

Back in the seventies, job opportunities were few in Saint Lucia. The common choice was to join the ranks of casual labour, mainly in construction and the banana fields. The banana plantation was favoured because it provided a higher income than an apprentice earned in construction work—but neither of these choices attracted me. While my decision to terminate my secondary education resulted from our economic situation at home, I needed to follow a path that would lead me to a career rather than just a pay packet. I saw this as a long-term strategy that would offset my sacrifice.

Being on the island's south coast presented the further challenge of finding suitable employment—my chances of finding work in the city were better because it was the central point for commercial activities. However, heading northbound meant high travelling costs; thus, the south was my only choice.

I prepared myself mentally and spiritually to explore employment opportunities. One of my discoveries was the prerequisite for shaping our destiny lies in tapping into our inherent abilities while developing our mindset relating to our faith in God's power through prayer—I favoured the Book of Psalms. The Psalms were instruments designed by the Psalmist to present their deepest emotions and situations to our Saviour. I detected reluctance from those with whom I touched on this part of the Holy Bible as if it were taboo. So, the question is, why was I continuously faced with struggles if I had such knowledge? My response was that these events represented the various sections of the track I was obliged to navigate to discover my strengths and weaknesses and understand the reasons for my existence; it was according to the will of the Almighty. My ability to defy misadventures would define my fate. I also knew that due to my experiences, perseverance and resilience were vital in contributing to my advancement.

I considered **P**erseverance and **R**esilience the initial two of what I refer to as my Seven Elements of Prayers. I applied this theory as I continued along my journey. My path was about to take a new turn when I started applying for jobs. At age seventeen, I had no work experience and could not conceal or disguise my youthful appearance. My first application was to one of the island's most prestigious, Caribbean-based life insurance companies.

Although Saint Lucians perceived the insurance business as lacking integrity, the people's belief did not deter me. I prayed fervently. There was no doubt in my mind about the limitless power of my God. I harnessed courage and made a decision that would conclusively map out my future. I knew I had aspirations and should not yield to the pressures. Therefore, **A**mbition and resisting the temptation to **Y**ield were my third and fourth elements of Prayers. My Bible, my pen, and my faith were my power tools.

The Chance to Prove Myself

While preparing my job applications for dispatch to various firms, I persistently and diligently prayed Psalm 65 on mornings at sunrise. I genuinely believed that praying this psalm was instrumental in my job-hunting results. The first response I received within days of sending out my applications was an appointment for an interview at the insurance company. This invitation was my first opportunity to test my preparedness for the world of work. Was I ready for this massive transformation, I wondered. Wait! I still didn't have a godfather in my corner. My life had been about struggle and strife, but I hoped I would get a break with this, my first job opportunity. I was determined to cast aside the apprehension that conflicted with the inspiring feelings of optimism.

My job interview with Peter Chalmer, who was the branch manager, was anything but straightforward. In Mr Chalmer's opinion, he was interviewing a boy to fill a man's role. He stated as much when he sought advice in my presence from his general manager, Mr Nigel Cadette.

With no regard for my feelings, Peter Chalmer pressed the telephone against his ear and stared at me with a smile. He started a conversation:

"Hey, Nigel! I have this young lad here whom I believe should be at school. He has written such a good job application, I thought it would be interesting to give him this interview. But I think he should be in a classroom."

Not hearing Mr Cadette's response, I presumed he suggested that Peter Chalmer allow me to prove myself. Peter Chalmer could not have known that as he and his manager spoke, I was mentally reciting Psalm 34. I always prayed this psalm in the mornings during my job-hunting mission, including on the morning of my interview.

My prayers paid off as if by some miracle. Peter Chalmer gave me a chance to prove my ability. He gave me the break that I was desperately seeking. Now that I had placed one foot in the doorway, I did not doubt getting my entire body through. Never would I allow my first job opportunity to slip away.

How I Kept Hitting My Targets

I overcame the first hurdle of keeping the employment door open, but the time for celebration was a long way ahead. My entrance to the world of work rested upon my ability to demonstrate my worthiness for this post. I had to succeed; there was no other option. I spent the first two weeks shadowing Peter Chalmer on his door-to-door sales pitches, servicing clients' policies and seeking new business. I spent time in the office learning about the various products and administrative duties. My training was comprehensive and engaging. I joined a team that welcomed me without prejudice.

Peter Chalmer told me during our conversations that I would be working alone from the third week. My reaction was one I presume many would have experienced on their first day in their new job: combined emotions of nervousness and excitement. Still, I knew that as my quest for divine guidance was ceaseless and that I prayed with every ounce of devotion, I conjured up the enthusiasm within me to succeed.

Finally, the time arrived. I was ready to take up the challenge, but not before I recited more psalms:

Psalm 65 became my daily prayer in my quest for success in my endeavours, and Psalm 47, seven times daily, boosted my confidence in interacting with others and enabling me to be well-received and beloved by whomever I encountered. I knew the various psalms I studied fluently; therefore, I prayed whenever I chose during my working hours.

My confidence grew as my anxiety gradually ebbed away. Peter Chalmer set my sales target for the third week. I was required to produce sales at the rate of two new customers daily, ten new customers for the week! Not a problem! By midweek, I had achieved my target. Peter Chalmer and the rest of the team were amazed. Mr Chalmer continued setting new targets. My abiding faith continued to serve me well as I was on course to closing the sales within the given time limits. Peter Chalmer contacted Nigel Cadette and told him about my performance.

Mr Chalmer revealed that Mr Cadette told him, "I told you to give the boy a chance."

My early success by no means automatically qualified me for a permanent position—I had to complete the trial period. Mr Chalmer gave me another target: finding ten new customers for the fourth week. Not a problem, achieved again! There was no stopping me. Eventually, after I completed the training, the company employed me. At the end of the fourth week in June 1974, I received my first pay packet in my new job; I became a breadwinner in the family. Regrettably, I didn't frame a copy of this pay cheque to celebrate its commemorative value. A secret I kept from the family was my intention to buy Mama her first gas stove with my first pay cheque. I deposited an amount from my salary on the brand-new appliance at a high street store and paid off the balance from my subsequent wages. I arranged for the store to deliver Mama's stove during my working hours because I knew this would add to the excitement. As I approached home from work one afternoon, I saw Silvie standing at the gate with a cheerful smile. She was waiting for me.

"Steve!" she called. "You bought that stove? How much did it cost? You got paid already?"

With a grin, I replied, "Hey, what are all these questions about? Where's Mama?"

Silvie continued, "You must have used all your money to pay for this stove. Oh, my gosh, thank you, Lord. We can now get rid of the coal pot. No more smoke in my eyes from blowing the fire." Silvie and I laughed.

Mama walked through the kitchen door to meet us at the gate. She joined in the conversation.

"Steve, what have you done? Why did you surprise us this way? I was going to send the driver back with the stove because I hadn't ordered it. Why did you do that?"

Mama was sad when she said, "You just started working and you've used your first pay to buy a stove." She asked, "When did you get paid?"

"That's okay, Mama. This is the special gift I planned when I got the job. So now you can ditch the coal pot."

"Oh no-no-no-no," Mama replied. "I heard you and Silvie talking about getting rid of the coal pot. I'm keeping my coal pot exactly where it is, so Silvie, don't get disaccustomed to the coals."

This small gesture was a big deal for the family. Mama kept her clay coal pot but ditched the firewood. Mama, Silvie and Phil enormously appreciated the upgrade, and I had accomplished the remaining elements of my Prayers, **E**ndurance, **R**esoluteness, and **S**incerity.

Charlo, a true Mentor

Once I had secured my position as a life insurance sales representative, Peter Chalmer wasted no time giving his final approval by driving me to the island's capital to meet the other employees and the general manager. I became a fully-fledged team member, giving me the *entitlement* to respectfully refer to my boss, Mr Chalmer, as Charlo. Charlo had thought of me as a kid but never expressed this in his actions. He was never condescending. He remained impartial and professional.

On my part, I was immensely pleased. I had proven my ability beyond doubt. The relationship that my manager and I later developed was one of friendship. My family warmly welcomed him whenever he accompanied me home. His visits allowed Mama to express her gratitude for the start that Charlo gave me by preparing tasty lunches that included stewed chicken backs with lentils, green bananas and rice, and a pint-size glass of freshly made lime juice. Whenever my manager finished his meal, he showed appreciation by leaning backwards from the table, placing his right hand over his mouth and casually letting out an enormous belch.

"Oh, excuse me! That's your fault, Mrs Ray," he would say with a contented smile as he took his handkerchief from his back pocket and wiped his bushy moustache. "You know I always enjoy your meal. Your food has filled my belly, way to the top. That was great, thank you, Mrs Ray."

"Oh, don't mention it, Mr Chalmer. It's always my pleasure. It's nice that you have enjoyed the lunch," Mama politely replied.

Charlo was sufficiently relaxed to visit occasionally without invitation. He would usually stop by with his new girlfriend on his way to or from the capital; Mama always had something to offer, whether cooked, to have at home, or uncooked to take away. He was a true mentor who guided me through a profession perceived as an unfortunate necessity during that era.

CHAPTER FOUR

Blessings and Rewards

If someone asked me for one descriptive word for the people's general attitude towards the insurance sector in Saint Lucia back in the 1970s, without hesitation, my answer would be *antipathy*. I realised that a stigma was attached to the industry, especially those that provided life and medical coverage. Anyone who chose this career plan had to have immense courage to face the many rebuffs they would undoubtedly be experiencing as they went from door to door seeking business. Venturing on this path allowed me to test my inner strength. I did not expect an exemption from any rejection or negative comments. In a short time, I began to appreciate Charlo's reasons for being reluctant to offer me this position when I attended the job interview. Thankfully, this opportunity enabled me to prove my capacity to withstand the bare-knuckle treatment.

While I managed my business territory that presented a mixture of knockbacks and embraces, I feel compelled to apportion a level of credit to Mama and Papa. I was fortunate to have been rewarded with the blessings of their unblemished characters. Some prospective clients' responses included, "I don't trust this insurance business, but I will buy the policy from you only because I know your parents well. They are respectable people and would not allow you to be in this business if it was bad."

Others would say, "Your dad, Mr Ray, was my tailor; he sewed my wedding suit. He's such a good man."

My potential clients uplifted me. I remember Aunty Millie, Mama's eldest sister, said, "Hey, never worry about what people think of you. Good name stands for a damn fool."

I can say unreservedly that Mama and Papa were no damn fools. Their blessings over the years were sufficient to funnel a share to me. *What a great gift,* I thought. I realised how great it was to be kind as I received many favourable comments. The hospitality that I received was generous, with one exception. Some individuals thought that what I encountered during a sales trip in their community was amusing, but my perspective was different. I am immensely thankful to God for the blessings of guidance and the shield that protected me.

Popo's Policy

I was selling an intangible and unpopular product that would likely benefit the individuals and their families who chose to listen to my presentation. It didn't matter how long it took to explain, even if it meant revisiting; I needed to be satisfied that the potential customers understood that they were making a long-term commitment once they purchased our product. Receiving a good reception from a client was a good indication that closing the sale was likely.

My working day began with a trip to the rural area of Anse-Ger. When I arrived at Mr and Mrs Popo's home, only Mrs Popo was present. Anse-Ger is a sub-district of Micoud about two miles south of the village. Many of the people of this small community were peculiar. They had established a reputation for not being too welcoming to whoever they considered an outsider. Their preferred option for settling disputes was that whoever delivered the knockout punch was the winner. The click of a finger would be sufficient to trigger a fight. Consequently, this community had become stigmatized for being intolerant and short-tempered.

I started conversing with Mrs Popo, "Good day, ma'am."

"Good morning, sir," she replied.

Once I introduced myself, she spotted that my name sounded familiar.

"Ahh! You must be the son of Mr and Mrs Ray?" Mrs Popo asked.

"Yes, I am," I replied.

"I have known your parents for a long time, though I haven't seen your mum in a while. How is she?"

"She's well, thank you," I answered.

As I completed my sales pitch, Mrs Popo stated, "Well, I believe insurance is good, but I've heard so many bad things about it. Although things are hard, I want to buy the policy from you because of your mother."

Even though I heard this statement from some of my policyholders, I was delighted to listen to it again and would welcome hearing it as often as my clients wished to repeat it. Having gone through the sales process, I closed the deal. I said goodbye to Mrs Popo and proceeded into the community. I stopped a short distance away to engage in conversation with bystanders.

Approximately 10 minutes after I left Mrs Popo's house, I heard an altercation coming from the direction of her home. There were frantic sounds of screaming and shouting. I immediately knew something unpleasant was happening as I listened to a male voice raging on, "I need to find that man who sold you insurance!"

I had no doubt that these were Mrs Popo's screams echoing through the neighbourhood. The Creole screams, "Soo-coo! Soo-coo! Popo car chewy mwea!" (Help! Help! Popo is killing me!)

Sadly, Mrs Popo's husband was thrashing her for buying the insurance. Straight away, I thought he would save some of his rage for me, which he would try to deliver once he finished with his wife. Mr Popo wouldn't know that I never failed to recite my prayers mentally during work. I always asked God for protection against all misfortune. I recited Psalm 22 daily.

Rufus, one of the people with whom I spoke after leaving Popo's home, told me,

"Garson (man), it sounds like he's just beaten up his wife for spending his money on insurance. Popo is an aggressive guy. Be careful with this man." Rufus continued, "I think Popo will be coming for you. I'm sure he will be looking for you."

I was concerned about Mrs Popo. "I'm going back to the house to give back the money," I told Rufus.

He repeated, "I told you to be careful with this man. He can be dangerous. Just stay away from his house."

"I am worried about his wife," I replied. "I certainly don't wish further harm upon her," I explained.

Rufus recognised my concern and reassured me, "Don't worry, Garson, as long as I'm around, Popo isn't going to touch you. Just don't go on his property."

I couldn't disguise my deep sense of guilt. I was anxious. *Holy Moses*, I thought. During that period, the ideal weapon for retribution for the people of Anse-Ger was the homemade fishing gun. I was not ready to die, but if death came, I was certainly not prepared to face the cruelty of a lingering and painful one brought about by the rod of a fishing gun sticking in my gut. Having a *guardian angel* in Rufus's image at my side was reassuring.

Rufus and I made it safely to the main road before Mr Popo caught up with us. Before Popo spoke a single word, Rufus told him, "Hey Popo, if you have bad intentions towards this young man, you better think again."

In an angry tone, Popo shouted, "All I want is my money, man! My wife gave my money to this guy, and I want it back!" Popo continued, "He has to return my cash, or else I will take it from him."

It was my business to handle the situation, but Rufus was happy to take over my case; he never gave me a chance to respond. He taunted, "Come on then. I'm holding the cash; you want to take it from me?"

While Rufus was shielding me, my only thoughts were that the nearest police station was about two miles away, should the situation escalate to a fight. Popo was a much older man who would have been no match for Rufus if the issue spiralled into throwing punches. It was amazing that a guy I had met for the first time was kind enough to defend me. Rufus did an excellent job by shifting Popo's attention firmly to him. Popo forgot his initial problem as the argument between him and Rufus turned into one about who would throw more blows.

The spectators, hankering for some action, cheered them on. The heated exchanges ended, and Popo quietly walked away to his home. There was disbelief among those present when they discovered that Rufus and I had never met before this incident. Later, some bystanders with whom I was acquainted informed me that Rufus, my newfound friend, had a temperament equal to Popo's; people from the community also feared him. Thankfully, this episode ended without combat.

To avoid having history repeat itself, I steered clear of Anse-Ger. This experience served as a further testament to my faith in my spiritual shield. It was one more hurdle I overcame through the power of prayers.

My Baby Had No Nose

Despite the intense competition, I continued making progress at work. The challenges continued but did not stop my awards from rolling in during the social events organized by our company. I cheerfully welcomed the recognition in many areas on the island where I worked.

Towards the end of my first year of employment, I was well-positioned to begin the search for my first car. Coincidentally, one of my colleagues, Gregory, owned what would become my prized possession. Gregory and I discussed the possibility of my eventual purchase of his blue Austin Mini. I knew nothing about the mechanics of vehicles. Therefore, I decided to take someone with me to inspect the car; if he gave me the go-ahead, I would purchase it.

My friend Albert, two years older than me, visited our home daily. Though he was my friend, he also tried to make his way into courting Silvie. With Mama around, that was no easy task. His daily greeting was, "Good day, Ma Ray."

"Good day, Albert. How are you?" Mama replied. Unfailingly, his response was:

"I'm all right, Ma Ray. I'm just sorts of passing."

Well, Albert had unknowingly created a new name for himself. We called him "Sorts of Passing," which stuck as his nickname.

Albert worked part-time learning at his brother's garage, so I assumed he had a fair knowledge of vehicles. He should have known a thing or two about cars, and I allowed him to prove the level of his competence. I inspected the beautiful 7-year-old blue vehicle, looking for something specific, but I had no idea. Albert's role was to guide me. He was to check the car and help me negotiate the price. Upon his advice, I agreed to pay Gregory EC$2,800.00, approximately US$1,030.00, for the car. This vehicle would be my reward for passing my driver's test on the first try in August 1974.

In early 1975, I paid for what was to become my first genuine possession. After completing the transaction, Albert and I got into the car and headed east to our village. Mama, Silvie, and Phil were anxiously waiting. For the Rosemond family, owning a car was a huge deal. The villagers perceived this possession as one more step up the social ladder and a nudge up the respectability scale. The neighbours came over to view my prized property.

Our relatives were surprised when they heard the news. As expected, Mama, with her usual quick observation and witty character, commented:

"What kind of a car is this?"

As we gazed at each other, Mama's question instantly brought a gloomy look to Albert's face. "It's an Austin Mini?" I replied cheerfully.

"Why did you and Albert buy a car without a nose?"

We all stared blankly at each other, wondering about Mama's statement. "What do you mean?" I asked.

Pointing to the missing grill on my beautiful Mini, "There, that's what I'm talking about!" Mama replied.

Ahhh, what a party pooper! I thought. My Mini had no grill, so I got it at a discounted price from Gregory. Nevertheless, I was not concerned about the missing grill. I was more concerned that Mama was fussing about it. If no one had noticed before, she, indeed, had highlighted it.

"You should not have agreed to buy this car even at a discounted price," Mama quipped. My trusted friend, Albert, immediately and sheepishly said goodbye, escaping the deafening silence as he walked away.

Aww! My mother's comments did not dampen my love for her. Mama was just too perfect. She never refused my offer to drive her wherever she wanted. Sometimes, she gleefully asked for my *chauffeuring service.* Silvie and Phil were never concerned about my car not having a nose. They welcomed the convenience of getting a lift from me rather than using public transport. Among those of my age group in the village, I was the only car owner and the most self-sufficient as I continued to accelerate my progress at work.

Jealousy Breeds Obeah

My confidence grew stronger as I never stopped turning to Psalm 47, which I read seven times daily, and Psalm 65. My dedication paid off when I repeatedly achieved my sales targets. I kept my Austin Mini for over a year, then decided it was time to change. I was looking forward to the day I would trade in my car for a better model—one with a *nose*. With my successful application for finance from the bank, I part-exchanged my Mini for a brand-new white Chrysler Avenger. This second car was my great pride and joy. Sure enough, Mama inspected the vehicle but found nothing wrong this time. I owned a brand-new car at age 19, making me the first person in our district to earn this accomplishment at this young age.

Notably, the *exclusive* group of people in the community with a vehicle at the time were the farmers who owned the most extensive banana plantations and a few government employees with modest incomes. Sadly, in Saint Lucia, many did not view progress as a reason for celebration. Instead, they saw it as a cause for resentment. Many had perceived my position as being aligned to the ranks of a *premier club*. So, was I unwittingly sowing the seed of displeasure through my advancement?

I was sure of one thing. My experiences up until that point had served to help me become more conscious of my surroundings. Before driving to work, I carried out routine checks on my vehicle. I looked for deflated tires, depleted brake fluid, oil leaks, and radiator water. Of course, there was no "Check Engine" light at the time; therefore, I had to carry out those precautionary checks physically. While going through the routine one morning, I opened my new radiator to check the water level. "Oh damn!" I shouted as I spontaneously pulled away from the vehicle. I was dismayed when a colony of black ants suddenly sprang out of the radiator. It was a shocking and inexplicable incident. I frantically ran to the house, asking for someone, anyone, to come and witness what had happened. Mama, Silvie and Phil rushed towards the vehicle, yelling, "What's going on? What's happening out there?"

Within a split second, all the ants had disappeared without a trace. The radiator was empty, and there was not a drop of water on the ground below. I had carried out the same checks religiously every other morning before driving off to work but I'd never imagined I'd find ants drinking a filled-up radiator.

The crowd that the event drew found it impossible to believe. I filled up the radiator to confirm if there was a leak; there was none. Mama informed Cousin Monnor, who lived a few doors away. He was a God-fearing man and a well-respected community member many turned to for advice. Like the rest of us, Cousin Monnor was baffled, and he remarked,

"In our part of the world, boys don't own cars."

I didn't fully understand his meaning at the time because Cousin Monnor often spoke in riddles when discussing unusual circumstances. We suspected that seeing a brand-new car belonging to the Rosemond household would not be a welcome sight for some community members. Among my colleagues in our firm's Southern branch, my much older mentors Charlo, Clint and Hunter were the only others who owned a car. We asked Cousin Monnor to clarify, but before he did, he asked me, "Are you wearing a lucky charm?"

"No, Cuz, I'm not," I answered.

With folded arms and a concerned look, Cousin Monnor said, "You see, Cuz, it's right to believe in the power of prayer, but God has also taught us to act within the boundaries of spirituality to safeguard ourselves. I will provide you with a lucky charm which you should always wear." I had never worn a talisman because I thought of it as a symbol inconsistent with my Christian principles.

Therefore, I thought charms were more associated with conjuring up opposing forces. I had always relied on my total allegiance to God through the recital of prayers. Cousin Monnor reassured me, "You don't have to worry, a powerful prayer is inside the pouch."

I was once again convinced that there was divine intervention. Seeing the ants and discovering the emptied water supply before setting off on what could have been a deadly journey was yet another realisation of how protected I was; from which I drew great comfort. My position perfectly symbolized the term *success breeds jealousy* and without reservation, I feel compelled to say that envy gives rise to Obeah on our 238-square-mile island.

Mama's First Plane Ride

At the start of 1975, Mama began planning her first holiday to England. She was hoping to be away on a well-deserved break for six months. The incident of ants in my car's radiator raised Mama's anxiety about our safety during her absence. She repeatedly reminded us to be vigilant and not forget to pray. Mama was no prophet, but somehow, she spoke as though she sensed some surprise heading in our direction; she was correct.

However, the situation was quite different; it was Silvie's turn to break the news. Silvie told Mama she was expecting a baby. Holy Moley! That was some luck! We only imagined how Mama would have reacted if this news had come about while she was in England. Oh yes! She would have been seething. The likelihood was that Mama would have criticized me and Phil for "Not keeping an eye on Silvie." How unfair!

Phil and I asked ourselves jokingly, "When and how did Silvie get away?" Phil was sharp-witted when he kidded, "Come on, Steve, haven't you heard of the saying, *where there's a will, there's a way?*" We laughed. The irony was that this happened even though Mama kept a firm grip on Silvie.

Saint Lucian society, back then, did not embrace teenage pregnancy or pregnancy out of wedlock. The older generation maintained conservative views on such matters because of traditional Christian principles. The widespread notion was that such conditions brought great dishonour to the family; it was a complete break from convention. Generally, the way out was marriage with the consent of the two sets of parents. Marriage, however, was not in the cards for Silvie. As far as Silvie was concerned, this cloud's silver lining was that Mama would be approximately four thousand miles away in London during most of her pregnancy, so she would not be facing what would undoubtedly be daily criticism. Papa Ray had planned Mama's holiday long before Silvie's announcement, but coincidentally, Mama would return in time for the baby's birth.

We promised Mama that we would be okay. We encouraged her to relax, enjoy her warranted break, and return home safely. In the meantime, Mama passed on the mantle to our 70+-year-old grandmother, Helena, whom we affectionately called Maam. While Silvie, Phil, and I were at home, Maam would continue to live at her house, but we would visit each other daily. Essentially, this would be our first taste of *independence*.

Maam's Crab and Callaloo

Maam was a calm, easy-going grandmother who adored a life with her twenty-one grandchildren even though the older ones were living in the UK and Canada. Sunday was the day we spent the most time with her. It worked out well for us because this was when she cooked her exceptional cuisine. From childhood, we always enjoyed our grandmother's cooking more than our mother's. Maam used her clay pot to cook her meals on firewood. We thought the clay pot added that unique aroma which glided through her home, leaving clues as to the simmering ingredients inside.

We would arrive at Maam's gate and immediately know when she was preparing our favourite mouth-watering crab and callaloo dish. Her scrumptious creole recipe included coconut milk, which we call Maapaa in Creole. Maapaa is made from dried, grated coconuts soaked, squeezed, and sifted to extract the milk. She added a selection of local herbs, young leaves from the dasheen plant, yams, and fresh green peas from her garden. Maam always cooked extra food because she knew her grandchildren loved her cooking, and they would surely stop by for their share. She spoke with a beautiful, gentle tone, mainly in Creole, because putting long sentences together in English was beyond her.

Funnily enough, she mixed English with Creole whenever we misbehaved, saying, "Stephen, par fer sar (don't do that) you blasted more-cos."

Having thought about it, I don't know what a "blasted more-cos" is; I guess Maam made it up. Even though none of us knew what it meant, we found it highly comical to repeat the expression at each other. Maam always had something to offer, and I seldom rejected it.

With her distinctive Creole accent, she would say to me, "A-A, Stephen, you're there, my child. Ahhh, I don't have much to give you today, but you can have some food." She would pick guavas from her tree, hand two or three over to me, and say, "There you are, my child, have a guava."

Sometimes, while she gently passed her hand under my chin, she would say in a loving, tender, and caring voice, "Awwe! Look at *you*, such *handsome* young man, but you sweet man, *empty* pocket!"

Maam used many funny expressions that always made us laugh. Upon leaving, she would say in the nicest possible way, "You are going my child? Poor jab... (poor devil) ...here you are. Take these five cents to put in your pocket."

Of course, even at that time, five cents would not buy much for a young man, but I cherished the gesture. The caring sentiments that she expressed mattered the most. Maam consistently demonstrated her love in some way towards all her grandchildren. She did her best to ensure we were fine, and we did our best to make her happy in return.

Our biggest concern was Silvie's pregnancy. How would we cope in a worst-case scenario? What support would Maam be able to provide in the event of an early birth? The time flew by, Mama's holiday was over, and in December of 1975, she was on her flight back to Saint Lucia. Would Mama's six-month stay in England have any physical, mental, or other impacts on us? Indeed, we did not expect any surprises after a short, six-month holiday.

Where Was Mama

The family, including Maam, waited eagerly to welcome Mama back home, but while no one could imagine what it would be, we all agreed that something would cause her to be unhappy upon her arrival. We knew our mum had an eye for perfection; she left no room for error. We all knew the time her flight was due to arrive, so we prepared for her. The home was immaculate after we cleaned up, beds made up, dinner ready, and chairs dusted. Predictably, Silvie's appearance had changed from how it had looked before Mama left. My only Uncle in Saint Lucia, Ted, was always available, and he too looked forward to welcoming his youngest sister, Mama.

Uncle Ted and I decided to stop for a drink at a nearby bar before meeting Mama at the airport; we did so while keeping an eye on the time. I had not been drinking alcohol very long, so in the past, after trying some samples, I chose whiskey—Uncle picked the same, so we sipped a little.

We eventually made our way to Hewanorra International Airport. Upon arrival, we stood in the waiting area for about one and a half hours until all the passengers had left, but we saw no sign of Mama. We wondered whether the immigration or customs department had delayed her exit.

"There are no more passengers in there," shouted an airport worker as he saw us waiting. Mama failed to show up. We were puzzled. Did she get on the wrong flight? We asked each other. Uncle and I kept wracking our brains about Mama's possible whereabouts.

Since there were no more arriving passengers, we drove to a family friend in our village to call our folks back in England, informing them that Mama had not arrived. Mary-Anne confirmed that Mama had departed on the scheduled flight, and she should have arrived in Saint Lucia. Even though Uncle and I panicked, he certainly thought the incident was worth making fun of when he said jokingly,

"I wonder if your mother accidentally opened the cabin door thinking she was heading to the toilet but landed in the sea instead!"

As serious as the matter was, I saw the funny side; it was ridiculously amusing. We immediately drove back to the airport, hoping Mama would be waiting, but it was too late. Fortunately, some taxi drivers at the airport knew my family. One of the drivers commented, "Stephen, you guys are very late. Your mum left in a taxi. Boy, she ain't gonna like that." It was evident Sylvester knew my mother well.

"What! A taxi? Taxis cost money," I exclaimed.

Without a doubt, Mama would not be pleased, and rightly so. Why would anyone blame her? Oh, what a nightmare. But why did we not see my mum at the airport? We continued asking each other. The question of getting drunk on one shot of whiskey? Not possible.

Not only did we look like the legendary comedians *Laurel and Hardy*, but we sounded like them, too. "Oh, Uncle, what a mess you got me into."

I wished I had a siren to place on my car as we drove back!

We finally arrived home. Silvie heard the screeching sound of my car pulling up, at which point she came to the door with a serious facial expression.

"Where on earth have you been?" she whispered tensely.

"We didn't see Mama at the airport, so we went back and double-checked," I responded.

"Mama is inside, and she's fuming," Silvie said.

I heard Mama's voice coming from the bedroom as we slowly crept into the house. A woman immediately walked out of the room and asked in a not-so-pleasant tone, "Where have you two been?"

"Hello, Mama!" I replied. *Holy Mackerel!* I thought.

"This was the same person I saw at the airport!" Uncle Ted said. "No wonder we missed her."

"But Mama, you look so different!" I replied.

I had never seen Mama wearing a wig before; at that time, wigs were not the typical attire. Within six months, Mama had transformed her appearance. She looked like someone had pumped her up, and this funny-looking wig on her head didn't help. If the Saint Lucia police were looking for Mama, this would have been a perfect disguise. I didn't recognize my own mother. Uncle was unable to identify his inflated little sister. Seriously, it was just hilarious. Understandably, Mama never managed to see the funny side of this confusion.

Now that she had settled down from her holiday, Mama turned her attention to Silvie, but this time, on a positive note. She came to terms with Silvie's pregnancy and was looking forward to the birth of her new grandchild as we welcomed the beginning of 1976. In February, Silvie gave birth to a beautiful daughter, Cindy.

She was welcomed into the family not as a niece but as our last sibling. Mama joyfully embraced Cindy more as her last daughter rather than as a granddaughter. She was a bundle of joy that became Silvie's only child and the most significant event in her life. Life returned to normal, and

I continued making strides at work when the firm expanded my work territory. I also established my first serious relationship, with Lynn.

Breaking with Tradition

Lynn and I shared similar backgrounds. She came from the southern coast of Saint Lucia in the village of Laborie. Her family enjoyed great respect and was of good standing in their community. Like my family, they were devoutly Catholic and conservative. Lynn was tall, slim, and charming, with a dazzling smile.

Most importantly, my parents and the rest of my family accepted her openly, just as her family welcomed me. Lynn worked at the capital city's office for the same insurance firm where I worked. She was bright and well-grounded. Our relationship gradually developed, but it had been no more than a year before the subject of marriage was floating around. Those around us thought we looked more like a married couple. A young bride and groom were what our parents would have liked us to be.

Lynn's dad, Mr Frans, had what I describe as a forthright conversation with me, kind of a future father-son-in-law chat during which he posed the question, "Stephen, why have you not spoken of marriage?"

I responded to Mr Frans: "Well, Lynn and I have never spoken of marriage. So neither of us is making such plans."

"If you decide to marry Lynn," Mr Frans responded, "I will give you sufficient land upon which you would build your home."

"I appreciate your kind gesture, Mr Frans. I understand, but respectfully, I'd rather wait until I am able to acquire our own," was my reply.

Mr Frans acknowledged that my simple reason for declining his offer was valid when he said, "I understand and respect your decision, Stephen, and it is good when a man is prepared to work to achieve his own. However, this would have been my gift to Lynn and you."

There was a good rapport between Mr Frans and me, and I thanked him for his understanding. While I saw nothing inappropriate about accepting a gift from Lynn's dad, I wanted to steer clear of any resemblance of even a tinge of enticement or incentive for my union with Lynn. Furthermore, I firmly believe in working diligently to achieve my goal. It is my opinion that self-determination generates feelings of accomplishment, contentment, self-esteem, and motivation. I was fond of Lynn but didn't think the time was right for the sacrament of marriage; I knew only Lynn and I would have to decide on mutual terms.

Nevertheless, Lynn's parents decided it was time to meet my family. By the beginning of 1977, Papa Ray had retired from England and was back in Saint Lucia permanently. I told my parents about Lynn's family wishing to meet them. They both agreed, and I confirmed the meeting with Lynn.

To the older folks, lengthy courting before marriage was not usually an acceptable custom. During courtship, people would generally perceive the formal introduction or meeting of the two families to be the first step towards matrimony. The meeting was not my idea, so I was not at ease while my family waited for my *future in-laws* that Sunday afternoon.

A Quickie Marriage in the Making

Mama and Papa seemed relaxed to entertain the marriage conversation as they repeatedly asked me about the subject. I knew they would not have objected to the idea. I was not looking forward to this *general* getting-to-know-the-family meeting. Furthermore, Mama was always candid during conversations. As she often expressed her opinion forthrightly, I was concerned that she would give the wrong impression. Papa passively sat while waiting in anticipation.

Okay, whiskey ready? Check. Are water and soft beverages ready? Check. Are snacks ready? Check. Is the house spotless? Immaculate. I had to create the absolute best impression, and I needed no one putting a spanner in the works. Are we all ready? All done. We had the scene set.

We knew Lynn had a large family, but we did not expect a turnout exceeding ten guests. With the arrival of sixteen, the gathering looked more like an engagement party without the rings. We hadn't prepared for that many visitors. We didn't think our whisky and beer would be sufficient. We worried about not having enough of anything to entertain everyone. We all started scrambling for chairs and benches.

Papa asked entertainingly, with his fast speaking tone, and in creole, "Sar-key motorcade sala? Campton car v-nee e-c-ah too e-sam." (Whose motorcade is this? Mr Campton is coming here; also, it seems.) Mr Campton was our Chief Minister at the time. Who would have blamed Papa for thinking that the Chief Minister of Saint Lucia was on his way to Micoud and was stopping by for a quick *cup-a-tea*?

Mama was calm when she commented, "Why did you not tell us that all the family was coming over so we could have prepared better for the occasion?"

During the conversation, my dad tried putting me on the spot by asking me in Creole, "So, key sar ou nee poo dee?" (So, what do you have to say?). I guess he believed that as the *future groom*, I should give a speech. I knew that Lynn was not expecting a proposal from me, so in response, respectfully, I applied the KISS acronym, *Keep It Short and Sweet.*

"There's not much I can say now, Papa, apart from I am not ready for marriage yet."

Surprisingly, no one reacted to my comments. There was silence for about forty-five seconds before Papa started a new discussion. The conversation continued for approximately one more hour, and our guests said their goodbyes. We were relieved that our concerns about our level of preparation were needless.

CHAPTER FIVE

Responsibilities, Expectations, and Adversity

Now that I had expressed my position on the wedding idea, I guessed I had brought the topic to a close. Hopefully, I had removed any doubt or anticipation about the subject. Immediately after, the guilt for not meeting the guests' expectations lingered. Nevertheless, the hospitality I received from Lynn's family during my visits was no less. Occasionally, Papa made those trips with me, which the family perceived as further approval of our relationship.

Papa's journey to Labourie was entertainment for him in a different setting away from the usual local environment, where I often drove him and Uncle Ted on Sundays. Being in a position to entertain these two senior citizens was one that I thoroughly enjoyed. Inevitably, there were instances when our opinions differed because of the generation gap.

Nevertheless, I was able to understand life from their perspective. I considered the occasions with them as mentoring sessions during which they offered much guidance while respecting my opinions. We three looked forward to these outings, except for Mama and Uncle Ted's wife, Miss May, who was not always amused when I returned their husbands. Both men beamed with satisfaction after a few hours of *joyriding*, good conversation with their mates, and of course, with good conversation came snacks and beverages. My closeness to Uncle Ted earned me the Creole nickname from his wife, "Tee-Papa" (Little Papa), which I welcomed as a great compliment. It was an honour for my aunt to consider me *a father to my dad and uncle.*

Even though Papa had returned from England, I continued my supporting role at home as usual. One of my chosen tasks was teaching Phil how to drive. Once he obtained his driver's license, I allowed him to move the family around whenever I was unavailable. Sharing my car with Phil was another way of demonstrating our unity, bond, care, and trust in him. Whenever the family visited from England, I would have the pleasure of being their island-wide tour guide. Chauffeuring them around was not a chore; we were family, and I firmly believed that was a way to build and strengthen our relationship. From time to time, I would allow them to use my vehicle while I hitchhiked or used public transportation. I cared about my family, so I assisted them and provided support without hesitation.

Kindness or Foolishness

I was committed to contributing to my relatives' well-being, though my assistance was not limited to relations. There were neighbours, colleagues, and community members, too. It was my privilege to assist those less fortunate than me or those who asked for my assistance in any way possible. The thought of gifts or rewards in return for my support never came to mind. Among the expressions Mama used, the one that stuck with me was, "If you do good, good will follow you." I also believe that the good or bad result of one's actions would not necessarily be immediate. Neither would it inevitably affect those involved directly with the original act. I substantiated this theory by referring to my parent's efforts that positively impacted me at the insurance company.

I was always in demand, and I made time for everyone. Party invitations came, and so did my first godchild. It was a pleasure to accept a request to be a real godfather for the first time. This first special privilege was soon followed by a second and a third. Mama brought it to my attention when she observed that whenever I responded to someone's request, my answer never included the words, "No, I can't."

As a young man, and perhaps in a naive way too, I enjoyed the attention. I was also eager to demonstrate my *gradual independence.* My use of the word "gradual" meant Mama was still in charge. Even though I had a key to our home, I was always conscious of her noticing when I came in from a night out of entertainment. I tip-toed slowly through the front door and into the sitting room. As I made my way towards my bedroom, which I shared with Phil, I would hear the sudden agitated voice coming from Mama's room.

"Stephen, where have you come from at this time of the night? You mean that's the time you're coming in?" I would not respond.

Often, the time to which she was referring was before midnight. Phil and I would listen to Mama's grumble, then chatted and giggled as we mimicked her.

My behaviour was no different from the average young adult aged 18 to 21, with weekend nights out of fun. Papa Ray became increasingly concerned by my growing popularity. He cautioned me about the number of people who came home asking for me. Consequently, Papa asked if I had switched my profession to being a counsellor or an advisor. He was disturbed that my kindness was bordering on silliness. Papa always wished me well, and his advice on this occasion was poignant. He suggested that I reduce the level or cease my social activities altogether; otherwise, there might be consequences.

Stout and Ganja – A Lethal Combination

There was no question about my understanding of differentiating between business and pleasure. I knew when it was time for work and when it was time for fun. I tried to uphold the sound principles I learned from home, school and work, and community members continued to view me as the young priest who was never ordained; they seemed not to have erased the idea from their minds. However, not long after my father's advice, I saw the writing on the wall.

I was fortunate to be surrounded by a group of buddies with whom I shared a similar background and never got into trouble with the law. We did the usual things young men would do purely for experiments spurred on by curiosity. One Friday evening, I drove with Kennedy, Paul, Greg and Josh, my closest chums, to one of our favourite entertainment nightspots approximately four miles from our village. The trendy drink for adolescents at the time was the 330ml bottled stout, so we drank a few that night. Consuming the alcoholic beverage alone was sufficient to give us the high we sought. However, we still went one step further, pushing our luck. In that era, the talk of anyone using illegal drugs was considered abhorrent.

Known for it particularly high potency at the time, our society had firmly associated marijuana, solely with the Rastafarian movement. Cannabis led to addiction resulting in disturbing psychosis in a few unfortunate locals, so it was viewed as a menacing substance. Unfortunately, the St Lucian community's lack of understanding of that religion's ideology led to derision—all sections of our society, including law enforcement, were hostile towards Rastafarians. Without any concern of such stigmatism and the risk of someone alerting the police, my friends and I decided to experiment with two *joints* of ganja that Paul, to our surprise, pulled out from his pocket. None of us asked about his sources, and neither was there any reluctance on our part to use the drug. For the first try in a dark spot away from the crowds, our group of five lit up and started to smoke. Until this moment, the thought of using cannabis had never crossed my mind. The outcome of sampling the concoction of stout and weed was that the knowledge I gained helped me understand the perils of using dope.

By consuming that cocktail, my senses were left *extraordinary*. I was disoriented. My consciousness of events as they were happening around me no longer existed, and I was desperate to return home. Kennedy also experienced the same bizarre and scary feeling. We both had lost our grip on reality.

Ignoring the advice of our other companions, Kennedy and I got into my vehicle and drove away. I was moving without a sense of direction; my condition was some strange mode of imagination or hallucination. Without control, I steered in reverse gear for four miles on winding roads, up and down hills, until we arrived in the village. Kennedy was silent for the entire journey; the following day, he had no recollection of what had happened. My exposure to ganja generated a sensation that seemed more like a bad dream. I could not answer or explain how I managed to drive back safely other than through spiritual intervention, which I praise and am grateful for. My friends and I heeded this perilous adventure and promised never to repeat it; so far, I have kept this promise, making this dreadful night the only time I used illicit drugs. Instead, I stuck with *the lesser of two evils,* cigarettes, eventually increasing the number I smoked to twenty a day. Cigarette smoking was a *trendy* habit I adopted from my work colleagues.

Trying out drugs reinforced my understanding of the possible undesirable effects of our decisions, whether through our own accord, pure enticement, or the power of influence. While I have previously described some benefits we can acquire by keeping on the right track, we must not allow complacency to set in by losing focus because Lucifer never rests; he is the king of mischief. Thankfully, I set aside the distraction and turned my attention back to lawful business.

The World of Obeah?

Are you astonished that someone with unwavering faith would endure what seemed like constant bewilderment? Well, that is the Devil's approach. He sows doubt in our minds to question God's power. Every soul matters to Satan, as he relentlessly attempts to compete with God. I agree that some situations we encounter can derive from our line of thought and emotions. For example, sometimes, we turn solvable situations into problems because of our approach to managing such conditions, only to inflict damage upon ourselves. There are instances when we tend to think deeply about events to the extent that we subconsciously conjure negative energy that consumes us through our imagination. Other deeds can also be so compelling that they are impossible to understand; they are simply inexplicable.

In my case, the intimidating episodes were unambiguous. My family was becoming weary from the frequency of events we faced. Oh how we wished Satan would take a break! He seemed determined to destroy our lives. However, we were mindful that emotions would not provide answers to managing our circumstances. It was, therefore, essential for us to remain calm and steadfast irrespective of our plight. It was through willpower that the boost of courage came. Inevitably, our situation turned into a *battle of wills*, and such conflicts were not for the timid.

The time was approaching 5 a.m. and the crowing cockerels began their calling. With a mighty yawn came the thought of *how frustrating*! It was time to wake up and start my day with the recital of my prayers, in which I thanked the Lord for allowing me to see the beginning of a new day. Coming from a devout Catholic family, my participation in the church as an altar server meant attending the 6:30 a.m. service daily.

The delightful smell of the fresh local coffee beans brewing in the coffee pot was a sure way of knowing that Mama Ray was already up. At nine years old, I was too young to have coffee, so I would have the bush tea Mama prepared from fresh herbs and leaves from various fruit trees before heading for the outdoor bathroom. The burning sensation on my back kicked in immediately as the chilled water I poured over my head from the patched-up galvanised bathtub using a plastic bowl streamed down my body. "Ouch! Ouch!" I groaned in discomfort. Thinking I was complaining about the cold water as I often did, Mama yelled from the kitchen 10ft away:

"Stephen, what is wrong with you? Stop keeping this noise."

"No, Mama, it's my back. I think I have cuts on my back."

I finished showering and went into my room. Mama came across to investigate. "Let me see your back," she asked. I turned around with my towel wrapped around my waist. "What have you done to yourself? How did you manage to scratch yourself like this?" I knew I couldn't have inflicted the abrasions Mama saw—three vertical parallel stinging marks to the centre of my back. Mama looked puzzled. "Come on, let's rub it with oil; it will soothe the burning," she suggested. As Mama dabbed the cuts using cotton wool with her homemade coconut oil, I recalled:

"Mama, this is the second time I've woken up with three scratches on me. The first time I noticed, they were on my right thigh some weeks ago, but I ignored it."

"Why didn't you say anything?" Mama asked.

"I just ignored it because I thought I may have scratched myself," I replied.

"Stephen," Mama responded. "It is possible that you could have scratched your back while fast asleep?"

With confidence, I retorted. "But Mama, I never grow fingernails beyond the tip of my fingers. How is it possible that I scratched myself so severely?

For what reason would I inflict these cuts on my body? And how would I make those lines so straight on each occasion? How would I place those marks near the middle of my back?"

These were all the questions I asked. Phil and I slept on the same bed, yet he was always unscathed. Was he the one inflicting those marks on me? I wouldn't bet on it.

I wondered why Mama didn't dwell on the subject. I couldn't help thinking this might be the beginning of something sinister as I had often heard conversations among the villagers on the issue of black magic. My siblings and I knew Mama withheld her true feelings of concern to avoid alarming us. We believed the only possible explanation was one of malicious intent. I had experienced this evilness irregularly for approximately four months before Mama informed Cousin Monnor of my anxiety—he later confirmed that these were the signs of witchcraft. He advised Mama:

"Cuz, I know of your strong faith, and you must continue to be courageous. You must understand that Satan never gives up, so you must continue to fight for as long as it takes. The Bible serves as a poison to those evil spirits, so I suggest you leave your Bible open alongside your bed once you have finished your nightly prayers."

Mama took this simple advice, and sure enough, my scratches disappeared. These incidents reignited our fears from the past when one of our older brothers faced his battles.

God Always Prevails

The demonic rituals of black magic were widespread on the island. This satanic practice brought terror in the dark to the innocent.

I was about seven years old, and I remember the occasions when the terrifying sound from John, who would have been eleven, would awaken Mama, Joe, Silvie, myself, and Phil in the dark of night.

"Mama! Mama!" Came the desperate cry, "I see a goat - I see a goat!"

Mama would rush to the bedroom where Joe, John, me and Phil slept—Phil and I slept on the floor. Silvie always slept in Mama's bed.

"Where is it? Where is it? Where is the goat?" Mama would ask.

"There, Mama, over there. It's a goat," John would cry out.

These events would last for about one minute, and then John would stop. He was the only one who ever saw the goat.

John's experience would leave us all shaking with fear while Mama would reach out for a bottle of holy water she obtained from the church and stored in her bedroom. Our mum would pour some of this water into her hands and sprinkle it throughout the house as she murmured a prayer before returning to bed.

Our Shocking Discovery

Whenever the Angel of Death attempted to unleash evil on our family, the goodness of the Holy Spirit conquered. God would allow us to go through the anguish not only to witness the level of our conviction in his power but also to remind us of the depravity in our midst. But he always provided the answers at the right moment; he always preserved us.

One morning, Silvie made a strange discovery while cleaning the kitchen cabinets. She noticed two tins of powdered chocolate, one loosely covered in the groceries. "Oh!" Silvie exclaimed. "Mama bought another tin of chocolate!"

Having two containers of chocolate wasn't typical, so her natural reaction was to check the contents of both cans to determine why Mama had bought a second while there was a substantial amount left in the other. We knew the extra tin had not been there for long because no one else had noticed it. By gently shaking the cans, Silvie realised the contents of one shook differently from the powdery shake. Shockingly, upon opening, she discovered a live frog inside; it was sickening.

Silvie was horrified as she shouted, "Mama! There's a frog in the chocolate tin!"

"What are you talking about?" Mama replied.

Immediately, Phil, Mama and I hurriedly went to the kitchen, and there we saw a sizeable live frog inside a 1.9kg chocolate tin, just as Silvie exclaimed. Mama's reaction was calm like it was just another day with yet another issue. Phil, Silvie, and I stared at each other with amazement as if to wonder what Mama would do. Mama kept the frog in its position, loosely covered but placed it outside the house. Soon afterwards, Mama contacted Mr Lloyd, an esteemed family friend and godfather of her eldest son who died in infancy, to seek his advice. Mr Lloyd always referred to Mama as Marcoomare, which is the term used by the godparents of a child to address the mother and godmother of the sponsored child, while Mama addressed him as Compare, meaning the father and godfather of the child.

"Marcoomare," Mr Lloyd whispered, "A frog in a tin? That is a dangerous sign. You must be careful how you dispose of that frog because frogs are associated with fire in the world of obeah." He continued, "Whoever placed the frog in your kitchen did so to make a fire that will engulf your home look like an accident."

"Fire?" Mama anxiously responded. "But Compare, how do we deal with this?"

Mr Lloyd explained, "Marcoomare, you must keep the frog in the tin just as you found it. Take it to the sea as soon as possible, where you will meditate for a few minutes in your special prayer. If you have a small bible, take it, and quietly recite Psalm 55. Close the tin tightly so that it does not open. Count to the third wave, then throw the container immediately into that wave. You should return home without stopping on the way or looking back. If you do as I have told you, you will know who placed the frog in your kitchen."

"But how will I know, Compare?" Mama asked.

Mr Lloyd repeated, "Marcoomare, there will be a huge blaze within three days, which will be impossible to control. If you do just as I told you, the owner of that destroyed property is the person responsible."

"Compare," Mama replied. "This sounds dangerous. By doing this, I will condemn myself to a life of guilt. God will allow us to discover the evil our enemy had intended against us, but to be responsible for someone's demise goes against my faith that God is my protector."

Mr Lloyd clarified. "Marcoomare, God has blessed us with the gifts of knowledge and wisdom to defend and protect ourselves. God will only punish you if you misuse his gifts."

Mama took the advice, and as her usual companion, I went with her to the sea. We safely positioned ourselves on the cliff out of the view of potential onlookers. Mama silently bowed her head for two minutes in prayer, then opened her Bible to read Psalm 55. After she completed the reading, she counted the giant waves that bashed ferociously against the rugged rocks below.

Micoud Coastline

Upon the third wave, Mama tossed the tin into the ocean and returned home. This experience was nerve-wracking. For no specific reason, Mama and I did not communicate after she dealt with the frog. We talked about the event only when we arrived home; it was an eerie feeling while we nervously waited to find out what would happen. The family never discussed this matter with anyone.

On Sunday, the third day, we were all on edge, expecting to hear of a disaster in the village. The day was over, and nothing had happened. Just before bedtime that evening at about 8:30 p.m., suddenly, we heard a commotion a few blocks away and screams of, "D-fay! D-fay! Kai Jacob pwee D-fay!" (Fire! Fire! Jacob's house is on fire!)

We should not have been surprised, but we froze; we simply stared at each other, dumbstruck. We waited at the front door to listen to the reports as the event unfolded. Those who witnessed the incident spoke of the intensity and speed of the destruction of the wooden structure. The flames beat back the villagers who attempted to put out the blaze, so the building turned to ashes before the fire engines reached. The owner, who lived alone, was not home when it started, but later arrived on the scene.

What had happened shook the village because it was unusual; we seldom heard of a house fire on the island, let alone in our district. The conversation continued among the villagers for many days, including rumours of a lighted candle causing the blaze. We heard no one talk about Jacob's account of how the fire might have started, but the neighbours told us he was traumatized. Jacob was a middle-aged gravedigger who lived opposite the village cemetery and was the best friend of Mama's fiercest opponent. We never expressed feelings or opinions about the matter openly, but without reluctance, I say we had no compassion, nor was it a time to rejoice. In our usual nightly gathering for prayer before bedtime, we thanked God for his protection and asked for his mercy the night after.

Mama discussed the matter with Mr Lloyd the following day, but he was not surprised, saying, "Mew tay de-ou sa tay cai fet, Marcoomare." (I told you this would happen, Marcoomare). "Ou ne poo continay pway-diay san dooboot, Marcoomare, paski Bondiea ca too-jou pwey-zer-veou." (You must continue to pray non-stop Marcoomare because God is always protecting you).

"Merci an-pil Compare, merci (Thank you very much, Compare, thank you)," Mama replied.

We were confident that we would find peace after this episode. We seldom saw or heard any more of Jacob, although we wished he would have understood that you can get severely burnt when you play with fire. We hoped he would have reflected and, in doing so, realise that we all have a choice in whom we serve. We chose the Almighty Father, and with the knowledge that we gained through his powers, we believe we were able to destroy the work of Satan. While Satan was hell-bent on our destruction, our tenacity to stand firm and defeat the beast was more powerful. God has always prevailed; he is our Shield.

Down but Standing

The beauty of choosing Christ as our Saviour is that we know he will never let us down; he will never fail us because the power of God is unparalleled. We must understand that the blessings we obtain from the Immortal Being are slow; hence, we must realise that he works on his time. Therefore, we must endure if we choose this route. It can be tempting to question God's supremacy or even his being. We let our guard down due to constraints; sometimes, we are too busy.

I consider these notions to be Satan's distractions. Giving in to disturbances means allowing ourselves to become the devil's instrument. He would be sowing the seeds of doubt about God's authority in our minds. Such miscalculations enable Satan to exploit our lack of faith. As I see it, through his immense powers and trickery, the devil will simultaneously provide the mirage of quick solutions for the same obstacles he creates. Accept his remedy, and you become entangled in his web.

I returned home from a night out in the early hours of one Saturday morning in 1976. I remember Mama leaving home for a church service at about 6 a.m. as I was lying in bed. I knew she would give me a scolding when she returned from attending Mass. Soon after she left the house, I decided to take my car to the garage for a pre-booked service, then made my way to the local market to buy freshly slaughtered meats, which I hoped would soothe Mama's displeasure.

Unfortunately, my "fresh beef" gesture didn't do the trick. Mama was more concerned about my early morning return home. She did not consider that I was a young, hard-working man who also contributed to the housekeeping. I did not allow my social life to interfere with my role at home or work. Understandably, Mama's uttermost concern was due to our past disturbing experiences. In addition, she saw some unfamiliar faces who visited me at home but was unaware they were business acquaintances from other districts. I felt she feared that my growing popularity would attract more negative attention.

While Mama was venting her frustration, there was a sudden burst of galloping noises on the road parallel to my bedroom window. People were shouting and screaming frantically with desperate calls.

"Ma Ray," someone shouted. "Stephen is dead. Stephen's car has crashed on the highway, and he died in the accident."

What is she talking about? I wondered.

"What is this all about?" Mama responded in a flustered tone. "Stephen is right here in his bed. Nothing is wrong with him."

The person responded convincingly, "No, Ma Ray, Stephen was driving his car, and he died in an accident on the Tromassee bridge!"

Mama was disgruntled when she retorted, "Stephen is right here in his bed; he is not dead."

Suddenly, Mama observed that my car was not parked in its usual space and asked where I had parked it. Immediately and chillingly, it dawned on me that Arthur, a village mechanic at whose garage I left my vehicle, may have driven my car from his garage and gotten involved in an accident. I panicked, ran out of the house, and headed in the same direction as the crowd. The news that I had died quickly spread throughout the district. While the family and I were making our way to the scene of the accident, people were shouting,

"Stephen is dead! Stephen died in a car accident!"

Was I devastated? It was numbing.

My feeling, and that of my family, was numbness and heightened anxiety. Upon our arrival at the site of the accident, we learned about a passenger on board. I was shattered to see the wreckage that belonged to me; my world instantly came to a grinding halt. We were all surprised that Arthur had crashed the vehicle, but he was unscathed, while Dave, the passenger, suffered a broken arm and other fractures. I do not recall talking to Arthur at the scene before the ambulance arrived soon after and took the driver and passenger to the hospital. The rest of the family rallied and gave me much-needed support. Mama, Papa, Silvie and Phil were all speechless. We all came crashing back down to earth. However, we understood that life had to go on.

I was down but not dead; I was still standing and needed to continue my work. There was one more dilemma. Arthur was not authorized to drive my car under the terms of my motor insurance, so naturally, the insurance company would not accept liability.

Finding a way out of this mess was imperative, particularly as I had not paid off my car loan. My family and I regrouped and began some brainstorming. We discussed our two possible options: to seek redress from Arthur, who lived with his parents, or to seek the assistance of my general manager, with the hope that he would influence the insurance company's decision in a positive way. I instantly dismissed the first without a second thought—we would be going into battle with an influential family without any chance of victory. This was the moment when I truly needed a Godfather in my corner.

My Half Loaf

It was beyond dispute that option one would not be achievable. While people perceived Arthur's parents as well-to-do, his father, Orlando, was not a pleasant character with whom anyone would strike up a sensible conversation. He was known for his crudeness and his repulsive attitude. Furthermore, I knew he was not obligated to entertain such a discussion. I thought the only way to hold Arthur liable would be through the courts. Going this route, however, would mean months and possibly years of delay. I foresaw no successful outcome from this approach.

Nevertheless, Mama took the lead and decided to speak with the parents. Not surprisingly, Orlando rejected Mama's approach outright when he declared, without any sympathy or empathy, "Madam, I'm not paying a black cent. I did not tell my son to drive that car."

I tried to be pragmatic. I wasn't disappointed because I didn't expect a different outcome. I communicated with my general manager, Nigel Cadette, especially since he knew my situation. He assured me that he would do everything possible to secure good closure to my plight. Meanwhile, I was grateful to my colleagues for their support in sharing their vehicles. The entire incident was a massive blow to my morale, but my resilience continued to carry me through.

This situation prolonged for a few months until I received a telephone call from Nigel Cadette. He informed me that the insurance company agreed to pay for my written-off vehicle at a much-reduced value even though they had no legal obligation. Such news was a huge relief; I was gratified not to have lost everything. At last, for the first time in my life, I finally had a Godfather, Nigel Cadette, standing in my corner.

Quitting Was Not Easy

I received a check from the insurance company for my loss. While I needed reliable transportation for my work, I hesitated to purchase another vehicle. Papa and I had regular conversations about life scenarios. My difficulty provided a further opportunity for Papa Ray to give me more advice about the cash I received from the accident. He suggested I invest in a plot of land in the village rather than buying my third vehicle. I did not envisage purchasing land as an option simply because I needed a vehicle for my job; indeed, my vehicle was my tool.

Although Papa's advice was intelligent, having a vehicle to carry out my work was equally crucial. I respectfully declined his advice, and he politely accepted my reason for doing so. After much consideration, I finally decided to look for the indispensable piece of equipment I needed to fulfil my job; I purchased a Ford Cortina 2000GT car in excellent condition. I was on the road again.

Having spent three years at the insurance firm by 1977, I began to find my job monotonous. I saw no further possible career advancement, at least not in the medium term. I had won all the awards for the taking and was confident I had nothing more to prove in this position. I had made meaningful contributions to our home, and it was time to examine other possibilities. I needed a different perspective; I turned my focus to travelling abroad.

It is indisputable that we will face some difficult choices in our lifetime. Options that we know will impact others in our circle. Regrettably, even with the likelihood that people will perceive our actions as self-centred, we choose the path we believe will lead us to a favourable outcome. This scenario became real life when I quit my job at the insurance company. I knew my position was secure at work, but I only realised how important I was to the firm when I was about to leave. As expected, my managers did not readily accept my resignation letter. The situation was delicate because the firm had been good to me.

The entire workforce, including the branch manager and general managers, tried to convince me to stay. Nigel Cadette came home and spoke with Mama and me to dissuade me from quitting. No matter how respectfully I presented my case, it wasn't easy saying no to a manager who had been exceedingly supportive in the past. As sad as it was, I had to look beyond that moment. I had made up my mind, and I was ready to explore.

An Optimist, a Realist

Driven by curiosity, I casually applied for a sales position advertised in a copy of a global newspaper by a realtor company in Quebec, Canada. Upon receiving a successful response, I submitted my resignation letter to my employer. I was fearless in wanting to discover the other side of the horizon, broaden my knowledge, and take advantage of any opportunity. I figured, either way, the travel experience would be of immense value. Once I finalized my plans, I contacted Simon, a friend who lived in Montreal. Simon had been in Canada for a few years, and we had remained in contact. We discussed my intentions, and he was gracious.

My first journey outside the shores of Saint Lucia was a trip to Barbados as a ten-year-old Boy Scout, but travelling to North America in 1977 was an eye-opener. Upon landing in Montreal, Simon picked me up and extended generous hospitality throughout my stay. In the meantime, I connected with my cousins in Toronto and Ottawa, who I featured in my contingency plan.

The group of recruits I joined included about six from multiple Caribbean islands. Like me, the Caribbean participants had travelled to Canada for the first time and had no experience with the position for which they had applied. It was a setting for good interaction. The atmosphere was pleasant because we identified with each other.

We all completed the orientation process, including viewing the many-acre land portions. We recognized the potential for terrific rewards. However, gaining such bounties would require monumental effort to close one sale. I was an optimist but also a realist.

By the end of the third week, several of us from the group had decided it wouldn't work out for us. We informed the management of our decision to withdraw from the programme. We suspected the company had been through the quitting scenario before because they seemed comfortable with our choice. My interpretation of their response was, *no worries, thanks for coming, we wish you well.*

Stephen N Rosemond

Pig Farming? Not for Me

From the start, I considered my journey to Canada exploratory. I was thrilled to arrive in this vast country and to understand the reality of the microscopic dot that my island was in comparison. I would first have to have my head examined if I were to expect to be the *shark in a swimming pool* like I was in Saint Lucia. Therefore, I was satisfied just by being there and manoeuvring my way, hopefully with the help of my relatives. Consequently, I activated my backup plan.

I followed up with my cousin Jimmy in Toronto and told him of my wish to spend extra time in Canada. Jimmy welcomed me into his home, and I was thankful for his goodwill. I enjoyed the many Toronto tours, including the memorable drive to Niagara Falls. I had stayed with Jimmy for less than one week when I introduced the talk about my desire to extend my visitor visa; six months would be enough for me to make up my mind about a possible permanent stay. I failed to understand how my cousin concluded that Canada was not the right place for me.

Jimmy and I came from the same background. Among Maam's many grandchildren, he was between the first and third. He had lived in Canada for many years. My cousin knew how the system worked in his adopted country but disagreed with my idea of exploring any possibility of staying there beyond my three-month visa. Thus, he suggested what he thought was best for me.

"Stephen," Jimmy started. "The family has so much land at Capwece, and you all are leaving it to travel abroad. Why don't you return to Saint Lucia and set up a pig farm?"

"What! A pig farm?" I asked, shocked. "No, Jimmy, pig farming is not for me. I won't even think about it," I replied with a burst of laughter.

In an instant, my dismay turned to amusement. My cousin immediately cheered me up; it was the best joke I'd heard in Canada, and it was on me. Why would I want to breed pigs in Saint Lucia? Did he think I would look better in a jumpsuit carrying a long shovel and a bucket to scoop up pig s**t? I hated being in the forest and disliked all aspects of farming. The temptation to ask Jimmy one question lingered: if pig farming was such a brilliant idea, and you know of the family's ability to undertake such a venture, why did you not return from Canada to take on that project? My thoughts were, *thanks for your suggestion, Jimmy, but I'll pass on that one.*

I figured further conversations with my cousin would be futile; it was time for me to move on. I focused on my next plan to contact my other cousin, William, who lived in Ottawa. William was happy to hear that I had moved to Toronto. He invited me to stay with him and was exceedingly hospitable after he picked me up at the coach terminal. I had not discussed my intentions before he introduced the talk about seeking permanent residency, just like he had done. William's thinking synchronized with my own, so it was a discussion I eagerly entertained. He suggested I accompany him to work on the construction site and would introduce me to the site manager. The manager advised that the project was nearing completion but would have me for about one month. I was grateful to have been engaged for that brief period.

While my cousin William did all that was possible to assist me in achieving my goal, Lynn's family, with whom I had been in touch and who also lived in Ottawa, did the opposite. We seldom had conversations that did not include persistent questions about my position upon my return to Saint Lucia. They astutely dismissed any talk of my wish to extend my stay in Canada; I understood their logic.

Frustratingly, I found myself in a revolving door—my situation was such that all except William believed they were qualified to determine what was best for me. I felt discouraged. It was nearing the end of 1977 when I finally decided to complete the three-month stay.

Test of Endurance

I knew my family back home was concerned about me. They were the most important people in my life and were eager to welcome me back. My brief stay in Canada was a wonderful experience. When I submitted my resignation letter to my previous employer, Peter Chalmer and Nigel Cadette told me that I would be most welcome back to the firm if I ever chose to return. Even though I had this option on the table, I knew it was best to move to new pastures. I opted to set off on my next job-hunting expedition. I had great confidence about finding new employment in Saint Lucia.

The results from my first job hunting experience gave me much confidence in my ability to achieve repeated success, my previous employment record placed me in good stead; I had the work experience to back me up, and I had developed critical skills to enhance my chances of employment, such as teamwork, written and oral communication, numeracy, planning, and organising.

In addition, my Bible was always close at hand. I turned to my prayers, Psalm 65. The rewards came about soon after I landed a job as a bookkeeper at the newly established Saint Lucia Flour Milling Company in the south of the island—walking into a new job so soon after my return was encouraging. I was excited to embrace this break, as it gave me a fresh outlook. I was eager to learn new skills, so this was a chance to settle down and concentrate on a career development path. This part of my journey also allowed me to test my endurance.

The Power of Evil

I worked well with my co-workers, particularly Angella, the financial controller and my mentor. The team also included our general manager, company secretary Lucretia, and quality control officer Dianna. I maintained a strong work ethic as I did in my previous employment. I had intended this position to be long-term as I had greatly enjoyed working for the firm. The atmosphere was superb. Using the company's vehicles was a privilege I enjoyed once I completed my three-month probation. This benefit was special to me because only the three departmental managers were entitled.

I had been with the firm for about fifteen months when my situation gradually changed. Angella began to raise her concerns about my performance. She pointed out mistakes that I had no clue how to explain. Such discrepancies suddenly appeared in my work; for example, I was puzzled when Angella pointed out that I entered the number 6 when it should be 8. I failed to understand how I achieved a total of 16 when I added 9 plus 12. It was absurd. The functions I performed in my previous employment were all about figures. I loved maths, and I was good at it. Indeed, I went through the competency exercise during the job interview. My tasks had not changed since I started with the firm; they were the same as I had previously performed efficiently; it was all mathematics.

What was happening to me at the Flour Milling Company was confusing. My eyesight and general health were perfect. I had not suddenly developed dyslexic tendencies and considerably reduced my social activities. I had not changed my working practices, and my attendance record was exemplary. I loved my job. My positive work attitude and team co-operation were no different from the outset.

The past turbulences I had experienced enabled me to stand firm and not yield. I tried to maintain a positive outlook while remaining vigilant, and I carried my trust in my creator. The only change that had taken place at work during this period was that our quality controller had resigned, and Trisha became her replacement and the new member of our team. Trisha and I knew each other because we came from neighbouring communities. It was common knowledge that her mother was a clairvoyant, or *Gardere* in Creole, who was reputed to have assisted people who came from afar. I had difficulty dismissing this as a possible link to my plight, particularly as Trisha had taken up her junior position at the firm's bakery some months before those events. Was it purely a coincidence? My family and I did not believe it was.

Lucretia first expressed her concerns about my predicament during a conversation.

"What a coincidence!" She remarked.

Most astonishing was that Trisha's conversation with me gradually reduced to a simple "hello" even when she made her daily trips to our office carrying pastry samples. I sensed a cloud of discomfort gliding over me whenever she entered the room. I also observed the changing attitude towards me from the general manager with whom I had previously had a great working relationship. Our interactions were lessening, and the atmosphere during our team meetings was becoming awkward; discomfort was setting in. Nothing was going right for me, as though the Angels of Darkness were hovering over me. It appeared the universe was slowly turning against me. It was all accentuated when my manager removed my privilege of using the company's vehicles.

"Was I not the same person who had quickly gained much approval from the entire workforce, including the manufacturing plant workers?" I asked myself.

The impression of rejection that bordered on ostracism was beginning to consume me to the extent of feeling insignificant. The pressure was rapidly building up until it became intolerable. The feeling of a hostile force shadowing me was overwhelming. Would it be surprising that one's confidence would rattle under such circumstances? It was a helpless and discouraging situation. My position at the flour milling company became highly strained.

The inevitable happened; the company dismissed me based on deficient performance. Subsequently, Lucretia, who became my ex-co-worker, informed me of Trish's promotion to my position. This event happened within seven days of my dismissal without the company advertising the job. Lucretia expressed amazement during our conversation.

"How could Trisha be promoted so quickly?" she asked.

There were all the signs of foul play. When asking myself why this should have happened to me if I had been so devoted, well, the answer was easy. While faith in the power of prayers can provide a sense of indestructibility, the power of evil can be merciless. I viewed whatever I encountered during my journey as the continuous testing of my endurance. I needed to maintain vigour no matter how bumpy my path was ahead, for I know that realising my true purpose in life also comes from the level of my tenacity. I never knowingly doubted the power in my petitions; regrettably, I had difficulty concealing my anguish on this occasion.

The experience of being terminated from my employment was problematic for me to accept. I had lost this battle. It dented my morale and nibbled at my self-worth, but I had to carry on; there was no alternative. The biggest frustration was that I was powerless to do anything about being fired. Even though employment laws existed, they made no difference; it was a carte blanche policy for employers. The psychological impact was awful, with the tension of being in limbo. My level of exhaustion was palpable.

The renewed thought of moving away from Saint Lucia had become rooted in my mind, but my immediate concern had to be about occupying my time productively. So, I was on the move again, searching for work. Within two months of dismissal from my earlier employment, I secured a job interview along the island's northwest coast from my application to Hess Oils Saint Lucia. I plainly stated at the meeting that I aspired to travel abroad and would do so at any given opportunity. The firm accepted my openness, and they appointed me.

Hess Corporation, an American-based global energy company, allowed me the chance to be a bookkeeper for a second time. I approached this position as a stopgap as the idea of leaving the island kept floating in my mind. At this stage, my migration ambition was more of an intention than a desire.

My Leap of Faith

My relationship with my older siblings in England was good. They knew of the challenges that I unceasingly faced in Saint Lucia. I informed them of my longing to move away from this environment, and they were empathetic. "But how would moving away be possible?" I pondered.

Lynn was expecting our baby daughter Jenny. This situation, which was of my own making further complicated my position. In the past, Joe and John's wife had initiated a conversation about a holiday to England for me, Silvie and Phil. This idea was a thank-you gesture for our hospitality to our sisters-in-law and their families when in 1976, they visited Saint Lucia for the first time. In 1978, they raised the topic and decided it would happen in the spring of 1979. There was no doubt that this was a welcomed opportunity.

It was also a decision I would struggle with because I knew I would not be making a hasty return if I ever set foot out of Saint Lucia again. The thought of taking such a bold step was daunting, yet I saw this as an opening to free myself from the smothering negative energy that encircled me. I saw no positive in my life during that period apart from the expected birth of my new baby daughter.

Despite the joy from the anticipated birth of our baby, cracks began to appear in my relationship with Lynn. She had a problematic pregnancy, and her frequent mood swings that derived from the stresses she underwent compounded the matter; her irritability had the most significant impact on our romance as far as I was concerned.

The sustained bitterness levelled at Lynn by her family was worrisome, yet she continued to endure. Being a dad for the first time was quite an experience. While the family's displeasure was predictable, I was oblivious to the psychological toll Lynn withstood. Regrettably, her hypersensitivity was not reassuring; consequently, my inclination to move away was not dampened. I didn't want to believe that I was capable of mustering the nerve to take any action that would harm the girl I cared about but, most importantly, our first child. Our baby daughter? The thought was heart-wrenching.

At that point, the burden of having no easy answers was overwhelming. Mulling over the certainty of being labelled insensitive by those with whom I shared mutual respect and care was consuming me. I felt I was undergoing an unimaginable change, some form of awakening;

I needed to maintain calmness. It was a matter of being submerged in my emotions or disconnecting from this quandary—having to decide on what was an exceedingly hard choice worsened my psychological woes. I figured moving away would present a greater sense of security, enabling me to get back in the saddle in search of some degree of physical and mental healing. These were such turbulent times that no matter how cautiously I manoeuvred, the outlook for an untroubled outcome seemed unlikely.

Notwithstanding the painful conditions, capitulating was an action I had resisted. Surrendering to those seeking my defeat—for those who tried to change my real destiny, would be their greatest reward. I had to endure and be resolute. I had to be sincere to myself even though the ones I would be leaving behind would dismiss my rationale. I continued to pray in my quest for courage, strength, and guidance to confront the new challenges that undoubtedly lay ahead. I never perceived finding streets paved with gold on the other side of the Atlantic, so I was conscious that my struggles would continue presumably in a different format.

Finally, it was time for me to face up to my decision. On this occasion, I turned to the infinite spirit for forgiveness. My three months of employment at Hess Oils was over, and immediately after, in

April of 1979, I was on a flight heading out of the island. Sorrow was what I endured throughout the 8-hour-long journey. I had left Lynn in Saint Lucia to travel two months after our daughter's birth in February. I would be honouring the responsibility of my child from a distance. My arduous journey away from a menacing environment was, without a doubt, my leap of faith.

CHAPTER SIX

Welcome to the First World

This journey was my third out of the Third World, and it was in the company of Silvie and Phil—it was their first off the shores of Saint Lucia. It was no secret to my family that I had intended to make the most of this break. I believe that God bestows the virtue of wisdom upon those who seek it. I think the gifts from our creator are not always as clear-cut as we would like them to be. They come more as a puzzle, sometimes like a dream. The task of unravelling and understanding the mystery ought to be our mission. Therefore, the onus is ours to identify, analyse, and utilize such blessings to accomplish our life's purpose. Not seizing a perceived once-in-our-lifetime chance [of an opening to the First World] would be an unfortunate misapprehension of a Godsend. My gift needed no further clarification; it was my moment.

I was determined not to fritter away the probability of achieving a better life outside the boundaries of this Caribbean Island. I received a God-given opportunity that I needed to harness fully. I found no easy answer when researching the options for a medium- to long-term stay in the UK. The educational route seemed to be the only plausible option. My older siblings also suggested that the college route should be my centre of attention. They advised me to further my education because they thought I could succeed.

However, pursuing this path required many financial resources, which were not accessible to me. Their earlier rejection of Papa's request for financial support with my secondary education and Phil's had become indelible in my mind. Even without Papa Ray's humiliating experience, I would not subject myself to such embarrassment by asking for help. Instead, I decided that the assistance I needed at the time was minimal, the kind that the average person would expect on a foreign trip—sightseeing and finding their way around in an unfamiliar environment. Fortunately, a friend in England would give me the holiday thrills of sightseeing. She was my tour guide.

Meeting the Family

I was fortunate to have had many friends throughout my school days. Although some had joined their families in America, Canada and England, we kept in touch as pen-pals. One such friend was Rose.

She was a beautiful, brown-eyed, energetic girl who joined her parents in England in 1973. Upon arriving in the UK, I informed her via telephone of my presence in London. Rose was excited to know that I was only about 200 miles away from where she was. This telephone call was the first occasion we had spoken in six years, and we agreed to meet at my sister Mary-Anne's home in North London.

The following weekend, Rose made the journey from her parent's home in Manchester and joined me as planned. Mary-Anne's husband, Corry, and I met her at the central London coach terminal. Upon our arrival at the family home, I introduced Rose to my sister and her family. Rose and I were excited to meet again after such a long time, and the ongoing chat was about the good old-school days. It was the first time she had admitted to doing all the teasing and chasing each other at school; we laughed about it as the memories of our school days were so vivid.

Rose graciously asked me to return the favour by accepting her invitation to meet her family in Manchester and spend a few days together there. While I appreciated her courtesy, I was uneasy about the idea. I knew of the resulting beliefs from meeting with one's family in the context of friendship, more so as Rose's mother was Saint Lucian. Nevertheless, I eventually agreed.

I remember travelling by coach to the northwest of England, enjoying the beautiful scenery of the English countryside while considering meeting Rose's family in a few hours. It was impossible to imagine the reaction from her people, even though I knew two of her brothers when they lived in Saint Lucia. I knew nothing about her mother apart from the briefing I had received from Rose; she had described her relationship with her mother as *not the best*. At last, I safely completed my journey. Rose met me at the coach station and reassured me that all would be fine; her people were looking forward to meeting me.

Too late for misgivings now! I thought. It was time to introduce me to her mother, Regena, and three brothers. The family extended a warm welcome and immediately offered the pleasantry of a *Great British cup of tea*. We got down to a family conversation that included, among other topics, my trip to England, Saint Lucia, my relatives in England, and their relatives in Saint Lucia. I presumed Regena had a fervent desire to *get something off her chest*. She brazenly changed the topic without signalling a diversion in the conversation with a pointed question.

Regena Popped the Question

"So you have travelled to England only to marry my daughter?" Regena asked with a shade of sarcasm.

"No," I responded, "My other siblings and I have travelled to England for a holiday for the first time to spend time with our family."

From then onward, the questions from Rose's mother about my background came in without a pause. Her most unusual question was, "Do you have a police record?"

"A police record!" I replied. "I'm sorry, but why would I have a police record?"

Regena must have seen the suddenly changed expression of astonishment on my face as the others looked uneasy.

I guess I should have asked her the question, "Do you have a marriage proposal questionnaire for me to complete?" At least that would have saved me from the interrogation. I was uneasy because I would have considered her line of questioning more pertinent if I had proposed to her daughter—or did she have suspicions about me? That is how she came across. One of my observations about Regena was that she seldom smiled throughout our conversation. I later realised that this was part of her persona. I presumed her motherly attitude was akin to a lioness protecting her cub. I suspected she was safeguarding Rose, who was her only daughter. For the second time, Regena popped the question.

"So, are you going to marry my daughter?"

Frankly, the word "marriage" did come up during the brief moment that we shared. Rose had alerted me about her mother's frame of mind. She had surpassed the typical St Lucian mum who *bubble wrapped* her daughter—she left no space for Rose to breathe. She had questioned Rose about our friendship and asked whether marriage was our intention.

"What was your answer?" I asked.

"No. We never talked about that." Rose replied.

Reversing the question Rose asked teasingly, "Well, would you want to talk about it?". She caught me off-guard but I saw the sparkle in her dazzling eyes; the conversation ended.

I was forthright in my answer to Regena when I told her, "Rose and I had only briefly and casually mentioned the word once. I did not propose to her."

She made it clear in her reply. "Stephen, I guess Rose told you we are Christian here. You will have to commit if you want to befriend her to the extent of being under the same roof, even during your brief visit."

But why was Regena pushing the idea, I wondered? To my knowledge, she knew no more about me than what I had told her.

"Well, Mrs Brown," I replied, "I believe marriage is a serious matter that the two involved must first discuss and mutually agree. We will inform you and all concerned if Rose and I choose to do so."

My response was not an attempt to lecture Rose's mother about the seriousness of this subject; I was not qualified to do so. Ironically, she had undergone the procedure twice before and was again in courtship—

That was the end of the discussion on this subject. Unsurprisingly, this conversation reignited my anguish; it was the definition of déjà vu, as I had recently turned down all attempts of getting me into marriage in Saint Lucia. I drew consolation from Regena's *cross-examination*; I viewed it as a compliment. The thought that I must have looked like husband material was comforting, ha-ha! My introduction to parents by their daughter seemed to conjure up the word *marriage.* I considered Regena's *lure* a matter of respect. I also saw subtle overbearing on her part.

No Time to Ponder

We were only meeting for the first time, but Regena seemed hasty with her questions about marriage. My gut feeling told me she thought I wasn't the right guy for her daughter. Indeed, I subsequently learned that she had conducted a background check on me through the Saint Lucia police force. I bore no hard feelings. I would probably do the same for my daughter.

Nevertheless, I was confident that my character was unblemished and that any report from the Saint Lucia police or another entity would substantiate that. I maintained implicit confidence in my prayers; this time, I sought hospitality. I turned to the reading of Psalm 27. With this psalm, you will receive hospitality if you repeat it constantly and with reverence during your journey.

Over the following months after Regena's interrogation, I realised that time was not in my favour as my UK visitor visa would be due to expire soon. I had to make up my mind about how to extend my stay and do it quickly. Restoring my stability was my objective, and the Saint Lucia environment was not conducive to that. I wanted to believe that the answer to my desire to remain in England was staring me in the face, although I was naturally concerned about the devastating consequences that would bear upon my loved ones in Saint Lucia, especially Lynn and my baby daughter.

In spite of all my emotions, the moment was approaching for me to confront my situation. I had no more time to ponder.

Time Would be My Saviour

Through our deep conversations and with time running against us, Rose and I braved the decision to inform both families of our intention for a low-key wedding, to match our limited finances. I was apprehensive about my parent's reaction to my announcement. I deeply regretted placing them in the challenging position of being "messengers" thus putting them in the line of the proverbial bullet by which to be shot.

Predictably, the effect of such news on Lynn and her family was horrible; it was painful. Apologies in any amount would not be sufficient. Nothing, done or said, would console Lynn and her family. My unqualified support of Baby Jenny that I promised brought no solace to their anguish; they wanted nothing more from me. I presumed it would have been more understandable and easier to accept had they received news of my demise. However, I knew that time would be the only deciding factor if there would ever be a healing process. Only such time would be my saviour.

Silvie, Phil and I were due to return to Saint Lucia during the second week of June, but inevitably, I cancelled my return ticket. I wanted Silvie and Phil to be present at my wedding; therefore, Rose and I set our wedding date for the 4th of June 1979. We had a modest ceremony, with the reception kept at Rose's family home. We would also use this address as our temporary residence until we could decide on our next step. It was time for us to travel to London for what I would consider a working honeymoon.

My life-changing journey, for better or worse, had taken a new turn, a course that I was determined to navigate through the certainty of tribulations. I was under no illusion as to the enormity of my expedition; I knew nothing would avert my attention from my goal of acceptable outcomes. I had a new status, and I had to carry on.

I Quit

During our honeymoon in London, Rose and I spent time strategizing for our immediate future. Our first action was to travel to the British Home Office in Croydon, South London, to declare our new status and seek permission for me to remain in the United Kingdom. We were interviewed and sent home with no conclusive result to my application; we weren't surprised.

The condition set in the meantime was that I should refrain from holding employment until I received authorization from the immigration authority. With a sense of calmness, we travelled back to Manchester. Rose returned to her full-time job while I stayed home. As Rose and I had mentioned, the plausible question kept popping up: How would I maintain my new wife or contribute to the housekeeping? Was I concerned needlessly? Not at all. Being relaxed about my wife or anyone taking on my upkeep was unimaginable. Such a proposition does not feature in my DNA.

As a young working adult, I was fortunate to have always provided for myself and others. I was now in an uncharacteristic position of dependency, though it was part of the process I had anticipated. The issues of sacrifices were those that often featured in our conversations. It was a matter of managing our circumstances in the best way possible. Furthermore, patience would be a critical factor in achieving any favourable outcome.

While waiting for a decision from the Home Office, I decided to occupy myself by seeking casual work despite the authorities' restrictions. Defying the immigration department out of necessity was a gamble I felt obliged to take. Engaging myself in some form of work activity was only one answer to the subject of my independence. My mother-in-law introduced me to Cleveland, a family friend in the construction trade; he invited me to his building site because I had expressed my willingness to try anything that would enable me to support Rose while keeping my mental capacity intact.

I welcomed Clevland's offer to take me out of the house and onto his worksite. My initial tasks were simple. I passed on bricks, held the measuring lines and tape, and passed the tools to the workers. The one thing I declined was to climb the ladders. Cleveland and his crew quickly realised that acrophobia, a severe fear of heights, was my weakness, yet they still persisted in trying to get me up the ladder. The memories of my limited time in such a conversely gratifying environment with my cousin William in Canada came streaming in. Cleveland gradually assigned me more tasks within my short spell with him. We worked for extended hours, which was strenuous, and I started doing the same heavy work as his other labourers. I was shifting buckets of concrete, pushing wheelbarrows laden with materials, and offloading supplies from his truck. Unfortunately, there was no boost in my pay to reflect this change; I spotted exploitation. I thanked Cleveland for his consideration, but informed him that I was unable to continue doing this work, and then hurriedly left the project site.

My Quickest Pay Rise Ever

I had no qualms about quitting this stint with Cleveland, even though my circumstances were tricky. I was confident I would find manageable or less strenuous employment, hopefully free from manipulation. I regularly scanned the local community newspapers for casual work while seeking updates from the Home Office about the status of my application. The response that I received from the authorities was always the same. "We are still looking into your application, Mr Rosemond."

As time passed, I became more anxious, exacerbated by the tense atmosphere at home. Worst of all, I was unemployed and stuck in the house with Regina, who was also unemployed—her jobless position didn't matter; she was in charge. I kept thinking that my unemployment situation was the probable cause of my mother-in-law being an eternal grouch. Rose and I had conversations about the situation. She reassured me that all would be fine. It was simply her mother's disposition, she explained.

Rose's eldest brother, Richie, who initially lived with his mother, Regina, was also awaiting permanent residency in England. The intolerable discord that existed between him and his mother, subsequently drove him to move in with a friend about half a mile away. Richie and I kept in contact and occasionally we would spend leisure time together, window shopping around Manchester City Centre. We also spent time at the local library, and general sightseeing. We developed a good rapport, and he explained the uneasiness he had endured before my arrival on the scene.

Richie supported Rose's description of their mother's temperament. He disclosed that neither of us was her favourite; Hilroy was the Jamaican family friend she favoured more than me. There were also whispers circulating among my family about my application at the Home Office. Mary-Anne was the first to inform me, followed by Richie, that the Home Office was delaying my application allegedly because Regena had reported to the department that my marriage to Rose wasn't legitimate.

"Why would she do such a thing?" I asked. I would not confront her with this hearsay, even on her best day. I managed the situation calmly but with sadness. I drew comfort from knowing that the Home Office would respond regardless and I prepared myself for any eventuality.

In the meantime, I continued my search for casual employment and found a job as a server at an Italian-owned take away fish and chips shop in Stretford, Manchester. This work environment was less strenuous than working my butt off on a construction site! I enjoyed the role of serving the customers with their orders of fish and chips, pies and sausages and every other product that we sold including light beverages. My duty became more exciting soon after the owner asked that I take charge of frying the chips, fish, and sausages—it was great fun. I increased the frying time of the potatoes, adding a touch of crispiness.

It was out with the old regular, soggy fries and in with the new, crispy Caribbean-style French fries. The change in the preparation of the fried foods attracted more customers, extended evening opening hours, and inevitably grew sales. My boss was impressed with my performance and rewarded me with what I considered the quickest pay rise that I had ever earned.

Breaking out of the Bubble of Insecurity

When I received my first pay packet from the fish and chip shop, Rose and I agreed to meet at the central shopping mall in the city. We decided to spend part of what I liked to refer to as my first "real pay" on something tangible, something for memories. Besides, we needed to start shopping for our household items. We were planning to find our apartment, irrespective of the response from the immigration department.

Rose and I decided to buy a beautiful dinner set. We took our new purchase home and shared our excitement and intentions with Regena. I remember Rose was not enthusiastic about disclosing our plans to her mother. However, we agreed it was best to be transparent as a family.

Furthermore, I saw our gesture as a mark of respect. In some way, I was expecting Regena to reciprocate with a favourable response. Well, Rose knew her mother, and I didn't.

My mother-in-law was far from impressed. She took no notice and maintained her daily cranky looks. If someone had been asked to decipher her posture, my supposition would be: "What the hell is this? We can't eat the bloody plates."

It was, in fact, quite embarrassing. Rose and I calmly took our sparkling dinner set and secured it under our bed, where it would remain until we moved out. This was the moment when I finally understood Rose's description of her mother; I needed no more evidence—Regena was no role model. As time went by, we received no news from the Home Office. I pressed on with my daily work at the fish and chip shop, and we continued to prepare in anticipation of our move. The tense atmosphere at home continued. Regena was unhappy with the housekeeping contribution she was receiving from her three employed children. Moreover, since Rose was married, Regena no longer controlled Rose's income as she did before.

Not being in control was a situation that Regena never accepted lightly; her love of money was unmistakable. I became extremely concerned as I continued to feel the pressure rising until I refused to remain in an atmosphere that had become stifled. We needed to move away from my wife's family's home and find our own. I embraced this situation as a necessary inconvenience, a chance to show my ability to stand firm even in this time of uncertainty. I knew I was occupying someone else's territory; therefore, I would not allow our marriage to endure the strain of living under such conditions. I needed to take my wife away from this environment and provide the best with the limited funds I had saved from my work. I was determined, and I would allow nothing to stop me.

Rose and I restated our intentions to Regena and informed the rest of the family of our plan to move out as soon as possible. Our flat-hunting plans got underway with our eyes set on London. We believed moving to London was wise—there would be more employment opportunities, and the prospect of earning a better income was also a factor.

In addition, we would be closer to the Home Office; I would be able to make the journey with greater ease. This joint decision was one that Rose and I were anxious to have materialized. The time was approaching for us to move into our unfamiliar environment, for better or worse. I was determined to break out of the bubble of insecurity. I would no longer allow the constant uncertainty to plague my life because I was unwilling to wait and see what our future would bring.

CHAPTER SEVEN

Leave it to God!

Saint Lucia has always been known for its interesting history and culture. However, converting such richness into sustainable development for the benefit of its people seemed to be an ongoing challenge. Like most societies, the wealth remained in the hands of the few, among which a limited number were indigenous. Those more enlightened saw the rewards of their labour, while others struggled throughout their lives.

Over the years, I listened to conversations during which my fellow citizens, who considered themselves less fortunate, repeated commonly used expressions to justify their setbacks:

"Why do we make plans when we don't know what tomorrow brings."

"I'll leave everything in God's hands because God is in control."

"Whatever will be will be because God knows best."

"I did not create this world. I will die and leave everything on this earth."

As for the fourth saying, I wondered how anyone would think otherwise.

I concluded that such gloom-ridden sentiments emanate from self-pity and resentment towards those trying to remove themselves from dependence. Moreover, I saw the elements of religious and political manipulation and exploitation of the populace, which appeared to have had the adverse effect of contributing to a culture of self-loathing.

I see nothing wrong with anyone seeking comfort or solutions during their time of need; whether such circumstances are self-inflicted is irrelevant. Nevertheless, I am aware of the paths my compatriots have chosen in search of answers to their plight; for example, they pray, then sit and wait, hoping that someone will deliver the packaged answers to their petition on their doorstep, or maintain their expectations and standards for basic survival needs. Therefore, they have no desire to empower themselves to achieve anything besides securing food, shelter, and clothing. The years go by, and nothing changes because their New Year's resolution is always, "Let's see what the New Year brings; I'll leave it to God." Or they surrender and cast blame; they've made less than favourable choices and can see no way out. They do not accept responsibility.

My belief in the power of prayer is indisputable. It is my irreplaceable source of inspiration, strength, and courage, but I do not subscribe to the above notions; far from it. My understanding of how things work differs; it does not connect to the concept of finding solutions by offloading my problems in God's hands and waiting. The teachings in Luke 11:9-13 King James Version Bible are what I favour: *"Ask, and it shall be given you... seek and ye shall find..."* Alongside my conviction comes the desire to be proactive, creative, and resourceful. I am not afraid to take the initiative. I understand the need for effort-driven personal and professional development, but most importantly, accountability and humility are imperative.

Trust No One

Going to seek my passport from the Home Office was a gamble, but this was the chance I was willing to take. My fish and chip shop employer knew of my circumstances, and he supported my intention to move from Manchester. I also informed my eldest brother, Hilbert, a popular member of the Saint Lucian diaspora in north London, of our decision. Therefore, I knew if there was anyone capable of helping us find rented accommodation in London, he would fit this role.

When I told him our needs, he referred me to a property owner who owned a single-bedroom apartment in north London. Fortunately, the landlord was a family friend who was kind enough to rent at a competitive rate. With immense relief, we moved to our new, quiet address to start our married life independently.

Rose and I started job hunting immediately after organising our belongings in our new home. I continued with my search for temporary work. Within the first month of our relocation, Rose found a job with a reputable local firm no more than fifteen minutes' walk from home. I found work at a local second-hand car dealership with the help of a fellow Saint Lucian, Leyonce.

Leyonce came from my village of Micoud; we knew each other well. He was a contracted supervisor at the firm, and I worked under his control, cleaning and polishing vehicles. Our Creole language was the link we shared, which gave us much fun during our daily tasks. We exchanged funny jokes and talked about Saint Lucia and Caribbean culture.

But no matter how pleasant my working day was, heading straight home after work was better than following him to the pub. I looked forward to preparing dinner with Rose while flicking through the channels of our black and white second-hand television, searching for evening entertainment. Our TV brought us much pleasure because we were proud to have acquired this item, among other small pieces of furniture. I was regaining my confidence because our new address was free from tension. In addition, I was able to meet other Saint Lucians living in our area. From my experiences, there was no uncertainty that being vigilant and seeking divine intervention was part of my daily ritual.

One of my requests for such intervention was overcoming fear. I made my appeal through the recital of Psalm 11. At the end of this reading, I reiterated my special prayer to the Mighty and Merciful God. The only God with the power to perform miracles was the one I trusted to secure my safety. I recited the Lord's Prayer after my special petition. I had to remain cautious, never taking anything at face value. Gossip can be a cruel act, and it was never far away. Therefore, I was careful not to reveal my business to anyone, nor did I disclose my true feelings or concerns. Those from the Saint Lucian community who knew of my background compared it to my work, cleaning and polishing vehicles, and drew their own conclusions. Some with whom I associated surmised my residential status was not legal; otherwise, I would have sought better employment.

Whenever people asked how I was getting on, my response was always the same, "I'm doing fine, thank you". Saying anything else would not improve my situation. I couldn't be sure that someone wouldn't inform the immigration authorities about my activities while awaiting their decision. Therefore, I trusted no one. Those in my arena thought life was generous to me and that I was stress-free, yet it was quite the opposite. I continued with the act of remaining silent while concealing my emotions of frustration.

I Needed No Sympathy

The respect my family gained from those who knew us in the diaspora was no less than how our people back in Saint Lucia viewed us. I never placed myself apart nor tried to be like any other; I tried my best to stay focused and not share my difficulties or anxieties. I saved face and used my coping skills to shield myself and manage so that those around me would judge me by my actions and not by my uncertain position in society. From this vantage point, coupled with my sociable personality, I had no difficulty adapting to the way of life in England. Yes, obtaining some basic information about cultural attitudes and behaviours was helpful, but I was fine in planning and organising my life; I needed no sympathy.

As I settled in London, I received invitations to various social events—house parties, pub visits, and even outings to betting shops. The problem was that these invitations came with a price tag. Thankfully, my previous work experience enhanced my knowledge of managing my financial matters; I was familiar with prioritising and saw that I had no money to spare for such pleasures. Throwing my hard-earned cash down the tubes was something I was not prepared to do. My precarious situation prompted Rose and me to save every penny we could afford. Though I had to keep a sense of optimism, preparing myself for the worst-case scenario about my residential status was equally important. Anyway, occasionally, I accepted the house parties that required us to bring a bottle because I wanted to avoid becoming a recluse.

My Commanding Tone in Prayer

Christmas 1979 came and went. I received no response from the Immigration Department. The year was coming to a close, and it would be my turn to make my New Year's resolution. In doing so, I prayed for the reflection of God's guidance in my actions. My emphatic belief in God's life-sustaining role throughout my existence was ceaseless. However, I knew my responsibility was to set my goals and work towards achieving them while my Spiritual Father led me along the way. I prayed so forcefully that my tone developed into more like commanding than requesting from the Most High. I prayed for strength and courage to overcome hurdles. The chances I had taken thus far and the results enabled me to attest that prayers without action are meaningless.

Furthermore, how can we achieve without a degree of self-confidence? With my intended measures, I knew there was an elevated level of risk. I had to pluck up the courage and determination; I decided that should my situation remain unchanged during the upcoming four-month period, I'd go get my passport from the Home Office to head back to Saint Lucia voluntarily. I chose the four months' limitation because this was the time remaining to complete my year's stay in the UK. Deep in my soul, I knew this was a huge gamble I would win. The pitiful compensation from temporary work and a fellow countryman's changed attitude towards me increased my determination to make such a move.

Leyonce's behaviour was increasingly contemptuous. I felt that because we had become close, he believed he could abuse our friendship by paying me whatever he chose, irrespective of my performance. Leyonce produced reasons such as, "We'll bring forward the balance of your payment," or, "The boss said some of the vehicles you cleaned up did not require much work." Worst of all, he would sometimes stretch his hand to me on payday and say, "Hold that man, we're expecting more cars tomorrow; it's going to be better." Even though I expressed displeasure, he knew I was restricted.

Leyonce was aware that I had no leverage to complain. My remaining self-esteem was slowly eroding, yet I tried to keep in mind my goal. My self-imposed deadline of April 1980 was drawing nearer, so I took a trip to the Home Office Immigration Department. The significant number of people ahead of me indicated I would be waiting in the prolonged queue for no less than two hours—such an abundance of time for negative thoughts to revolve in my mind. Judgment day was finally upon me; I would not fail. I refused to lose!

Psalm 34 was among the many psalms I had memorized, so I softly repeated that psalm, followed by the Lord's Prayer throughout and up to the point before it was my turn to be interviewed. I was confident and calm. I was focused and convinced I would return to Rose with a stamped passport. My number was called, and it was my turn to state my case.

"Good morning, sir. How can I help you?" the interviewer, a gentleman, asked.

In a composed manner, I introduced myself and then explained my situation.

"It's almost one year since I have been awaiting a reply to my application for my residential status in the UK. Due to my difficult circumstances, I am no longer willing or able to continue waiting under these conditions. Therefore, I have come to collect my passport to return to my country."

His facial expression was one of surprise—I presumed he had never encountered a bold applicant like me before.

"Oh!" Replied the interviewer. "I'm sorry to hear that, Mr Rosemond. Please hold while I check. I'll be with you in a short while."

The official went to the back office while I waited for approximately fifteen minutes, which seemed eternal. He returned with my file, opened it on his desk, pulled out my passport with a letter, and said:

"Congratulations, Mr Rosemond. We have given you permission to remain indefinitely in the United Kingdom." The date was February 1980.

My eyes lit up, my mouth opened wide, and my hands placed on my cheeks. I could not believe what I had heard.

"Really! I can stay? I can work? I don't have to return to Saint Lucia now?" I exclaimed.

He replied, "Yes, Mr Rosemond, you can stay and work. Congratulations"

He firmly shook my hand and wished me well. Our meeting was over.

I had no words to explain my feelings; that moment was exhilarating. After waiting a long time, the end came without further questioning. I immediately headed to the telephone booth to give Rose the excellent news. She was ecstatic.

At last! I was free from the psychological burden; the immigration department had finally removed the invisible iron chain around my neck that had weighed me down. My initiative and the vital ingredient of prayer had ensured my success—God had answered my prayers decisively, so I could start putting my life back on track. My Lord and Saviour would bestow the grace that would contribute to the formation of my destiny.

My Lucky Dip

My first business in trying to restart my life was to find valid employment. I tested the waters by submitting job applications in response to advertisements in the London newspapers. Within three weeks, I continued from where I left off in Saint Lucia after receiving an invitation for an interview to fill in a bookkeeper's position at a menswear manufacturer in the East End of London. Although it was a small firm, a family business with low wages and no job security, it was a suitable way to get my footing in the job market. This opportunity provided me with a regular income, and it also served as a confidence booster. I was, therefore, content to hold on to this position while I continued my search for more stable employment.

My further job applications led me to interviews at a North London Hospital, the London Postal Service, and a Public Transport Network. My success in employment interviews continued when I managed to secure all three positions.

I was in an excellent spot to choose the best of the three available jobs. Having considered my options, I respectfully declined the hospital's offer. For my remaining choices, it was more challenging to decide on the best. They were both equal in terms of their employment terms and conditions; they offered what I sought. My priority list included job security, good promotional prospects, various insurances, social benefits, a reasonable income, and a good retirement plan. To pick my choice, I did a lucky dip. I drew the Public Transportation Network, and I went along with it.

At last! My first day of stable, long-term employment in the UK began in February 1981.

My Indispensable Lesson

The day arrived when I took up my position with the other recruits at the company's training centre. The induction began with us being issued with staff uniforms; this was my first surprise. I wore a boiler suit or overalls when I worked at the car dealership, but other than that, I had never worn a formal work uniform. I began to wonder if I had made the right decision in picking this job. I leaned on the side of the general belief that wearing a uniform at work was always associated with manual labour. During the theoretical part of the training, a facilitator aged in his mid to upper 20s conducted a lesson on customer care and effective communication.

Initially, I considered the lecture uninteresting. From my perspective, I had surpassed that level based on my past work experiences. I kept thinking, "Who the heck is this young guy trying to teach me how to communicate?"

I thought I was occupying a seat that would help someone else. However, listening attentively, I recognised the gaps in my knowledge and understanding of customer care and effective communication. By the end of the morning session, I backtracked from my original thoughts. I instantly removed my *Caribbean man thinking cap*, which I had worn for the previous year and replaced it with another that formed an utterly irreversible mentality.

From that point onward, I took a great interest in the remaining training topics; I was ready to learn. This lesson was indispensable; it was an eye-opener. Once again, I equated myself to the proverbial sardine in the Atlantic Ocean. This unforgettable experience reminded me that I was beginning a new life that needed a new attitude. I embraced the opportunity to develop my skills and immensely appreciated what I learned during my training.

Upon completion, the company assigned me to a train station located in the heart of London to work through the standard probation period of three months. This bustling environment was where I started my practical training and accepted my work schedule. Even though I was wearing a heavy grey blazer and a black cap, which I didn't like, I was somewhat excited...until I read the work roster.

Caught in the Act

I was demoralised after discovering that a significant part of my duties was sweeping the entire station, including all public areas. I could only presume that the facilitator had shared our roles and responsibilities during the induction process but I had to admit that that part of the lesson never attracted my attention. It was a rude awakening to realise that cleaning made up approximately 30% of my duties. It seemed to me that there must have been a mistake in allocating my responsibilities, and I immediately told my supervisor. I informed him that no one had mentioned sweeping when I applied.

My supervisor uttered covertly, "You proud twit, I'll have you do all the sweeping." He took pleasure in telling me,

"Hey matey, if this is the job you applied for, this is what you do."

I thought, what the heck can I learn from pushing a broom?

I was angry with myself. The result from my lucky dip appropriately turned out to be my unlucky sweep. I saw no way that I would spend one month doing this work. From starting as a white-collar worker to becoming a blue-collar sweeper! No way. I called Rose to share the news, which disheartened her.

Rose supported and encouraged me. I expected nothing less when she suggested I hold on until I move to a suitable position. I was aware of the better opportunities within the firm. Therefore, I knew that there was ample scope for progress. I calmly waited while manoeuvring toward the promotional ladder. I informed my group manager of my disappointment with my new job. Alas! It was my turn to sweep. My heart was racing. I kept thinking, *what have I done to myself?*

This job was supposed to be the beginning of an exciting life ahead! It turned out to be my first nightmare. I was stuck. I had to think of a technique to avoid the black folks going through the station and seeing me perform this task. How on earth would that be possible when thousands commuted daily? I swept the station in a panic, and every time I saw an Afro-Caribbean person coming down the stairs or around the bend, I sneakily but safely hastened to a corner where I placed the broom and moved away.

I continued doing this until, lo-and-behold and with no time to escape, I was caught in the act by Eileen, with the broom firmly in my hand. Oh no! Eileen was a close friend of the family.

"Hello, Stephen!" she said.

"Oh, hello, Eileen, how are you?" I responded.

She went on, "So this is where you work? That's what you do?"

Damn it, now she's rubbing it in, I winced.

"Isn't it obvious that's what I do?" I mumbled. With a forced smile, and then I replied, "Yes, it's all part of the job."

I knew from that moment that my family members would know about my new public sweeping job; they got the news before my shift ended. When I arrived home from work, I received my first call from John about my new role. He jokingly asked if this was the new career path that

I had chosen. My brother was amuse when I told him of my trick and how Eileen caught me. When I showed how I reacted to Eileen, Rose found my action hilarious.

"You'd be lucky not to be cornered," she commented. She continued, "It was inevitable that your hiding streak would be short-lived."

We laughed about it whenever I returned home. Rose teased me by asking how many black people I had hidden from during my shift—no offence, I did not want to be seen by one of my own, wearing a heavy uniform and pushing a broom in a public setting. This life experience denoted Mama's guidance about honest work.

My Blessing In Disguise

Time passed, and I continued to prepare myself for any opening of a better position. My manager told me I would qualify to apply for promotion or transfer after my three-month probationary period. I was going through the longest three months of my life. That test period was yet more that I had to endure. I was eager to get it over with, and immediately after it was over, I submitted my application for a non-uniform clerical position. Yes, I got the job. I was out of uniform, and the only sweeping I would do from then onward was in our home.

Upon reflection, I considered my position as a Railman a tremendous advantage. I was blessed to have had the opportunity to start my new career from the lowest grade. This position taught me much about the organisation's structure, technical and operational procedures, rules, regulations, and more.

Most importantly, I empathized with those going through the same process. My feet were firmly on the ground, and my sleeves rolled up. The time had arrived for me to continue marching on, leading to my tomorrow. But how smooth would the route be ahead? It didn't matter! I was ready.

CHAPTER EIGHT

Family Start-up

Moving forward with Rose had to begin with the natural progression of building our family. We had discussed this crucial matter as we agreed that there was no more uncertainty about our immediate future. Rose and I decided it was best to start at a young age, in our 20s, rather than wait until later. Having a family of two children was something that we both wanted. I received permanent residency status in the UK in February of 1980 and in November of the same year, our first child, Charlie, was born. We continued to work diligently towards meeting our financial and other needs that would facilitate our next move.

All the items on our "things-to-do" list were a priority; however, it was not too difficult to determine which one we should position as number one. Before baby Charlie arrived, it was okay for us to live at the home of a private landlord and share a kitchen with another tenant. Not surprisingly, the situation was different with our new baby at home; we needed more space, so we focused on obtaining better accommodation; it was top of our list.

We were keen to move one step up the ladder from a private landlord's property to moving into our own apartment. We applied to our local housing authorities, and within one year, the offer of a two-bedroom, newly built apartment came from a housing association. Our buddies thought we were the luckiest couple because we had relatively swiftly achieved this milestone, but they would not have known of the sacrifices I made by waking up before sunrise on mornings to give thanks and praise through prayer. Psalm 65 was what I continued to read incessantly.

Our new address was on the east side of the City of London, close to the heart of the capital. It all turned out to be perfect because I was closer to my place of work. We had our privacy and no longer had to tread softly to avoid disturbing our next-room neighbour. It was a relief to move away from the messiness of our disorganised co-tenant in the kitchen and the bathroom. I will leave it up to your imagination to figure out what it was like to walk into the bathroom after our scruffy male co-tenant had used it—no offence to male readers intended. The joy of moving to our apartment was nothing short of exhilarating.

An Obsolete Tradition

Once we moved to our new address, we had fewer visitors and fewer distractions. It wasn't difficult for me to discover that the previous social events were unimportant. In addition, I saw little value in building or strengthening relationships with my older siblings. Despite my reduced interaction with them, their yearning to draw me into their discussions appeared ever-present. I inferred from their behaviour that they probably valued my opinion; however, there was one problem.

Hilbert behaved like his senior status in the family automatically qualified him as the leader. He believed no one had the right to challenge his *authority*. Had this been a political scenario, his appropriate title would be "The Dictator." Do as I say and not as I do. Yes, I knew that Mama was strict. She instilled discipline. I also remember that Mama would pass the baton to the older sibling to take charge in her absence. She gave us all the necessary tools that should enable us to maintain mutual respect and lead independent lives.

While Mama did an excellent job that benefited me, and I shall forever be grateful for that, her approach had a downside. In my estimation, she unintentionally induced fear into her children. The behaviour of the older siblings was equivalent to being intimidating, causing fear among the others of being open and honest. They appeared to be worried about expressing their opinions. The anxiety festered in Mary-Anne, Joe and John, allowing Hilbert to assume a commanding position. My three siblings had difficulty detaching themselves from the old notion that Big Brother was in charge. Worst of all, whoever didn't comply with Big Brother would be denounced.

Mama and Papa longed for peace, unity, tolerance and care in the family; such were the pillars of our upbringing. I believe that while we must always hold on to discipline and mutual respect in all circumstances, those to whom we extend such courtesy must not lose sight of the keyword, mutual. They must not misconstrue our civility as a recognition of their power or dominance. Instead, they should maintain awareness of the need to reciprocate to earn such esteem rather than expect or demand simply because of one's position.

In Hilbert's presence, no one would openly endorse anyone's objection to his views, effectively giving him a free hand. I respectfully took a different stance whenever it was necessary. I was not troubled about not having any support if my opinion differed from his. I didn't apologize for the times I needed to stand alone, even though I paid the price. It was a sacrifice that I was willing to make to break away from this past rule.

It was Evolution

My agreement for togetherness as a family was beyond doubt. However, I considered the non-compromising approach no longer relevant because we all went our separate ways with our families. Furthermore, I observed that this old method led to intimidation and exploitation among the siblings; Mary-Anne, Joe and John always capitulated to Hilbert. Conflict was also another factor that this custom brought about. Joe and John's objections about Hilbert and Mary-Anne slowly developed into unhealthy relationships. To further illustrate this absurdity, John did not dare to turn down Hilbert's frequent calls to join him in the pubs, even though his wife repeatedly warned against such invitations.

I presumed John enjoyed those regular social events, but why was he complaining to all of us except Hilbert? He moaned that Hilbert was using him as an alibi for his indiscretions. Joe complained about Mary-Anne's incredible appetite for tittle-tattle, often about the family, including Hilbert. Joe protested to John and me but not Mary-Anne and Hilbert about her insincerity. He did not attempt to check up on, or corroborate, Mary-Anne's account of her stories.

Joe and John criticized Hilbert and Mary-Anne for changing the phrase *Blood is thicker than water*. From our family's perspective, it was the reverse because Hilbert and Mary-Anne always showed more appreciation towards non-family. In Joe and John's opinion, Hilbert and Mary-Anne consistently displayed concern about their friends' well-being more than they did for the family.

While Silvie, Phil and I had an open, honest, and friendly relationship in Saint Lucia, we were all aware of the friction among our older siblings in England. Therefore, it was no secret that such harmony did not exist among them. I observed a degree of self-concern, notably in Hilbert and Joe. My mindset was not in sync with that of my older siblings. What I regarded as evolution, they saw as a disconnection from tradition.

Joe's Frenzy and Profanity

My older brothers and sister were rooted in redundant habits; they failed to understand the importance of consensus. Why should they expect me to comply with their suggestions when they consistently disregarded my opinions and preferences? If I disagreed with anyone's ideas, they looked upon me as indifferent. During family gatherings, they would lecture me on the pros and cons of living in England. I considered the lessons more of a refresher training course in the school of life. I learned: that nothing in life comes without a price; to watch my back and protect myself from the exploitation of my compatriot; that my allies would choose to be supportive in handing me meals rather than advising me on meaningfully steering my way through the system. I interpreted their unsolicited advice as taking the easy, rather than the best way out.

I appreciated their concerns; however, there were times when I felt forced to revert to the shell of my ten-year-old body. I couldn't understand the big deal about passing my driving test on the first try. The thought of attempting more than once never popped into my head. Nevertheless, they all heaped praises on me, which I welcomed. Hilbert volunteered to advise me on the vehicle I should buy. The following was his recommendation.

"Stephen, you've passed your driving test, and I know you will be eager to buy your first car. My advice is, don't buy a car other than a Ford. They're cheap, and they're good cars."

During that era, the motoring public viewed the Ford vehicles as unenviable due to their mechanical breakdown frequency. However, compared to their competitors, their more affordable price attracted many. I remember the numerous complaints from John about his Ford Cortina car. John's frustration about dealing with mounting problems triggered my thoughts: "If Hilbert was genuinely concerned about my welfare by recommending this brand voluntarily, why does he not own one himself?" Instead, he had recently purchased a highly reputable Swedish brand. I needed no time to figure out an answer. My eldest brother ceaselessly displayed his overbearing role. He placed himself on the pedestal; no one else should assume or be perceived as challenging his self-appointed position. The other siblings gave him carte blanche, whether through fear or respect I don't know—my inkling leaned towards the former.

Rose and I continued with our efforts to meet our needs. We subsequently bought a used Japanese car. My decision to determine my own choice of vehicle did not go unnoticed. I was astonished to learn of the blowback that resulted from our transaction. It was ridiculous! It was childish, notably, when I received the first illustration from within the family about my refresher training, nothing in life comes *without* a price. It was apparent that some discussion had occurred among my older siblings about my vehicle purchase because Joe knew about our newly acquired possession before I told him.

One mid-morning, there came a knock on my door. "Who could this be?" I asked myself as I walked towards the door. Through the peephole, I saw my frowned-face brother Joe waiting. With such a look, I knew immediately that the purpose of his visit was not social—I opened the door.

"Hey Joe, it's a pleasant surprise. Come on in."

"Yeah, it's just a quick visit. I won't be long." Joe replied.

"So, what's been happening?" I asked.

My brother started explaining the reason for his call:

"We all know you came here on a holiday given to you by my wife. Since you chose not to return to Saint Lucia, we believe it is fair that you repay us the fare."

This incident came without a hint or warning. I had no reason to think or anticipate Joe would raise such a topic—I was taken aback. I thought this was his way of drawing me into the discord that existed in the family long before I arrived in the UK.

"But why have you waited so long to raise this subject?" I replied.

"We had to think about it seriously before asking," said my brother.

"Well, Joe," I answered, "I'm aware that my ticket to England was a present from Elma. However, I never knew we had a special clause attached" I continued. "We all know why I received a free ticket, but in any case, I thank both of you again for your kind gesture. Anyway, I can't give you a response right now."

In ending the conversation, I made no promises to appease my brother. Instead, I thought otherwise as we reached the door on his way out. I spoke once my brother was outside our apartment; the door partially opened but secured with the door chain.

"Joe," I said. "I pledge to repay you immediately upon winning the football pools."

The football pools was, at the time, what the National Lottery is today. Yes, it was a good strategy that I used in saying goodbye to Joe.

My brother was seething! He looked stunned, his eyes opened widely, with creases across his forehead. Oh my! What have I said? I realised I had shown a red flag to a raging bull. Joe immediately kicked my door in a frenzy while using profanity; I instinctively slammed my door shut. The truth is, I had always intended to deliver on my promise.

Regrettably, I had not been lucky enough ever to win the pools. This episode marked the end of my relationship with Joe for a considerable period. It was also the beginning of my exclusion from other family events. In effect, I was on the way to being ostracised.

The Business of Putting Together

This trivial and insignificant situation with Joe, which looked like a conspiracy, is just one example of what it took to assign me to the family's *black book*. A few months had passed after Joe and I broke ties when Hilbert's father-in-law passed away in Saint Lucia. I was unaware of the sad news until Mary-Anne called me and asked,

"Why were you not at the wake last night? Everyone except you came to Hilbert's to sympathize with the family."

"What wake?" I responded.

"Didn't you hear of Mr Henry's passing?" she replied.

"No, I didn't hear about it. No one told me," I answered.

"It wasn't nice that you were the only family member missing," Mary-Anne said.

From her tone, I suspected Mary-Anne was putting me on the defence.

"Why should you suggest blame on my part if no one told me?" I asked.

In my final statement, I expressed my disappointment and frustration, and in doing so, I added, "Well, Mary-Anne, whoever attended did so because those who knew notified them. Do you know of any reason why no one informed me? Let's consider my non-attendance a blessing."

"Why do you say this?" Mary-Anne asked.

"Perhaps you guys figured I wouldn't feel too comfortable in the crowd," I boldly replied.

I guess I had a knack for hitting sensitive spots when I communicated. My response to my sister aggravated an already weakened bond. My older siblings saw this as another good reason to throw me to the wolves. It never took long for the word to spread. They construed my non-attendance as a non-cooperation and lack of respect, and drew Mama and Papa into what I termed the silly saga.

Meanwhile, Mama and Papa's health took a downward turn, so our broad support became critical. Whenever Mama requested assistance from us, the one she contacted would ask the other siblings and me to "put together". For example, if Mama asked Joe specifically for assistance, Joe would feel the compulsion to have all his siblings contribute. Hilbert and Joe most frequently took this miserly stance. Their logic was, "I'm not the only child." I went along with putting together. However, while I joined in with the collective contribution, I also continued to help Mama and Papa voluntarily whenever possible.

Hilbert had returned from a trip to Saint Lucia, where he saw Papa's condition. He determined that we should all contribute to what he predicted would be our dad's last trip to England. With our situation more akin to a dysfunctional family, I told

Rose of my intention to terminate my agreement to contribute collectively towards Mama's upkeep. However, before I withdrew, I agreed to Hilbert's request to put together for Papa's holiday.

My older brother was fortunate to have been an employee of a UK international airline. With his position, he was privileged to travel at concessionary rates wherever the airline flew. His conditions of employment also included discounted travel tickets for his family and close relations; we all chipped in towards our father's reduced-priced fare. The pettiness of the matter was that nobody else would have contributed if only one could not afford it. Such a situation inevitably became a cause for arguments. It caused friction, consequently depriving our elderly parents of our cooperation in their needs.

Nevertheless, I decided it was time to disengage from the collective contribution approach once we had secured Papa's ticket. I informed the family of my withdrawal but added that I would continue to provide whatever was within my means to my parents. Despite my circumstances, they knew I never waited for my parents to ask before volunteering. In the meantime, I was committed to supporting my toddler daughter Jenny in Saint Lucia.

Stephen N Rosemond

My Role Was Big Brother's Spotlight

There were no longer any ties between Jenny's mum and me; therefore, my contributions to our daughter were through Mama. Sometimes, I sent it through Hilbert because of his frequent trips to Saint Lucia. Several years later, Lynn informed me of Hilbert's generosity towards our child. He never told her that the items he delivered were coming from me. I can only presume that he did this to portray the image of being the most caring uncle in the world. So Uncle Hilbert was taking on the role of Jenny's daddy. Hilbert supporting my daughter? He loved the spotlight, and he knew how to get it! Sadly, generosity was not part of his personality. Ironically, he did not do what he was pretending to be doing for my daughter, for *his* own two daughters.

Amid all the family drama, the anticipated change in my circumstances occurred when I became the sole breadwinner. My position was anything but easy. Once Rose and I started our family, she resigned from her job. She would remain a proud and busy stay-at-home mum until our situation permitted us to do otherwise. I was energized and willing to work all the advertised overtime hours on the roster. I also religiously scanned the company's weekly internal publications for better opportunities. In 1983,

I secured a position on a 16-week training course. Once I completed the course, I was placed on the promotions waiting list and was looking forward to commencing my new role as a Relief Clerk.

This new position fell into the category of middle management. Primarily, Relief Clerks managed a specific number of locations within the firm. Occasionally, they would take charge of the entire operating department within their assigned area. The company established its promotional structure on length of service status rather than suitability or merit. Therefore, even though I had secured a position, I would be waiting for approximately two years before getting the job, which was not unusual. I was near the bottom of the qualified prospective Relief Clerks' waiting list. In the meantime, I continued my regular duties as a Cover Clerk, earning a reasonable income.

My wages included: travelling time between my home station, where I signed on for duty and the site where I performed my task, key money, for returning the office keys the following day at the location where I had worked a late shift the previous day, enhanced payment, for working on my off days, Saturdays, and public holidays, an additional payment for working unsocial hours before 7 a.m. and after 9 p.m., and double time for Sundays.

My weekly wage added up to a fair sum.

Rose and I remained focused on building our future while our love blossomed. Our second and what we had planned to be our last baby was on her way. In February of 1983, our beautiful and energetic little princess, Tasha, was born. Our small family was complete. We had achieved the family makeup we had longed for and were blessed to have accomplished it.

A Hard-up Family

With our family of four established, Rose and I were on the move again. We had applied for more suitable accommodation from the housing association during the same year of Tasha's birth. Once again, we were fortunate when the housing company offered us a semi-detached house. This new offer surpassed our apartment size, but there was a snag. The location was way out of London in a new town, Milton Keynes, Buckinghamshire, approximately 74 km (46 miles) from London. The journey from London took up to an hour and a quarter by train. We had to think about this offer carefully. It was a real test.

I knew that it would be no joy ride to commute that distance daily, but I thought this was a small sacrifice to endure to achieve the end goal. Indeed,

I was willing to face another to settle down with my family.

Working shift patterns meant my morning shifts started as early as 05.00 hrs, and my evening shift finished at 00.50 hrs. I would have to prepare my mental and physical strengths to cope with at least 10 hours per day away from home, travelling time included. There were, however, some positives to offset the negatives; such as having a cleaner and more secure environment to raise our young children. Also, the cost of living in Milton Keynes was more affordable compared to London and we would be financially better off because I would be earning London wages while we would be doing most of our spending in Milton Keynes. We immediately saw this as an opportunity that would enable us to realise our dream of eventually buying a home, which was what we aspired to do.

Once Rose and I accepted the offer to move, I immediately applied to my workplace for a transfer to a more convenient location, nearer the train terminal for boarding to Milton Keynes. We settled in our new three-bedroom home with a beautiful back garden. The space was fantastic. It was the first time in the kids' short lives that they could enjoy the convenience of playing in their backyard. One inconvenience at our new location, though not a big deal, was that our next-door neighbours were not the ideal ones we had hoped for. Al and

Kath were a lovely but over-friendly couple with four teenage children who would have welcomed our invitation to spend a weekend at our house—or even a whole week.

They became accustomed to the extent of borrowing almost everything from us. Their request started with garden tools and steadily moved on to cooking oil, salt, onions and sugar. We understood the garden tools, but groceries! We didn't expect them to return the groceries. They were indeed a hard-up family. Al had chronic asthma, which stopped him from having a job, while Kath...well, let's just say she stayed home all day and, we presumed, chain-smoked.

Rose and I broke the habit by politely declining after no more than three tries; we responded that we hadn't gone shopping yet. They had no way of knowing that we also struggled, although our situation was not as dire. We never disclosed our business to anyone and managed without anything beyond our means. Like all caring parents, we prioritized the kids, keeping them happy, healthy, and secure.

Mutton Dressed as Beef Steak

We provided the kids with whatever little luxury we could afford. We catered for birthdays, Christmas, and public holidays. We all enjoyed the trips to the funfair, but their gifts included bicycles, roller skates, and anything that would make them happy and that we could afford. Rose and I wanted nothing else other than to be able to save towards purchasing our first home. We scraped the pennies because we were determined to move into the next property as owner-occupier. We were keen to achieve this within a reasonable period, aiming for five years from my acquiring full residential status; effectively six years of marriage.

Furthermore, London was our target for purchasing a property, so we knew that we would have to double our efforts because of the higher prices; we sacrificed as much as possible to go the extra mile. We tightened our belts and joined the march toward homeownership. We never spoke of holidays away from home because we knew that was beyond our reach. Our wardrobes had plenty of space, and our meals were basic but nutritious.

When we needed to go grocery shopping, we would head to the market nearer closing time to buy our vegetables because then we received bargains at the food stalls. The market traders always accepted a cut-price rather than a no-price, particularly on weekends. We purchased the lowest-cost foods but enjoyed delicious meals at all times. All those we had previously entertained knew Rose was super in the kitchen. She was creative with her food preparation. She also produced the most delicious meals with the minimum, and the cheapest ingredients. We made fun of our regular purchase of mutton breast, one of the most inexpensive cuts of meat. We minimized our inhibitions by buying from different butchers rather than patronising the same one whenever we shopped.

Leg of lamb and lamb chops were strictly off our menu. As for the beef steak, such luxury was beyond our means, though we ate it regularly. Have I aroused your curiosity? I assume that you're asking how that was possible. I can assure you I am no magician, but turning mutton breast into beef steak was well within our ability.

We sat at the dinner table and thanked our Lord for providing us with the delicious meal we were about to consume. We needed to do no more than pretend that our cheap mutton breast was beef steak. It was that simple! Our mutton breast pies, mutton breast stew, mutton breast casserole, mutton breast fry-ups with chips, and baked mutton breast were terrific. Oh yes! Rose was the chef who did it all. *What would our cholesterol levels have been had we gone for a medical check-up?* I wondered.

Nothing would stop us from placing ourselves on the housing ladder. The question was how we would climb over the broken rungs we were sure to encounter on our way up.

CHAPTER NINE

Climbing the Ladder

I remained resolute in believing that a better tomorrow is probable with spiritual intervention. Why should I think otherwise? All the evidence was there, and I never doubted there would be more to come. I also believe that blessings manifest in all forms, sometimes staring us in the face without us realizing it. Rewards can come through the simple, normal circumstances we encounter—for example, I have had inspiring conversations with total strangers from whom I learned something new at work and during my train commute.

Many of us take our good health for granted. We fail to appreciate it as a godsend. The onus is on us to recognize and convert such blessings into positive outcomes. We will materialize these with resourcefulness, determination, tolerance and resilience. We must have unwavering self-motivation to receive our share of good fortune while applying humility. The devotion we employ through our worship is crucial. Therefore, we must understand that the power to cultivate our inherent riches exists in us.

I had achieved what some people in my orbit thought was beyond my reach. Why did they believe that my aspirations were out of my league? I suspected those with such an opinion were underrating my ability; those were the ones who rendered no real value. Therefore, the burden was upon me to communicate with God, asking for enlightenment in understanding the real reasons for their presence around me.

I have always believed that it is wiser to demonstrate my talent through my actions rather than through words. I planned and organized. I set myself *SMART* (Specific, Manageable, Achievable, Realistic, Time-bound) targets. So, I proved many people wrong through my initiative and spiritual conviction.

Strength, Courage and Cash

In 1984, Rose and I submitted our application to our housing association for registration under the homeownership scheme. In its revised housing legislation, the British Government introduced a new programme, *The Right to Buy*. Under this scheme, tenants like us who rented from the housing authorities obtained the legal right to purchase either the home we lived in or on the open market. One requirement was that tenants needed no less than two years of occupancy in the public housing sector. We saw this as the perfect opportunity to guarantee us a share in the bricks-and-mortar investment.

The authorities attracted potential buyers to this scheme through rental rebates, which they structured based on the length of one's tenancy. We did not expect a massive discount because we had just reached the minimum occupancy requirement of two years. Another attractive element was that buyers would use their rebate to buy the home they chose anywhere in the country. The minimal discount we believed we would receive under this scheme did not deter us; we were ready to take the plunge.

Once we received confirmation that our application was in line for assessment and we were free to begin the homeownership process, we were on our way to achieving our goal. These times were exciting but challenging. Rose and I knew nothing about the process of purchasing property. Our rebate was enough to cover our deposit, but we had to cover the conveyancing cost and other associated fees. Despite having minimum cash, we had sufficient courage to take us through—there was no turning back. The realization of owning our home in England brought us tremendous joy. Yet, with this excitement, there was a scary feeling. This vast undertaking would be our first; it was a giant leap forward. I was the only breadwinner with a wife and two toddlers, so I knew it wouldn't be easy. We presumed securing a mortgage offer based only on my income would be challenging. I had to remain optimistic but realistic. Strength, courage and cash were what we needed most. I knew we would be treading a thin line. Would my figures add up? One thing I knew for sure was that failure was not an option.

I'd be Damned Not to Know

My next move was to secure a meeting with a bank manager to assess the chances of qualifying for a mortgage. Within seven days of my appointment, I received confirmation of a favourable assessment result through the post. My figures indeed added up. I was so excited that I decided to share our good news with my youngest brother in Saint Lucia, as I had an excellent relationship with him. Since Joe and I had recently made up, I wanted to build on our reconciliation and emulate my relationship with Phil by sharing my news with him, too. I started by asking Joe about buying a property, as he had already bought his own.

"Hey Joe, what's up, bro? You know Rose and I are thinking of buying a property in London. I guessed you'd be able to put me on the right track in searching for properties and prices in London, your area, and recommending a lawyer. You know, this kind of stuff."

I knew the East End of London where he lived was leaning towards the lower price tags on the market. I remember the pause before the response which Joe delivered in his usual unpolished, and this time, dissuading tone.

"Man, I don't know, but when you buying house in England you have to have money you know. Without money, you can do nothing."

Well, I'd be damned if I didn't know that much! I never expected such a thoughtless response, I was dumbstruck. Based on my brother's reaction, I imagined he wouldn't have observed the pause after I had taken a deep breath before responding.

"Oh yeah, of course! I completely forgot. Sure, I have to have money to buy a house, Joe. Yeah, I'll be fine, no worries. Never mind, I'll take care of that, we'll talk again. Take care."

I never mentioned that I needed money in my short exchange with my brother. Did he not think that I was aware of that fact?

The encouraging response that I was expecting from Joe never came. I never received a subsequent call from my brother to inquire about my progress. Therefore, in my opinion, this demonstrated his disinterest in my affairs. Was I too naive to believe my brother bore no hard feelings towards me? Should I have presumed he was still remorseful about his wife's gift that he had previously demanded from me? I figured I had resurrected the old memories. I would not allow such sarcasm to dampen my spirit. On the contrary, I was more determined to accelerate.

I started house hunting by registering with various estate agents. This part of the process was punishing, as the internet was still in the making. My working hours and property viewing time were exhausting. While exploring, I often spent an extra two hours in London after work. I managed my time by searching one day and viewing all by appointment another day. My system worked out fine.

Once I eventually found a property that I thought would be suitable, I arranged a second viewing with Rose and our babies. We finally decided on a property we liked; I had gained Rose's blessings just as I had envisaged. As first-time buyers with minimal resources, it was an okay-sized family home with three bedrooms and the necessary facilities. Most importantly, we were stepping onto the home ownership ladder and moving toward a better future.

My Dying Lawyer

Rose and I stood solidly with each other as we continued with our sacrifices to turn our dream of owning a home into a reality. We pushed ahead with our planning and organising. We contacted the firm of solicitors who were recommended to us by the estate agents. We had some funds saved for our new purchase, and Benny and Andy, a couple of colleagues, were on standby to assist with our anticipated relocation. We were ready to press on to the next stage. We submitted our application to the bank for the mortgage, and a few weeks later, we received approval.

While it was a fantastic opportunity to purchase a property through the Government's right-to-buy housing scheme, we realised that the three-way transaction added much time to the process. Not only did we have to wait for the vendor's administration to be completed, but we also had to sit out the delay by our housing association; the hold-up was sometimes frustrating.

Rose and I were mainly concerned because the three solicitor firms blamed each other for the ongoing setback. The most worrying thing of all was that the deadline for the mortgage offer was fast approaching. We would have to repeat the application if we allowed it to expire. We held our breath in anticipation for what appeared to be an unending period. The cause of the delay eventually emerged.

Our lawyer had been ill for some time and passed away. This information was relayed to us by his office. The estate agent later freely confirmed the details of the lawyer's passing; he had died of AIDS. The news was exceedingly sad.

Yet, at the same time, a little part of me couldn't help thinking why nothing worked smoothly in my life. Why am I constantly being tried? Of the thousands of solicitors in the UK, why was one with a terminal illness assigned to us?

My Desperate Moment

The lesson I gained from my adversity was to unreservedly accept that whatever happens in my life, good or bad, I should never waiver in my faith. Upon receiving the news about the solicitor, Rose and I went through the natural feeling of disappointment and unease. Nevertheless, we stayed calm and continued; we prayed that something better would come up.

With all that was happening around us, I kept in close contact with my family in Saint Lucia, who updated me about Papa Ray, whose health was continuing to fail due to his severe condition. The latest information my siblings and I had received from Silvie was that Papa's situation was slowly deteriorating. Mama was also in poor health and was incapable of assisting her husband. Phil was playing his supporting role, but sadly, Silvie carried the weight of caring for our mother and our father.

My siblings and I arranged a meeting to discuss our parents' situation. We agreed that we should all try to assist in one way or another. We had long abandoned the *putting together* idea but had to revive the topic because it was a critical moment.

It was May 1985, six years since I had left Saint Lucia. No one was accountable for the timing of our father's condition, but the situation was incredibly distressing for me. Hilbert suggested that the seriousness of the matter justified our travel to Saint Lucia to relieve Silvie. We all provisionally agreed to the idea but would later confirm when we met at Hilbert's home. Being able to contribute would pose some financial difficulty due to my pending transaction. Thoughts were racing through my mind. I explained my economic circumstances to my siblings and asked them individually, "What would you do if you were in my position?"

The answer I received was not at all surprising.

"It's up to you," they all agreed. Well, I guess that's a reasonable answer.

John said he was broke and could not contribute despite our prior agreement. Joe was no different. He gave his usual reason for not helping: he had too many bills to pay. Mary-Anne, who had immigrated to the USA some years earlier, had decided to travel to Saint Lucia to assist. Hilbert agreed that he would make the journey, too. It was, therefore, my turn to state my position. I knew, despite our cash flow situation, the result of my discussion with Rose would be supportive, but I chose to delay until she and I had had the opportunity to discuss the matter in detail.

Rose and I conversed deep into the night. We prayed and asked the Lord for guidance. My imagination that someone, from somewhere, was somehow putting my loyalty to the test was vivid. There were only two options from which to choose: to go ahead, carry on with our plans for our family home, and follow in the footsteps of Joe and John—after all, like them, I had no cash to spare—or to use part of the cash my wife and I had saved to acquire our home to visit my dying father and seriously ill mother.

Hilbert's Callous Remarks

My wife and I agreed that I should go ahead and see my dying father. For me, this was an emotional moment twice over. First of all, there were tears of sadness because I imagined how tough it would be if Papa passed away without having the chance to say goodbye. Secondly, I wept at the realization that my wife supported me at such a tough time and was willing to place our future on hold. I telephoned my other siblings, but I asked Hilbert again before I announced my decision.

"What would you do if you were in my position?" He responded without hesitation, "I would go ahead and buy our home."

I replied, "Well, we are putting our home on hold. Rose and I have decided I will make the trip."

To Hilbert, this was a bold statement which exposed the dissimilarities in our attitudes to life.

"Stephen," Hilbert responded, "I am very proud of you, although I was not expecting anything less from you."

He also expressed deep disappointment with Joe. His sharp criticism of Joe's endless complaints about having bills to pay was unflattering. From that instance, Joe earned a new name; we called him Mr Bill. Hilbert then turned his attention to John.

"Well," he stated, "Since John spent all his money at the pubs, he should seek a loan from the pub to visit his dying father."

His opinion of his two younger brothers was not empathetic; instead, it was disparaging. In my view, Hilbert's remarks about John, in particular, were callous. John was seldom in the pub without Hilbert; they were joined at the hip when it came to a trip to the bar. Hilbert's remarks and John's declaration of his finances confirmed what I had suspected was John's vulnerability. Was John doing all the spending at the pub while his older brother and leading drinking partner enjoyed the fun at his expense? I wondered.

"When are you going to book your fare?" Hilbert asked.

"I am ready to do so now," I replied.

"Okay," replied Hilbert, "let me book the ticket for you at work. I'll get you a discounted fare to Saint Lucia. Give me your details, including your return date, and I'll arrange it."

I agreed to meet at his home, where I handed over my details and payment for my ticket. I appreciated my brother's assistance immensely as it represented a substantial saving. Our next meeting was at the airport's departure lounge. Hilbert, his wife, and I were heading to Saint Lucia. I would be spending two weeks with my family.

Papa's Welcome Respite

When I arrived home for the first time since leaving six years earlier, my welcome from my family was moving and exciting. Mama was speechless as she embraced me, and Papa was stretched out in his bed, gazing at me with an expression as if to say, "Welcome back, my son!" Momentarily, we all reached for a face rag and dabbed our eyes and cheeks—but why? Papa was still with us! It was tears of joy. I was flattered that Hilbert sang my praises to the entire family about the hard choices Rose and I faced in deciding on my journey.

The affection and attention I received were overwhelming. We all expected Papa to pass away on the night of our arrival, but his apparent inner feelings overpowered his physical appearance; he was not ready to leave us yet. I was pleasantly surprised two days later when I visited Papa in his room to hear him slowly whisper his first words to me.

"Stephen, I heard what you did. God will bless you, my child. You will find a bigger and better house when you return to England. God will bless you, my son."

Later that day, our dad was sitting up in his bed. To our surprise, he asked us to take him to the living room, where he sat on his favourite chair. It looked like the Lord had given Papa a welcome respite. We were all thankful for the extra time with his children as we cherished the moment. My two weeks' visit had come to an end and I was lamenting my father's condition, yet joyous, during my eight-hour flight back to England with Hilbert, to be returning to my wife and family.

Stephen N Rosemond

The Manifestation of My Father's Blessing

On the afternoon of July 4th, 1985, within two months of my return, I received the sad news of Papa's passing. Our beloved father was gone, but I was comforted that I had the opportunity to speak with him. Most importantly, I was encouraged by his last blessings. The words that my dad uttered to me during my visit were so inspiring. I knew that we brought some joy to him before he left us.

I did not attend Papa's funeral, nor did anyone expect my presence. I gave Phil the suit I had intended to wear at the funeral service; he would wear it as a gesture of my attendance. With Hilbert's travel privileges, he had no problems making a second journey to attend the burial. Although there was no obligation on my part, I made an added financial contribution; I gave Hilbert £200.00 to pass on to our mother. In our subsequent discussion, Mama expressed satisfaction with her children's participation in our dad's passing. A special thanks went to Hilbert for his "kind gesture" of an additional £200.00 toward the burial expenses—this information warranted a pause; it had me wondering. Knowing of my brother's attitude, I felt obliged to prolong the conversation by asking Mama:

"Did he pass on the £200.00 to you that I gave to him for you?"

"When was that?" Mama replied.

I wasn't surprised. My mum confirmed that Hilbert never informed her of my deed. By the end of our chat, her mood had changed from composure to dismay.

My trip to Saint Lucia meant that Rose and I had lost the chance to buy the house we had initially wanted but we readily regrouped. We resumed our search for a suitable home as we got back on track. During what looked like an endless search for another property, my father's loving words kept ringing in my ears; we never lost hope. Deep within me, I was confident that Papa's blessings would come to life. I looked toward finding that bigger and better home that he had wished for us.

In December 1985, Rose and I found it. In March 1986, we moved into our new home in East London with our two adorable kids without any hitches. The property was just as Papa described, with far better features that included: a newly remodelled kitchen with custom-fitted cabinets, stainless steel cooker, built-in oven, dishwasher, and microwave, three sizable bedrooms a through lounge, a porch, a storage room and a cellar

The new package came with the same price tag as the previous home, and the quality was unparalleled. This episode, to me, was no blessing in disguise. Instead, it looked like a prediction, a miracle, a vision. I regarded this experience as the manifestation of my father's approval.

We processed the entire transaction without any setbacks, for which Rose and I were genuinely thankful. Upon moving into our new dwelling, my first action was to recite Psalm 61, followed by my prayer for the blessings of good fortune to our home. Our neighbourhood was quiet, nothing like Back Street, although I hoped the nearby residents would be as welcoming.

Floop

I was exceedingly grateful for all the blessings I had gained thus far during my six years in England. During our search for a property, the estate agent had recommended to Rose and me the most favourable part of the borough; we were happy to heed his advice. There was a good mix of young, middle-aged and elderly in the neighbourhood. We were only the second Afro-Caribbean people living on our road, but we were pretty distant from the elderly couple before us. We tried to fit in with our friendly greetings and the occasional 3-minute chat with anyone who cared to accommodate us—there were not many.

Among our immediate neighbours, Eve, an elderly widow who lived opposite, was the best. She was friendly and caring and never resisted a conversation, more often initiated by her. Next to Eve was an elderly couple whose names we never knew throughout our sixteen years in the area. They owned a yellow car, so I called the husband "Yellowman". The husband and wife stared blankly at us. They seldom said hello but nodded their heads in response to our greetings. Most important was our next-door neighbour, a lovely couple, Chrissy and Tariq, who were a similar age, twenty-nine approaching thirty and had four young children. Unlike Cath and Allan, our neighbours in Milton Keynes, Tariq, a South Asian, went to work daily while Chrissy, a Caucasian, was a stay-at-home mum. Rose and I were happy to share our home-grown vegetables with them as we developed a harmonious relationship—just as we had hoped. Within one year of knowing the couple, they added a new member to their family. By the end of our fourth year as neighbours, the number had further increased. We never observed Chrissy's pregnancies because her physique was always the same.

Rose and I had arrived from a shopping trip one afternoon when Tariq and Chrissy were making their way into their home—Tariq was already halfway through the door.

"Hi Chrissy, hi Tariq," we greeted. They responded in kind.

"How are the kids?" Rose asked.

"Oh, they're fine," replied Chrissy. "We've just come from the hospital," she added.

"Oh, what's wrong? Is everyone alright?" Rose asked.

Chrissy replied, "Yes-yes. Everyone's fine, including this little one."

"Which one?" Rose questioned.

"Tariq's gone in with her," she replied.

Rose and I were startled as the conversation continued; Chrissy made the most astonishing remark. She proudly explained. "I went in this morning to have the baby, and everything went well. The baby came out so quickly; it was just, floop!—and it was over."

Well, to Rose and I, that was funny. We imagined it as a straightforward open-and-shut case. This child was their seventh. I was surprised when the couple continued to increase their family size because I had previously only tied the big family tradition to my people in the Caribbean.

Echoes of Mr Isaac

Tariq and I would converse, often talking about sports; like me, he loved cricket. Shockingly, rather than disclosing it, he allowed me to discover the hard way another sport he enjoyed.

Rose and I suddenly started hearing cooing sounds in the early mornings from the back garden. We initially paid no attention because we thought pigeons were hanging out in the trees. Unfortunately, the sounds persisted, and bird droppings appeared on our translucent conservatory roof; it was disgusting and required washing down. This situation was annoying with what looked like bird diarrhoea or (*lar-jee-jit*, as we would say in Saint Lucia), in our garden regularly. We later discovered the birds were sheltering in Chrissy's garden. Within one month of our initial observation of that unsavoury matter, the bird diarrhoea had landed on Rose's washing on the line. The nuisance quickly escalated into a problem requiring immediate attention. I decided to have a candid conversation with my neighbour.

"Hi Tariq, I'm sorry to trouble you, but I needed to inform you of our concerns about some pigeons we noticed you have caged in your back garden."

"Oh, yeah, Steve. I never mentioned it before. These are my racing pigeons. I kept them at my brother's for a while but decided to keep them here now."

"But why bring them here, Tariq? They're really a bother because they poop all over my conservatory and in our garden where the children play. Worst of all, they've even pooped on Rose's laundry on the clothesline. And when they're not out flying, their constant cooing causes a disturbance."

"Come on Steve, they're my sporting pigeons. They're meant to fly."

I genuinely hoped to come to some amicable resolution, but Tariq's subsequent reply blew me away. I heard echoes of Mr Isaac's reply to his wife—"I did not tell the goats to eat your food," when she complained about the goats eating her vegetables.

I was not amused when Tariq mockingly stated, "Steve, they're pigeons. I can't tell them where to shit."

"Tariq," I replied. "You're being unreasonable. Why not leave them at your brother's?"

Tariq was sarcastic when he declared: "Where do you want me to keep them? In my bedroom?" I saw shades of discourtesy in Tariq's attitude; I was peeved but remained calm.

"Come on, Tariq," I replied, "You can't keep them here. Two weeks is a reasonable time for you to relocate them. How about that?" I asked.

He responded, "Steve, I can't relocate them, and I certainly can't stop them from shitting."

Our conversation ended. Now, this condition was parallel to what took place in Back Street. I had been relieved to have moved away from the early morning cocks crowing, only to end up to persevere, hoping that someone from the local authority was bound to intervene or another neighbour would raise an objection.

As time passed, our hopes faded—I began to feel haunted by the ghost of my past third-world environment. "How was it possible to end up in a neighbourhood in a developed country in the heart of a community where such an enterprise was allowed?" I asked myself. I may not have taken immediate action but I promised myself that at the appropriate time, and irrespective of the time it took, I would end what I saw as a total lack of consideration. Meanwhile, my wife and I focused on transforming our property to our liking.

Killing Myself to Develop New Skills

Now that we had joined the homeowners club, we had to prepare ourselves for all the tasks included in the privilege. The trouble was that Rose and I had no clue where to begin, even though we knew how we would like to start. I started by equipping myself with several DIY manuals, including ones for plumbing, tiling and painting. I ensured I had the appropriate tools before engaging myself in any project. Using a knife as an alternative to a screwdriver is not my definition of working proficiently.

Getting my hands dirty in London home.

My critics interpreted my DIY efforts as, "Stephen killing himself". My perspective was that opportunities presented themselves for me to develop new talents and expand my capabilities in the interest of my family. To this day, many people, family, and acquaintances alike, portray me more as a pen-pusher. While this depiction has an element of truth, I won't turn away from an opportunity to get involved with practical work to get my hands dirty. Rose and I did the painting and decorating, and we welcomed the offer of help from Rose's older brother, Cheddy, a registered electrician, with whom she had a great relationship. He undertook the renewal of the electricals.

Those who later visited expressed admiration for the work that Rose and I had done. I was humbled when folks with some knowledge appraised our new competence level as a "professional" standard. With our confident approach, we completed the jobs satisfactorily and within our means. The goodwill gesture from Cheddy was of immeasurable value—the financial benefits of savings on labour charges, and with Christmas fast approaching, we considered it our special gift. These circumstances further demonstrate that alongside prayers, we require initiative as well as a passion to achieve what we want. The power to bring our desires to life lies within us.

A No-cooking Day

We were excited about celebrating our first Christmas in our new home with our two children, which would be extra special. There was no better opportunity to give thanks and praise to God, beginning with attending the midnight mass on Christmas Eve for the first time as a family. One of the valuable lessons I learned as a family man regarding Christmas was that kids are only concerned about their gifts from Santa—Rose's only concern was obtaining more than the mutton breast we had for a long time funnelled into our bellies. I thanked God I was also able to provide much more. Rose had all the trappings she needed to ensure a very merry Christmas.

We continued our celebration with enjoying a healthy breakfast and opening gifts as we played beautiful Christmas melodies. Rose and I were unprepared for the kids paying no interest in the dinner Rose had so wonderfully arranged. Well, it was Christmas Day, their gifts entranced them, and we allowed them the freedom to entertain themselves—they survived on snacks for the day, which allowed Rose and I to declare Christmas Day a no-cooking day. We subsequently had our festive meal on Boxing Day. From then onward, we designated Boxing Day as our day for Christmas dinner, and it has remained so ever since.

The Flintstones' Turkey and the Caterpillar

We went one step further in keeping with our Saint Lucian tradition when, the following year, we invited family and friends for Christmas dinner. However, they were confused when told we would be serving the dinner on Boxing Day. As might be expected, no one understood why the change of routine until we explained; they loved it. With lots to eat and drink and the best of Caribbean music to dance to, everyone enjoyed our Boxing Day party. Our parties usually extended late into the night; so we would always make sure to inform our next-door neighbours of our gatherings beforehand and to offer an advanced apology for any disturbance. We always ended our festive season on the first of January with a New Year's Day dinner-turned-party at a family member's or friend's home.

On New Year's Day, my family and I arrived at the home of our middle-aged friends, a couple named Angie and Dennis, in the middle of the action. Everyone held on to their glasses as we revelled, the kids enjoying their snacks and having fun with the other children. Angie and Dennis spoke mostly Creole; they saved their limited English for special occasions.

"Come on everyone, grab a seat if you can. Izz time fuh dinna," came the call from Dennis. My family and I were among those who sat at the 8ft long table, all decorated with a selection of meats, including turkey, pickles and sauces, vegetables baked and boiled, salads and everything that could fit. It was an eat-all-you-can buffet.

Angie walked in from the kitchen, "Please, everyone, mek sure you all enjoy. Donn be shy," she said. We all started to tuck in. Angie targeted our six-year-old son Charlie,

"Go on, Charlie, you can have the torky leg. Donn be afraid," she reassured him. Angie decided to serve Charlie, placing the turkey leg on his plate as Rose and I looked at each other with a grin.

"Oh dear, that's a lot for Charlie; he won't eat all this meat," Rose told Angie.

"No-no, it's Crismos; let him have his torky leg. He'll be okay," Angie replied.

Not wishing to create awkwardness, Rose allowed Charlie to continue. What no one knew was that little Charlie had a thought that he would share with his sister, who was sitting next to him. Tasha giggled after Charlie whispered in her ear. I suspected the joke was about Charlie's turkey leg because I had never seen such a giant one like this before.

"Hey, what are you all saying? Stop giggling before you choke on your dinner," Rose warned softly.

With Tasha continuing to giggle and pointing at Charlie's turkey leg, she told her mum quietly:

"Charlie told me he would keep this Flintstones turkey leg to knock me out with if I trouble him."

Our Charlie was spot on. The size of the turkey leg reminded us of the funny television series from the 1960s. The leg of a stone-age turkey being served by the prehistoric Flintstones family. Rose and I saw the funny side, but that wasn't all. Our little boy had a good sense of humour and a very sharp eye, too. There was a hidden addition to the vast amount of protein laid out on the table. We hadn't reached the salad bowl when Charlie wisely pointed to a tiny caterpillar crawling between the lettuce leaves. Rose discretely scooped up the leaf complete with the insect still on it and discarded it in the bin without saying a word. The downside to this stomach-churning discovery was that it instantly doused our appetites.

We have never before revealed this incident, and maintained our friendship with Angie and Dennis for a long time. Yet, while we continued to exchange visits, Rose and I limited our acceptance of foods to snacks whenever we visited. The celebrations season was over; Rose and I reverted to our routine. My journey as a *Third-Worlder* was entering a new phase.

CHAPTER TEN

Does Success Breed Jealousy?

Having gained first-hand knowledge of the phrase *patience is a virtue,* I had no intentions, nor have I aspired to experience another—*success breeds jealousy.* In this case, it is more proper to describe such success as perceived, as I termed it. These outcomes do not allude to our finances or level of material capacity. It is not quantifiable or apparent to us, the beneficiaries. We see ourselves as ordinary citizens going through struggles, yet folks would place us on a high pedestal. Their explicit acknowledgement of us is what I view as perceived success. "What do you mean?" I hear you ask. The answer is plain.

We have made little effort to acquire the qualities that make us who we are. In effect, we are unconscious of the optimism that we reflect. We are respectful and, in some way, unique. People look up to us as intelligent, and we are gaining the attention of others; they listen and take notes when we speak. We become a magnet for envy for reasons unknown to us.

If we recognize such reactions toward us, it becomes our responsibility to cultivate positive responses. Obtaining favourable results would be based on our initiative-taking, creative, assertive, and forward-thinking abilities. Couple these together with humility, and we will achieve the God-given blessings of success.

Some folks around Rose and me believed we were well underway to achieve our life's pinnacle, even though we knew such realization was a long way ahead. I suppose people would judge us based on their standards because our aspirations and progress exceeded their expectations of us. While they continuously struggled to remove themselves from their burden of setbacks, they regarded our strides in offloading our difficulties as self-centred.

Our steady improvement became an attraction. Our allies didn't know our aims and didn't grasp our strategies; therefore, they misconstrued our ideas. We did not seek validation but among the approvals that came our way, beneath the surface of many, there were plenty of witticisms. "Wow, we'll have to visit by appointment only," one family member remarked. Another quipped, "Where did *you* buy this *expensive* piece of furniture?"

My family considered our standards too ambitious and way beyond our reach. I regarded those with such judgment as setting their success bar at a mediocre level with low expectations; therefore, our basic position was an enormous achievement from their standpoint.

In contrast to their view, I saw a determined mountain climber aiming for the summit. To sum it up, my interpretation of success through blessings is like a beaming light shining through you, yet invisible to you. Let me expand on my personal experience.

I consumed one of the cheapest of meats, mutton breast, for quite an extended period. Yet, individuals around me thought my diet consisted of beef steak. Trust me, I only ate steak in my imagination, and it was of the most tender varieties.

My appearance was never reflective of my actual budget or social status. I never revealed where I shopped for clothing. Yes, I was just another shopper at the ordinary high street shops and the Sunday market stalls, but some believed I shopped at London's West End high-end stores. It didn't matter what outfit I wore, the people saw a positive image.

During the earlier days right up until the 1980s, it was customary for people to borrow cash from their colleagues and relatives when buying property; I stayed away from that practice. Even though seven years was a long time for me, my family did not understand how we purchased our home within that time without approaching them for financial help, considering our years of instability. By sacrificing, overcoming repeated setbacks, and with determination, we fulfilled our goal to the surprise of many.

No Goodwill for Family

Once we settled into our new home, Rose and I concentrated on building on our accomplishments. Although it was not urgent, getting our finances back on track was necessary. We expected this would be no easy feat because I remained the sole income earner. We agreed to mitigate our circumstances by Rose finding full or part-time employment. However, this would only be possible by employing a babysitter or childminder. Once we had examined the possibilities, we concluded that part-time work was the way to start. Rose successfully applied to one of the major local supermarkets for employment.

We didn't have far to go to find a carer for our kids because Joe's wife, Elma, was a registered childminder. At that time, she had other children in her care but was short of her maximum capacity. We believed she would have welcomed the opportunity to care for our toddlers, so we proposed the idea. We were delighted when she agreed to our proposal; of course, we weren't seeking a free service, nor would we have accepted one.

Rose started her part-time job as a retail assistant. We adopted the following simple routine. Rose would take the kids to Elma's and head off to work. I would pick them up after I finished work. After two weeks into the practice, Elma informed us that she would no longer be able to care for our babies. Her explanation of being "overbooked" did not add up because she had discussed the proposal with us in detail before agreeing. This situation was an inconvenience but it was no surprise. Why should I expect our efforts to work uninterrupted by involving Elma and her husband?

While my sister-in-law had no hesitation in caring for our toddlers, it was quite the opposite with my brother, Joe. Some years later, when cracks began to appear in Elma's marriage, she revealed the truth. Her husband did not want her to mind our infants. His objection echoed the usual petty arguments on Elma's account:

"Stephen went buying a house. He thought it would be easy. Just leave him with his mortgage and let him find someone else to care for his children."

My brother demanded that his wife stop, and so she did. My older siblings' mindset was unfortunate as they directed their tendency to dispense goodwill toward comrades while overlooking family. Rose and I revisited our plans. It was a blessing when we found a suitable babysitter without disrupting our programme. Lisa came to our house while we were at work, and her fee was more affordable. Joe had unwittingly assisted us because his decision had achieved the opposite effect; it was a blessing as my wife and I were the winners.

My Guiding Principles

If Joe intended to make me a victim, he would have been disappointed. I didn't feel sad about his actions; they didn't matter to me and I didn't lose sleep over them. Joe had proven once more to be one of the opposing forces in my sphere. I was duty-bound to adjust my emotional attachment to my older siblings. I dismissed all expectations of any meaningful reconciliation. And I strengthened my resolve to navigate towards my goal, irrespective of the hurdles I would meet.

Occasionally, we may ask ourselves why our folks treat us with disdain despite our selflessness towards others. Please do not despair, for the solution lies in the incredible power of prayer. We must trust that God is our defence. He assigns us our Guardian Angel, forever present whenever the enemy sets out to inflict harm. Our invisible shield provides security and preserves us from potential dangers. This powerful force enables us to distinguish the good from the bad and identify our foes among friends. Our confidence becomes so plain that we feel invincible, never fearing further encounters.

In time, I developed a mental attitude that would enable me to manage distractions. I translate someone's jealousy towards me as an endorsement that I am moving along the right path. Adopting a new but positive mindset isn't easy. It can be unfortunate and sometimes painful to others. However, this circumstance regarding my brother's objection boosted my confidence to continue discovering my true purpose. Whoever bears the grudge exposes their weakness. I continue being who I am and not who those around me want me to be. I will not allow people to characterize me by being the person who becomes "one of them" for the sake of being well-liked. Intimidation is not a force that drives me to self-isolation. Should my adversaries want a battle, their results would be frustration. They would have been oblivious that they were, in fact, fighting themselves and would be the glum losers.

Psalm 44 was the prayer that I used to boost my resistance to ward off ill intentions toward me.

I continuously try to be pragmatic in my approach. While possible defeat is a factor that I consider during planning, failure is not an option that I envisage as a final result, even though it is inevitable that we will all, at some time or another, fail no matter how careful we are. I also recognise the need to be mindful that practising what, in general, we consider morally and socially unacceptable is another way to lose. We stand to lose respect, dignity, and social standing; I tried diligently to make these my guiding principles.

Nothing Short of Betrayal

The affection I obtained from my beloved parents was not in short supply; my mother kept her confidence in me. She did not doubt that I would always be her pillar. Of course, my closeness to Mama was no secret, and to prove that point, in 1986, Hilbert thought it was right when he gave me a nickname. He bestowed a new title upon me, which I approved with humility; he labelled me "Mama's King." It was my honour to accept unreservedly.

I would never object to such acclaim if my brother believed it suited me. How bizarre! Hilbert had intended this new title to be a price I should pay. Instead, it became a prize I appreciated. It turned out that he was creating an atmosphere that would bring about resentment toward me for reasons that were not too difficult to imagine. It looked like he was sparing no effort to disrupt my focus.

I regarded attending to Mama's well-being as a privilege, irrespective of the time or place involved. Mama's health was not improving, and in 1986, while Hilbert was on one of his usual ten-day trips to Saint Lucia, he and Silvie accompanied Mama to one of the island's hospitals. Following the medical assessments, they overheard the discussion about Mama's prognosis: amputating her leg. Hilbert and Silvie were alarmed by the thought of Mama losing a leg, and they objected. My two siblings are no medical practitioners, but they thought their mother ought to have a second assessment—a great judgment. Hilbert believed there was a better chance of Mama obtaining advanced treatment for her condition in England. There was urgency in organising her trip and Silvie informed me of the situation. Once more, Hilbert used his favourite phrase, "put together," for Mama's journey to England. Pitching in on this occasion was a desperate need, therefore, no objections ever surfaced. Mama would be travelling with Hilbert, so my older siblings and I agreed to chip in to get Mama on the flight. Hilbert and his wife, Catherine, had established that Mama would reside with them upon her arrival.

Regrettably, the two got into one of their typical arguments on a late evening, four days before departure. It was sad and shameful when they drew our mother into their fray, especially as our mother was grieving the recent loss of her husband. We had never known her to intervene in matters that had occurred in the past between that couple, and Mama always had a special affection for Catherine because her travel privileges enabled her to visit often with or without her husband. She chose to stay with Mama even though her parents lived in Saint Lucia. Yet, in an outburst, Catherine reversed her decision about Mama's trip and told her she was no longer welcome at her home in England. Hilbert was either unable or unwilling to let his wife withdraw her statement. Of course, this submission was characteristic of him.

The incident between my eldest brother and his wife was like something from a soap opera. Spouses set the scene, intent on creating a conflict. Their vicious plan was to drag the helpless mother-in-law into their dispute. Unable to defend herself, the mother-in-law becomes the victim. The couple achieves their goal of giving their mother the push and evading their commitment to her. Mama's visit to England was about to derail because she talked about cancelling her journey. Silvie, in a heartbroken mood, relayed the events to me.

"Why should this become Mama's crisis?!?" I declared. "Why should Catherine make such an irrational statement and Hilbert not oppose her behaviour, despite all agreeing to the plan?"

Our sick mother had three other married sons in England with whom she was expecting to spend time during her temporary stay. She was looking forward to joining us and being among her many grandchildren.

This incident was cruel. It was no surprise that it dampened Mama's spirits. She no longer wanted to travel. Silvie continued to inform me of the situation as it developed. I liaised with Joe and John to discuss the matter, but I didn't discuss the issue with Mary-Anne because I thought doing so would have been pointless. Furthermore, she wouldn't be involved in Mama's upkeep in England since she had moved from the UK to the United States some years earlier and remained Hilbert's staunchest ally. Joe and John weren't surprised by Catherine's outburst, but they were astonished that their eldest brother had said nothing to overrule his wife's callous behaviour.

While my two brothers agreed that our eldest sibling and his wife's actions were deplorable, they did not suggest an alternative to Mama's accommodation. I introduced the conversation and spoke about the options for caring for her. Understandably, they wanted to discuss the matter with their spouses before committing. They would inform me after their discussions. Shockingly, neither Joe nor John decided to accept Mama at their homes or commit to sharing the cost of her maintenance. Their response indicated that the spouses had rejected the proposal to share and care. I was sad and embarrassed once again—for Mama. I considered it humiliating.

The final decision about Mama's well-being remained with me. I would not have allowed my mother's hopes of seeking medical attention in England to be dashed. I would never backtrack on my promise to her. Regardless of our situation, Rose and I would welcome Mama into our home and allow her to stay for however long would be needed to complete her medical care. I considered our mother's rejection by her three daughters-in-law, supported by her three sons, nothing short of betrayal. Mama never wavered in showing an unshakeable commitment to her children. In return, my older siblings reciprocated by dishonouring their mother.

Our Five Gallon Bucket

Playing the unpaid servant role for many years was the prime example of Mama's devotion. Whenever our siblings visited us in St Lucia, she prioritised them over me, Silvie and Phil. They were served ahead of us with the best from the menu. They slept in our beds while we slept on the floor. We were their messengers. Without a second thought, we would have washed their feet if they had asked us, and Mama would have allowed us to do so. They only needed to click their fingers for help, and we would be at their service.

When they were preparing to return to England, Mama used the paltry cash she scraped together to purchase gifts for them. Those gifts included local rums, cashew nuts, fried fish, yams and spices. Mama, Silvie, Phil and I spent hours roasting, shelling, and peeling the skin off the nuts, ensuring they received the best from the selection; of course, we suffered the consequences. For many days, our hands would remain discoloured and flaky from the oil produced from the roasted nuts shell because we didn't have the luxury of wearing protective gloves. Silvie, Phil and I shared whatever bits of broken pieces of nuts were left.

Mama interpreted our level of attention to our visitors as "being pleasant". She welcomed all with abundant generosity that bordered on ridiculousness. While she never neglected us, she gave her children who arrived on holiday priority; that was Mama. That was her true loving and caring nature. Silvie, Phil and I were never bitter, as we cooperated to the fullest. However, reluctantly and with the benefit of hindsight, such consideration reflects the relics of servitude from where I stand. When Joe and John visited with their families, there was no lack of excitement as we looked forward to having all the siblings back in our childhood home together—but there was a glitch.

Back then in St Lucia our three-bedroom dwelling consisted of a kitchen measuring no more than 9ft x 12ft, our sitting and dining area wasn't any more spacious, and outside was a toilet Mama fitted with a 5-gallon empty butter bucket. Our house was heaving with life. On one occasion, Mama, Silvie, me and Phil were overjoyed to welcome Hilbert, his wife, and two daughters, Joe, his wife, son, and daughter, and John and his wife; they holiday stayed for three weeks. Regrettably, Papa Ray was the only one missing. Throughout his sixteen years of residence in England, Papa visited no more than three instances during Easter. Imagine fourteen people using one 5-gallon bucket as a toilet daily—I accompanied Mama to the seafront every morning at about 4 a.m. to dispose of the contents. The diagonal posture of Mama's shoulders as she walked, her left shoulder slanted while carrying the load in the right hand, clearly indicated that she was not moving feathers. The stench was comparable to the weight.

I was the innocent boy who always trailed Mama, walking against the early morning breeze. I had the misfortune of sniffing the disgusting odour that blew into my face. One morning, we were on our way with our unsavoury container, loaded to the total capacity. We encountered an older man from the village named Lé-couze (pronounced *Lay-Cooz*). Lé-couze was a bit of a comedian, yet sarcastic. We greeted him. He responded and remarked in our Creole dialect with a playful smirk on his face:

"*Ware! Poor jabb. Kaii saar-laar nee bonn-daah! Zor jaarr shahyea kar-kar!*" (Well, well! How sad. This house has many backsides! You guys have carried lots of poop!)

It was hilarious! What else could it be? Mama could give no response other than, "Yes, and you can say that again."

Lé-couze's observation was spot on. Even though we seldom saw him while we carried our load to the sea, it was clear that he watched us every day doing the trek by peeping through his window. Mama and I laughed it off because there was no other sensible thing to do. These were all part of Mama's sacrifices for her children.

Mama's Desperate Moment

My circumstances with managing my new role at work, refurbishing my newly acquired home, managing our childcare, and getting by on a shoe-string budget were difficult. Despite all that, if my older siblings thought I would crumble because I needed to take on Mama as an additional responsibility, they were mistaken. I agreed to take our mum into our care with Rose's usual support. Rose and I needed to answer the immediate question, *How would we manage our limited space while maintaining comfort for all?* We agreed that my mother would share a bedroom with our toddler daughter; we were prepared to accept her with open hearts and arms.

Our mum, Hilbert, and his wife travelled to England as planned. They drove her to my home, which was unorganized but clean. Rose and I made the necessary arrangements to ensure we would all be happy and comfortable throughout Mama's stay. Without remorse, my older siblings didn't just take a back seat in caring for our mother; they disappeared from the scene. I had proven my resilience several times and was ready to prove it again.

My wife and I cared for Mama without help from her other children during her six-month stay in England. Without any doubt, I saw this as a deliberate act to try to *punish* me. Was *dumping* Mama into my lap during a challenging period tied to my title and privilege of being Mama's King? Once again, if my older siblings intended their actions to be a punishment, they were blessings, thanks to God. This opportunity enabled me to honour my mother at this point once more.

This friction was a needless spark to demonstrate my unequivocal devotion and commitment to our mum. I was able to provide for my home while still ensuring her welfare. This time of need was Mama's desperate moment. I was able to deliver that need, yet these were sad times for our mother. Once again, I got the cold shoulder from my older siblings because I stood up for what I felt was right. To me, this was history repeating itself.

CHAPTER ELEVEN

Mama's Testing Times

Within a few months of her arrival, Mama's health progressed from using a wheelchair to being able to walk unaided. Notwithstanding her four older sons being nearby at the time, I was the only one willing to help our mother on her journey to recovery, which saddened me. As awful as it may sound, I often pondered why my mum bothered to have so many children if they bore such stony-hearted tendencies toward her. In deep reflection, I envisioned the time my chances of survival as an infant were poor. My thoughts drifted to Mama's composure levels as I lay at death's door in a hospital cot with my mum sitting beside me, holding my tiny hands while pleading with our Creator and Saviour to spare me the fate of two of my older siblings who had died as toddlers. I asked myself, was my role in Mama's well-being the more significant purpose of my existence I was fulfilling? My survival as the sixth of seven living siblings had been profoundly meaningful.

Having a large household in the past was the norm; in our village, there was one couple who had fifteen children. So, in comparison, we considered a home like ours, with seven, average. Apart from conforming to our Christian belief in the context of family planning, one other reason for having so many offspring comprised a simple word—investment.

In that era, the number of children by a couple equated to the parent's insurance policy value. It was customary for my parent's generation to be proud of having many children because it drew much applause. They relied on the older children to help care for the younger ones and contribute to the general upkeep of the home. Parents regarded their offspring as their guaranteed retirement fund. They instilled in their children the worth of conforming to the bible teachings, the fifth commandment: *Honour thy father and thy mother.* Of course, that was proper; it was customary in our upbringing. However, I presume those with solid family values gave credence to this teaching. It grieves me to reveal the evidence pointing to the contrary, the deficiency of such virtue in our circle. In today's world, some readers would consider family feuds to be trivial. However, in our time, it was taboo. Still, nothing stopped our division from becoming a talking point in the community.

Mama spent 14 days at an East London hospital, and during that time, Joe and John visited her, their wives excluded. In addition to the previous disappointments that Mama experienced, another would soon follow when she pointed to her dilapidated pair of bedroom slippers and requested a new pair from Joe.

He responded, "You already have one pair of slippers. What will you do with another?"

Joe didn't see the need for his mother to replace her battered pair. He denied her request. During Mama's hospitalization, her children delivered no courtesy or gestures that would have indicated their appreciation, remorse, or care, not even a gift of flowers. Rose and I were thankful the circumstances that Mama braved did not exacerbate her medical condition; instead, she made a speedy recovery.

The good Lord blessed her to receive the best medical care. In addition, without any doubt, Mama's quick recovery was also attributed in part to her nutritionist who prescribed implementing a strict diet with the utmost care and attention. Rose's skills in food preparation ensured that Mama received the required nourishment. She also received immeasurable love and attention from her grandchildren, Julie, Dan, Matt and Bob. Our daughter, Tasha, was almost four years old but was already wise enough to include her granny as part of her collection of dolls. She helped Mama in the shower, combed her hair, and fed her. Oh! Mama enjoyed the pampering.

Julie, Hilbert's daughter, also gave tremendous support and visited at least four times per week. She organized Mama's post-hospital care visits, medical appointments, and daycare centre visits through her position as a nurse; her contribution was immense. She had this special affection for Mama because of Mama's critical role in her upbringing. Mama embraced her as a granddaughter and played the father's role, too. After completing her education in Saint Lucia, Mama pleaded with Hilbert to pave the way for Julie to exit the island. Her numerous appeals paid off when Hilbert brought his daughter to England, affording her a new beginning. She remained eternally grateful to Mama for the transformation that followed in her life. Dan, Matt and Bob, Hilbert's sons, also retained excellent memories of their time spent with Mama while they lived in Saint Lucia during their childhood.

Mama's recovery was also boosted by receiving visits and telephone calls from many of her Saint Lucian pals from the diaspora. Yes, her popularity extended to England. Once she was on the mend and started to move around with a cane, she received many invitations, which she was always happy to accept. Of course, my mum was an extrovert, and in her better days, she loved the attention. The visits she received from her friends brought her much comfort.

Regardless of my mother's total contentment in our home, it never escaped her thoughts that her older children placed the total weight of her responsibility upon my shoulders while they looked away. Furthermore, while Mama continued receiving telephone calls from many friends, her daughter Mary-Anne never contacted her from the USA throughout her six months to inquire about her or wish her well. Our mother endured feelings of abandonment from the lack of cooperation and unity among her children.

In all the sadness, I managed to bring a smile to my mother's face when I reminded her that her children should have been the insurance policy to deliver her a proper retirement—"But did you read the fine print, Mama?" I asked.

Mama chuckled, then replied, "Stephen, you will never change. You always make me laugh."

Time to Say Goodbye

It was Mama's 67th birthday, and I was fortunate to have her celebrate this event with us. We were determined to give her the birthday party of her life. All the invitees showed up except Hilbert, John, and their families. Joe showed up for a brief moment and left before we served dinner. Joe had always been peculiar in his ways. He arrived at the house with our cousin Tom, whom we had also invited. Rose and I hadn's requested contributions from anyone towards Mama's celebration; why should we? The event was our idea. However, it was nice of Joe to bring a bottle of whiskey.

The issue with his gesture was that he left the bottle in the car parked outside our home. He left the gathering but never brought the bottle in. Tom informed me of Joe's boastful statement about not taking the bottle from the car because "Stephen thinks he has money". Nobody told him to organize a birthday party for Mama, so let him face his party bills." I dismissed Joe's assertion once more. Had he asked me for a bottle of alcohol or any other beverage to take away from our leftovers, I would have been happy to oblige.

The time for Mama to say goodbye was fast approaching. We had become accustomed to enjoying her company and knew we would miss her dearly. Her recovery was remarkable, a real blessing. I was grateful to Rose for her invaluable role in Mama's healing; I remain convinced she treated her mother-in-law as she would her biological mother. The experience was indeed an opportunity that yielded mutual benefits, though the care we provided to Mama was nothing compared to the blessings she later showered upon us in return.

Still, I had my loving wife and two beautiful children on whom I would refocus my attention.

They were all I had and all I needed. I would spare no effort to provide the best of whatever was within my capacity to make them comfortable in our new home. We continued with the refurbishment of our property we installed double-glazed windows, replaced roofing tiles, refurbished the front porch and put in new fencing.

I was not averse to borrowing from the banks, but if I chose that route, I had to be comfortable about meeting all the conditions without doubt or fear. Therefore, we capitalised on attractive borrowing facilities to manage the renovation. We saved on labour charges by completing the interior decorating ourselves. We were grateful for the support from my cousin Jamie, who, despite having travelled from Saint Lucia for further studies in the UK, still found time to assist with erecting the new fence.

The strenuous home improvement tasks were complete, but there was still more work around the house: domestic chores. Working shift patterns meant I would be home alone on several occasions. The kids would be at school while Rose went to work. However, I never had a dull moment. I was intent on making effective use of every spare second I had.

I was determined to achieve my objective by exploring several ways to advance myself however possible. Notwithstanding, modern technology was not a topic I was well-versed in; providing myself with the necessary skills was one that I saw as imperative. Therefore, to stay abreast of the rapid technological advancements of the mid-1980s, the first action I listed in my plan was to equip myself with a personal computer.

How to Accomplish My Goal

I once considered myself a social butterfly. However, socialising disappeared gradually from my to-do lists as I felt it was no longer a priority. My vision for our future was clear. I first needed peace, stability, and contentment to achieve an untroubled home. I knew I needed to compromise and make some adjustments; I was easy-going. I needed to play my role in the home based on the skills Mama had taught us during our upbringing. Since I needed no reminders of my responsibility at home, it all flowed as second nature.

Let's look at the subject of compromise. I grew up in the era of men assigning the role of managing household affairs to women. I viewed this practice as outdated; to me, it was a shared responsibility, and I was happy to play the part. It did not matter whether Rose was at home or work; I did my housekeeping duties. I never allowed my wife to come home from work and engage in domestic work while I was indoors. Correction! Except for preparing the meals, which she appreciated. I have never embraced cooking and never volunteered for that chore; I'd much rather wash the dishes! Rose was happy to prepare the meals before she went to work whenever possible. Thankfully, on the few occasions I cooked, I don't recall the meals making those who ate them sick.

Soon after we were married, I discovered Rose was not as outgoing as I was, she was the opposite, so this is where we had our differences. In any case, from my perspective, this wasn't a matter of concern. I was able and willing to make the necessary changes that ensured mutual respect and understanding—in my opinion, maintaining the status quo would be equivalent to combining business and pleasure. I chose to embrace my marital responsibilities because there was no question in my mind about which of the two I should give priority. I placed my desire for entertainment on my list of non-essentials. My preferences did not go without notice or criticism. Of course, the chitchat caused me no harm.

My cousin Jamie was the first to comment, "Stephen, even though you're now married and have a family, it doesn't mean you should change your personality."

I didn't dismiss his opinion because I saw some truth in the statement. However, getting my priorities right didn't equate to changing my personality. But how valid was Jamie's view? I wouldn't embrace his idea because he didn't have the same experiences that I had. He did not have a wife and family of his own, so from that standpoint, his understanding of my reasoning was lacking.

In response, I drew reference to those within our circle. I cited other relatives who had adopted his concept and had achieved less-than-favourable results, such as a failing marriage. I saw nothing they had gained that gave credibility to Jamie's suggestion. In my estimation, it was an implicit statement that suggested I continue my usual way of life even though my circumstances had changed.

IBM – That's all I knew

In the 1980s, owning a home computer wasn't typical as people viewed it as a luxury item. I saw it as a necessity. While on a two-week break from work, I chose to stay in bed until mid-morning one day, contemplating my way forward. I wanted to use every minute of my spare time to educate myself and learn new skills. What I had not yet included in my development plan was costs.

A voice kept telling me, "Stephen, get a computer now. Get the computer, and you will learn as you go along."

I started figuring out the best way to acquire a home computer.

I never questioned my ability to learn computer skills, but I was concerned that affording one at that particular time would be challenging. However, the cost of the lost opportunity in not buying a PC would be losing what I felt would be the chance to give our kids a head start. I was confident they would be fascinated and learn how to use the machine. I jumped out of bed, telephoned Rose at her workplace, and told her,

"Hey, Rosey, I'm going to buy a computer!" Stunned, she replied:

"What!"

I told her again, and she responded,

"Why? How are you going to afford it?"

Now, for the affording bit, I hadn't prepared an answer. Rose being passive about the idea was as good as approval, so I made my way down the high street. My mission was to find a piece of equipment we had never mentioned in previous conversations. I told the sales assistant that I wanted to buy a computer. He began with the questions,

"Which one?"

"What brand?"

"How much do you want to spend?"

"What memory capacity would you like?"

"What's your reason for buying the computer?"

Oh, s**t, I kept thinking. I had no answers to any of those questions!

All I wanted was a computer. I told the assistant that I wished to purchase an IBM. My sole reason for that choice was, well, I hadn't heard about anything else! All I knew about computers were those three letters, I-B-M. I told the sales assistant the truth about my total and absolute ignorance of the subject and that I needed help to become a proud computer owner. When my inquiry was over, I was delighted to leave the store with my package containing an Amstrad PCW 9512. I was amazed to see the difference between the low price I paid and the high price I had expected.

I later equipped myself with some of the "For Dummies" computer manuals, and from there onward, our two young children, my wife, and I started using computers. There was a bit of a hiccup, however. This machine was more of a word processor that operated from MS-DOS. Nevertheless, I never looked back. Having a new PCW in the home was a big step forward—I became familiar with the programming language, MS Basic, which I used to design my work; it was fascinating.

This Man is Never Free

Following our reconciliation once more, my brothers and I exchanged visits. We agreed to call ahead before visiting. However, there were occasional impromptu visits, which was fine for me. I always welcomed them, offering whatever we had and engaging in conversations. But why couldn't my siblings avoid making my activities their talking points? They seldom commented to me about my undertakings, but they did so among themselves and to our relatives:

"Every time I visit Stephen, he's always doing housework. This man is never free."

However, in his usual laid-back manner, John uplifted me when he remarked, "Man, you're always busy. Each time I come round, you're always on a computer."

No doubt, John's statement had undertones of objection. However, I considered his remarks most complimentary. Essentially, he was telling me that I was making clever use of my time.

Our approach to disciplining our children was another matter that came under scrutiny. While Phil was on a short visit to England, he agreed with Hilbert and John that Rose and I were too firm with our kids. Surely they could not have been comparing us to Mama's parenting style? I appreciated Mama's inflexibility, which may have been appropriate in her time, but Rose and I chose to evolve as time dictated. We nurtured Charlie and Tasha in grasping the ideals of accountability, tidiness, and responsibility—qualities that should remain unchanged.

Above all, I never agreed with the idea of corporal punishment. As caring parents, we were very protective but not obsessive. We set limits on do's and don'ts and explained our reasons to the kids for doing so. We praised them for their excellent behaviour and performance and highlighted their shortcomings. Oh yes, we yelled, and they listened, but we avoided zero tolerance. I was very transparent about my shaky relationship with my older siblings, and as the children grew older, I tried to explain to them the harmful effects of family feuds. Rose and I expounded on the many advantages and the importance of siblings maintaining a healthy relationship. We were firm whenever the need arose yet lenient on other occasions.

My brothers believed our firmness would be counterproductive to our children's development. According to them, we were making our kids foolish. They commented that we disallowed our children to join in conversations when they visited. It was my brothers' prerogative to hold an opinion; it was ours to disagree.

One of the house rules we laid for Charlie and Tasha was that they must say hello to our visitors, have a brief chat, and then to leave the adults to their conversations. Likewise, before we left for visits to anyone, Rose and I instructed them clearly about their behaviour, including what we expected from them and what to expect from us.

"What should you do when you get to Uncle John's house?"

They would respond, "Say hello to everyone, sit down, and behave ourselves. Don't run around in the house or touch anything."

All the criticism came as no surprise because nothing I did went unnoticed. People's opposition or criticism motivated me. It drove me to be better. I listened to their comments with interest and selected the good from the bad.

While I never chose to isolate myself from the outside world, I relished spending every minute teaching myself how to use my new machine. I was also determined not to allow peer pressure to dissuade me. I continued doing what was best for my family and me.

Despite my many earlier setbacks, I included one item in my long-term plan: my eventual return to Saint Lucia. My continuous battles against evil deeds were demoralizing to the degree of giving me the temptation to forsake the place of my birth. However, being born Saint Lucian was my identity.

I hoped I would return someday before reaching the age of sixty-five, which was the state retirement age for men at that time.

This long-term plan was an event I considered would begin to emerge once Charlie and Tasha started to gain a sense of independence. Rather than applying a time-bound aspect, I avoided the delusion of many of my fellow Saint Lucians. By my reckoning, those who had made the journey to England intending to fast-track their return to the Caribbean within five years were over-ambitious.

As I write, hundreds are still waiting to return and others never lived to realise their goal. I used the age of my youngest child as my gauge, and upon calculation, I would be back in Saint Lucia at age fifty-five. That would give me a minimum of thirty-two years of residency in the UK. Setting myself such an aspiring goal would require immense discipline to achieve.

The Caribbean Man's Major Pitfalls

Upon my arrival in England, it was incumbent on me to note, understand, and learn about the country where I would start a new life. Like all civilizations, the UK was not exempt from society's woes. There were opportunities, but the talk of prejudice was routine. This issue had been irrelevant to me until this journey. While I never allowed social inequality to preoccupy my thinking, I did not dismiss its existence. Those within my inner circle tried to prime me, and there were reported cases of racism on the news. However, I resisted engaging in the conversation to avoid distractions that could have negatively altered my perspective.

One of my earliest observations was an imbalance in the economic development among certain sections of the communities. During a family and friends group discussion, I expressed my views. Without wishing to diminish the accomplishments of my Caribbean folks, I made what I knew would be a controversial comment,

"Many of the Windrush migrants from Saint Lucia seem satisfied that there is no more to achieve in England than buying a home."

Sure enough, there was unanimous disagreement with my views.

"What else is there to achieve?" they asked. "The whole idea is to purchase your home, so once you've managed that, what else do you expect?"

"Well, I can't ever imagine anyone disagreeing that purchasing your home is a monumental achievement," I responded, "but the South Asians seem to have figured out other opportunities. What about starting with further education? And how about setting up Caribbean businesses? Aiming to invest in our country to aid its development could be a good plan."

Please, do not misconstrue my statement. I would never suggest that any of these would be easy to achieve. Neither would I ever undermine my fellow countrymen and women's successes. Notwithstanding the social barriers we faced, countless of us had made good strides. However, it crossed my mind that the other minority groups had made multiple inroads into the social and economic structures through diversification. Many Saint Lucians I knew, and those I had met at various Caribbean functions, had immigrated to England in the 1950s and 60s. My older siblings, for example, were between the ages of fifteen and nineteen when they travelled to England; I just wondered whether they could have been more strategic in their planning.

In all the areas of England where I lived, I observed many non-European businesses were owned mainly by members of the South Asian communities. These included pharmacies and doctors' surgeries, general retail outlets combined with post offices, travel agents, estate agents, grocery stores, restaurants, wine stores and more. I also knew of importers, wholesalers, distributors and manufacturers. In contrast, in the Caribbean communities, I saw no diversity. There was a saturation of hairdressing salons and barbershops; the cultural differences were conspicuous.

I was eager to identify the reasons for such dissimilarities between these two communities. Therefore, in striking up conversations with several of my South Asian colleagues, and to some extent through social dialogue, the word that repeatedly surfaced was "united." The support structures they created were missing from our community. For example, using the hierarchical system, they accommodated as many family members as possible at one residence to ensure eventual home ownership.

Every working member contributed financially to guarantee each loved one would eventually move into their own property within a 5-year term. They extended this system from residential ownership to commerce. They chose blood relatives to hold key business positions while generally selecting those from their neighbourhood for menial work; this scheme uplifted their communities. Nevertheless, the public services offered scope for making headway from secure employment to anyone who chose that route.

Like hundreds of my fellow Saint Lucians, I settled for employment in public service. Well, I understood why public service employment was so attractive. There was good pay, good prospects, *a job for life* and a good pension. I mean, that's what I saw when I chose my first official job.

Nonetheless, I longed for employment beyond having "just a job." How simple would it be for me to accomplish my goal? Of course, my boldness would be a determining factor. I never expected my ideas to be smooth sailing, and I knew it would require total commitment and lots of sacrifices.

My 20P Win Yankee

One most noticeable characteristic of the Saint Lucian community was in the line of entertainment—there was no shortage of weekend partying. The most popular was the *bring-a-bottle* house party. The pub gatherings and the betting shops were what I considered addictive recreational centres. I saw these as entertainment magnets that led to the decisive defeat for some; they were the traps. I referred to the bars and gambling shops, or bookies, as the Caribbean man's major pitfalls.

This social factor was one more of the differences I observed between the other minority groups and us. We seemed far less progressive, with shallow goals and a low collective achievement bar. It was as though pleasure was all we lived for once we had provided a roof over our heads. Denver, who came from my village in Saint Lucia, suffered a devastating blow to his livelihood and family by choosing the bars and bookies.

I didn't understand how resisting those poor choices was so challenging. Having witnessed these unfortunate situations, I wondered why someone could not avoid such compulsive behaviours. So, although I never anticipated any difficulty, there was no better way of knowing but to experiment, and that's what I did.

I learned how to place a bet on the horses from Geoff, who had married Rose's mum and had become a new family member. Geoff's favourite wager was selecting four horses he forecasted would win their races. He put what he explained was a 20p win Yankee plus accumulator at a total cost of £2.42p, including the tax. This particular stake presented the opportunity to win significant sums, providing that all the selected horses won their races and their winning odds were high. For the first time, I placed my wager.

The first three of my chosen horses won their races. As the fourth horse, whose odds of winning at 33-1, took off on its race, with Rose sitting at my side, I expected her to feel the vibration from the throbbing of my heartbeat, I was sweating. At the end of that race, I was relieved that I was still breathing. Because of the close margin between the two first horses to cross the winning line, there was a slight delay in determining which won.

The winner won by a "nose," and my horse was declared second.

I walked briskly to the betting shop within walking distance to present my first-ever winning ticket. As if in a caring stance, the attendant paid me off while stating,

"Oh! You're the unlucky guy! Had your last horse won its race, you would have been a wealthy man today."

I stared at him with a smirk and thought, what a load of horse manure, an enticing invitation to try again.

I presumed the clerk was telling the truth because of the winning odds on my last horse. Now that my first-hand experience was complete, I understood the psychology of gambling; I needed no further evidence that investing at the bookmakers was not a good choice.

The Joke We Could Not Share

Apart from the potential financial perils of gaming, I would spare myself the risk of a regular accelerated heart rate. I knew of the destruction that stemmed from gambling addiction. Such risk-takers placed bets on the dogs, horses and whatever else was listed in competitions at betting shops. They believed they would one day win sufficient sums to recoup all they had lost—such an unfortunate delusion. As for the bring-a-bottle parties, I can't recall attending any boring ones.

The joyful atmosphere among family and friends who met at my cousins' home in the west of London was like having a piece of Saint Lucia in London. Cousin Wallie, one of the most senior in the family, and his wife, Felicia, both in their late 60s, were hooked on these social events. The ones I attended were exceedingly entertaining and action-packed. The mainly Creole conversations, dancing to the sounds of calypso, reggae and zouk music, and the variety of Caribbean cuisine that included black pudding and souse, would ensure we stayed on our feet. I never met anyone as funny as Cousins Wallie and Felicia during my stay in England.

It was summertime when Rose and I arrived early one Saturday evening at one of their parties—the lively atmosphere had begun as the invitees arrived. There were about twelve guests ahead of us. Keeping with the Saint Lucian custom, the ladies stayed inside while the men gathered in the back garden, where they played dominoes and chatted until the party got into full swing. The timing of our arrival was perfect as I had the opportunity to witness a most unusual back-and-forth between Cousin Wallie and his lifelong friend, Lambert. As the game progressed with the four players, each player made an emphatic point simultaneously with every domino slammed. Wallie's repeated point was more of a command directed at his best friend, Lambert. In Saint Lucia, the players use expletives during the game. Wallie's language was unique. With a stern look, he stared at Lambert and uttered two simple words— "Stop it!" We all knew of Wallie's outrageous sense of humour, so we thought he was adding a new feature to the game. Lambert slammed his domino and forcefully said, "In your mouth!" Wallie banged his domino on the table on his second turn and, still without a smile, "I told you, stop it." It was Lambert's turn to lay his domino; not knowing that Wallie was dead serious, he said, with a giggle, "No way!" as his domino hit the table. Cousin Wallie immediately stood up, pointed at Lambert and demanded: "I want you to stop touching my wife because if you don't, she'll get to like it, and she'll want *me* to do it to her too."

Cor blimey! How many drinks did Cousin Wallie have? I wondered. Is he serious? We all burst into such howling laughter that some ladies came out to join in the fun. "Hey, what's the juicy joke? Give us a taste," one shouted. Of course, this was a joke we couldn't share. Cousin Wallie had inadvertently immediately ended the game—we all forgot about dominoes as we joined the party inside.

Vodka and Vodkanese

Felicia made an announcement: "Come on, everyone, enjoy yourself. Plenty to eat'n 'drink, so be happy."

Being jolly was one of her qualities, but we suspected she had already had one or two shots of vodka and coke, her favourite tipple. As she moved to the calypso beat, Wallie, holding firmly onto his glass, moved in to embrace his wife as they danced.

"Come on, darling, let's show them how it's done," Felicia told her husband as she rotated her waist with her buttocks nearing the floor. It was hilarious.

"Oh yes," replied her husband. "No one can do it better." Clearly unsatisfied, Wallie shouted to the DJ, "Great tune DJ! Hit it one mo time." We boosted their energy by cheering them on. My cousins took over the floor, twisting and wining away.

"Both of you will be complaining about your waists tomorrow," a guest commented.

"Oh no, we won't," Felicia replied. "Tonight Wallie and I will be having twins, and you know what we'll call them?"

Wallie jumped in before anyone guessed, "Vodka and Vodkanese!" he shouted.

No one was expecting this response. There was a roar of laughter from the crowd. "How appropriate!" a guest commented. How else could my cousins demonstrate their unquenchable love of their favourite drink but name their children after it? But hang on! *How is this going to be possible?* I thought. Cousin Wallie must have forgotten about his earlier dispute with his best friend!

Safeguarding Myself

Regarding the pub visits, I enjoyed having a pint of draught lager. However, I was more satisfied with taking home a six-pack from the off-licence. I got much more for less in comparison. Uncle Eddie, my staunchest support, was a frequent visitor at the bar and, at the weekend, would invite me for a drink. I occasionally accepted his invitation out of courtesy because he had been terrific since I moved to London. My uncle always encouraged me to keep on the right track. He always offered sound advice, and we enjoyed each other's company. I needed no more lessons to recognize the stumbling blocks in those common gratifications, so I safeguarded myself. I looked in the direction that led to a path to building the foundation of our future.

CHAPTER TWELVE

Reaching My Ultimate Goal

I was under no illusion that my journey ahead would be simple. The route I chose was one I needed to navigate without deflection. In appreciating the need for inspiration, I turned to Psalm 65. Our life was on the right course as Rose and I maintained an excellent relationship. The kids were progressing well in school, and my employment situation was stable.

In 1987, I received a telephone call from Mama informing me of a plot of land for sale measuring 30ft x 60ft in our village. The asking price was EC$8,000.00 which equated to approximately £1,600.00. Rose and I hadn't yet reached the position even to consider such a proposition. The timing wasn't the best, as no more than one year had passed since we had moved into our new home. Nevertheless, we didn't dismiss the idea of owning a piece of Saint Lucia. Once we did the maths, we were satisfied that this offer was within our capacity; we decided to pursue the deal solely for investment purposes.

I figured the return on this investment would sit pretty well, irrespective of when we would decide to cash in. Phil executed the purchase on our behalf, and we were thrilled to own our first plot on this Caribbean Island. We hoped this milestone would be the first of more opportunities to come.

There was increasing optimism about Saint Lucia's economic activities during that period. The general conditions that existed from the mid-1980s onward were favourable. Foreign investors set up assembly plants to export and sell products from the island on the international markets. There was also limited manufacturing, but agriculture was the backbone, with the banana industry at its peak. Along came rapid infrastructural developments that spread throughout the island. The towns and villages were expanding at a quick pace. Large estate owners demarcated their landholdings for residential development, and the citizens sought to acquire a slice of the economic pie. In certain areas, landowners were selling a minimum of 5,000 square feet of land for as little as EC$0.90, which equated to approximately 18 pence per square foot. Phil informed me of the scope for further investment. Who would not wish to sacrifice and grab a few thousand square feet of land for such an attractive price?

Once again, Rose and I conferred and agreed that a good game plan would be to seek the sale of our earlier purchased property in the village and reinvest in a more attractive one of greater value.

We put the plan into action through Mama and Phil without delay, and in 1988, we found a buyer and sold for EC$12,000.00. Following this transaction, in August 1988, we bought 23,000 square feet of land at the cost of EC$19,000.00, equivalent to approximately £3,900.00.

This business was quite an achievement for us. Phil described the location to me, but I was familiar with the general area. In any case, I was eager to see our investment, so Rose agreed when I expressed my wish to visit Saint Lucia.

A Promising Future

It was 1990, five years after my first visit back to Saint Lucia when I decided to go on an actual holiday. I was ecstatic to be returning home once more. Seeing our acquisition gave me a sense of security and achievement, inspiring me to keep moving. Even though this trip was a deserved break from work, I yielded to the temptation of making my fourteen-day trip a working holiday. I wasted no time in exploring the possibility of a business associate. I was willing to consider any feasible trading idea or proposal. During my short stay, my mates introduced me to Freddie, an attorney and businessperson.

Freddie, who owned several boutiques on the island, needed a reliable business partner in Europe to do his bidding. I saw this as an ideal opening, even though I had no experience in importing / exporting or international trade. If I decided to pursue the lead, I would need to familiarize myself with this field of work.

Freddie and I had thorough discussions on the matter, and he appreciated my honesty in disclosing my inexperience in his line of business. Nevertheless, he offered a proposal, and I accepted. This encounter marked the beginning of our business relationship. I was thrilled to become his buying agent. Our partnership was most convenient because he was also qualified to undertake whatever legal matters I would need to manage on the island.

My two-week trip ended. I was back in the UK, and my position changed from having free time to contemplate my way forward to being occupied with a fledgling import-export business venture. My ideas were shaping up and our future was looking promising.

Hunger for Knowledge

Within one month of my return to England, Freddie tested my ability by faxing over his first assignment.

I was to source an assortment of beauty products, consolidate the cargo, and ship the consignment to Saint Lucia. My execution of this initial order would determine the sustainability of our connection.

Without the benefit of the internet, I managed to perform the task uninterrupted. My telephone, fax machine, and Amstrad PCW 9512 were sufficient tools to guarantee efficiency; it was exciting. Freddie signalled his approval with the many orders that followed, effectively sealing our association.

He continued to place larger orders, bringing me into direct contact with manufacturers and other stakeholders in the import-export business. These significant requests meant an enhancement in my business activity. This condition didn't require a second thought; I was gratified. I was willing to continue providing this service for as long as needed. I was eager to educate myself in that trade, and nothing would stop me.

Apart from being self-taught in international trade from manuals I purchased, I spent much time visiting our local public library. My hunger for knowledge took me one step further when I enlisted in a correspondence course with the Business Management Association (BMA). In September of 1991 I completed the course and was awarded a Diploma in International Trade.

Alongside Freddie's project, I saw one more opportunity that I felt was viable. I saw the opening of a modest business proposition involving Mama and Silvie.

A Win-Win Proposal

Mama and Silvie set up a 14ft x 14ft corner shop in the newly extended and refurbished family home. Nonperishable goods formed the bulk of their inventory. Throughout this period, I never ceased my contribution towards Mama's upkeep. So, whether it was 5, 10, 15, or 100 British pounds, I made it my duty to subsidise her care. Why not convert this cash disbursement to an investment? I thought. My outlay would be much more substantial, but the potential rewards would be worth the risk. I discussed my view with Rose and suggested the idea to Mama and Silvie. Following our detailed discussions, we were all on board and agreed on a simple partnership.

My subsidies to Mama would take the form of purchasing inventory items for her corner shop. Silvie provided lists of things with a long shelf life and produced a quick turnover. I would oversee the financing of inventory purchases, sea freight, customs clearance, and transport for delivery to the shop. In return, their contribution would be a total commitment that included clearing the goods from the customs department, arranging transportation to the shop, and skilfully managing the business. They needed no finances. Like most businesses, my initial outlay would be the most sizeable. If handled in good order, the shop would self-sustain and provide an income for all; we would all be winners because Mama and Silvie would determine their income based on commission on net profits. This would provide an excellent incentive for them to do well and they would have access to a regular cash flow, reducing Mama's potential feelings of hopelessness. Moreover, their business would be more meaningful as they would carry a broader range of goods and expand their customer base. This venture would enhance Silvie's skills as she would be responsible for dealing with the Customs and Excise Department because of the added dimension of importation. And of course, there would be no financial risks to Mama and Silvie, and I would be converting expenditure into investment.

Mama and Silvie saw no downside to this proposal, so they accepted. The final aspect of this venture was to agree on how Mama and Silvie would manage our finances. Once we had established this part, the first order from Silvie was underway.

Building Our Capital

Our share from sales was of no concern to Rose or me because there was always mutual and total trust between Mama and us. We were satisfied that the business continued working as planned. Rose and I required Mama to deposit our share of income from sales in our Saint Lucia savings account.

In Freddie's case, our business contract was different. Initially, our transactions were on a Proforma basis. Once I had arranged the trading terms with our suppliers, Freddie would provide the funds noted on the invoice I prepared. As our relationship developed, we relaxed our trading terms. There were occasions when I advised him to deposit one part of the payment in our Saint Lucia savings account and forward the balance to our UK bank via telegraphic transfer. Freddie was unaware of my reasons for this payment arrangement, but our profits were what I required him to deposit in Saint Lucia. Sometimes, depending on the invoice value, I requested that he deposit the entire amount in Saint Lucia.

Silvie informed me of concerns about clearing and transporting her goods through the Saint Lucia Customs Department as time progressed. She hinted at frustration in what she believed was the complicated part of the undertaking. She raised concerns about the elaborate procedures in clearing the goods at the Customs and Excise Department and arranging the transportation to the shop. The importation process in Saint Lucia was renowned for being clogged with bureaucracy and nepotism. I needed to convince Silvie to view the situation as an opportunity rather than a challenge. Still, I accepted that she was entitled to express her sentiments and decide the best way forward.

Moreover, while Mama never complained, there was one among us who did—Hilbert believed our mum had nothing to gain from our dealings. He didn't know about Mama's agreement with me, yet he suggested I was the only one "reaping all the rewards."

"You're hustling to prop up Stephen," he commented to Mama.

Beelzebub Proved Me Right

I regretted not being able to escape the constant scrutiny from my older siblings. Hilbert was unaware that his immediate family and other relatives shared one common opinion. We all agreed that all the evidence was visible that he instigated family feuds. We all concurred upon one word that best described his disposition—arrogant.

We would often find his indelible fingerprints in all unfavourable circumstances. Just as he had attached a name that he thought was relevant to me, his antagonistic behaviour earned him the most fitting pet name. I called him *Beelzebub*, one of the many aliases of the devil. Sounds pretty harsh, right? Yes, but nothing else was suitable. It was the best I could think of, so I polished it to "Bellzie," which sounded better.

Bellzie added one more act to his long mischief list—he successfully talked Mama into dropping our project. He unwisely, wrongfully, and jealously told Mama, "You're killing yourself for your King. You're helping him get rich quick." Bellzie advised Mama to quit our partnership because, "There was too much stress involved in this work".

Unfortunately, our trading venture halted as Mama and Silvie's enthusiasm waned.

Mama reverted to her much scaled-down retail shop until, some months later, Bellzie intervened once more. Her eldest child persuaded her that he would fill the gap that, "Stephen created". He enticed his mother with the incentive of avoiding the process of clearing the cargo from the Saint Lucia Customs Department.

Bellzie was privileged to have concessions on travel and limited cargo shipments as part of his company benefits, hence the charm. He was popular among the baggage handlers at the airport in England. My brother was also well-known in Saint Lucia; therefore, he had no difficulty getting his goods through.

For my part, I bore no hard feelings. Bellzie acknowledged my resourcefulness and entrepreneurial acumen. He proved my scheme was valid by his actions and behaviour; to me, it was humbling. Too bad my brother failed to realise that there was room for the entire family if we had allowed unity to prevail. Had they chosen to do the same as a united team, we all would have been winners. In the meantime, my business relationship with Freddie continued for a couple more years until he folded his enterprises.

The Brother Who Shared My Goal

The end of my business connections with Freddie did not diminish my enthusiasm. I had gained an immeasurable amount of knowledge and experience in international trade. The experience of communicating and negotiating with importers and distributors was worthwhile. The confidence that I gained reinforced my resolve. Phil and I maintained communication as there was no let-up in our "near-perfect" relationship.

Whenever I visited Saint Lucia, it was like the return of the good old days. The sentiments of brotherly love Phil and I shared were unmistakable, as we spent many hours discussing various topics, including our shared aspirations. During our first family holiday, Rose expressed displeasure about the lengthy periods I spent with Phil and I acknowledged her concerns.

My family and I were on holiday when my favourite brother was conveying the impression of having acquired a broad knowledge of events on the island, which was very intriguing. He had gained momentum as an electrician and was quickly promoted to a supervisory position in electrical installation and maintenance on a major hotel project in the north of the island. From his involvement in the building industry, Phil recognised the gap in the market between the supply and demand for general construction equipment, particularly electrical supplies, which arose from the wide-ranging construction programmes in the private and public sectors throughout the island. We saw this as a great project worthy of consideration; therefore, we agreed to explore the feasibility of us plugging this gap.

Soon after our holiday, Phil informed me of the result of his big breakthrough pertaining to the first and highest bid he had submitted to the Government of Saint Lucia. He won the contract to conduct the electrical installation work on the construction of one of the most prestigious academic institutions in the south of the island. I was thrilled upon receiving the news as I saw this as an excellent opportunity for him. Following his victory, Phil sought my assistance in executing the project. He later travelled to the UK to select the necessary supplies.

Before my brother travelled to England, he sent me his inventory list. I was committed to ensuring that his journey would be productive. I began the process of sourcing reputable suppliers for high-quality standards and competitiveness. Unlike nowadays, I did not have the luxury of sourcing online document templates; therefore, I designed various trade forms and paperwork that would allow him to project a professional business image. By the time Phil arrived in England, I had arranged meetings with the relevant distributors. I also obtained companies' profiles and various other information such as comprehensive price lists, trading terms, and delivery.

To my brother, this mission was a learning curve. He gained a much broader insight into managing a business on a larger scale and the opportunity to connect with his new suppliers.

I applied to use up some of my holiday time from my employer to accompany Phil, driving him around to meet the traders. We wasted no time completing our activity list. Phil completed his tasks ahead of schedule, allowing time for increased leisure with other relatives and friends. It was evident that his journey was a resounding success. He had achieved his objective and did so within budget. In addition, he enjoyed the warmest hospitality Rose and I managed to afford, including a shopping spree for his family.

As he prepared for his return journey, he reassured me that he would refrain from the established blasé attitude of doing business in Saint Lucia. Instead, he would commit to conducting his operations on an enterprise level. I was confident that this experience had primed my brother to prove his ability, and he would continue developing his entrepreneurship skills.

I once aspired for a "Rosemond Brothers" business partnership to evolve someday. I knew this was no longer possible among the older siblings, who had never displayed their will, ambition, unity or aptitude for such a pursuit. However, I envisaged this aspiration advancing between my favoured brother and me. He was the one with whom I thought we shared a common goal. The end of Phil's agreement with the government was approaching when he informed me of some other uplifting news. The authorities further recognised his ability when they awarded him a new contract for the electrical maintenance of all the educational facilities from the east to the south and across the island's west coast.

Building the Pillar Upon My Corner Stone

During my lone visit to Saint Lucia in 1995, I discovered a piece of prime land on one of our highroads, comprised of 28,000 square feet, for sale by the owner. I was curious about what looked like an attractive deal so I decided to pursue the lead. Following my inquiry, I informed Rose of my thoughts. However, on this occasion, she was not in agreement because, in her opinion, I needed to slow down on business activities.

"We don't need any more land," she stated.

Phil informed me that the seller was desperate to sell this property, so the chance of him accepting an offer was possible. Despite Rose's disapproval, I proceeded to make an offer. After I negotiated from a position of strength, just as Phil had predicted, the seller accepted my proposal.

I persuaded Rose that we were striking a good deal at EC$3.57 per square foot and that purchasing this additional property would be the right decision. The activities on the island pointed to the value of properties moving upward. Rose and I had accumulated substantially more than the deposit the local bank required from us to finance this purchase. Without further consideration, I assigned the matter to Freddie, who had remained a friend, and whose services I retained as an attorney. Freddie eventually completed the transaction after I returned to England. He forwarded our documents, and Rose and I became the proud owners of a second treasured piece of real estate in Saint Lucia. The location of this property was ideal for any business setup. Considering the ideas that Phil and I had continuously discussed, I had no doubt this investment would serve its purpose well.

In England, Rose and I continued as usual. News of our acquisition soon became the topic of speculation. Interestingly, my sister, Mary-Anne, was curious about my ability to acquire these properties in Saint Lucia.

She asked Mama, "How is Stephen financing the purchase of all that property?"

Mama's response to her daughter was great and very appropriate.

"How would I know? Why don't you ask him?" she replied.

Of course, Mary-Anne never posed the question to me. I guessed she was not versed in the bank's role in business matters.

Now that we had wrapped up another property deal, the pathway to my goal looked clearer. My confidence in strengthening our financial position in Saint Lucia was progressively taking shape. I was now building the pillar of my cornerstone, and I would not be turning back. We had paid off the first set of land we had acquired, and the balance on this second purchase was negligible. All the transactions I executed in Saint Lucia were in Phil's presence. For all I knew, I had sufficiently proven to Phil my seriousness to dispel any thought on his part that I was bluffing.

We granted Phil the Power of Attorney; therefore, he was privy to our business. Phil and I had agreed that this was the beginning of our intended long-term business partnership. Although Phil and I both had other commitments, including raising young families, we both pledged support for each other and longevity to our unity, while acknowledging that spending the rest of our lives discussing business schemes would have been unreasonable and imprudent.

Yes Means No

My experience thus far was a testament to the fact that nothing in life comes without a measure of sacrifice, in my case, lots of it. I was privileged to be enriched with God's guidance from which my unyielding confidence in my ability to lay the foundation of our future derived.

I believe understanding challenges as anything other than part of living would be unwise. Therefore, emboldening ourselves to adopt the right mindset to advance our purpose is pivotal. I needed no added lessons to know I would not achieve my goals overnight. I was also aware that facing difficulties head-on is a required skill for effective management.

In my judgment, my approach to how to move ahead was straightforward. Therefore, my methodical way of not attempting to rush things should not be misconstrued as withdrawing from the process. My efforts to avoid whatever plans I had discussed with Phil becoming a fancy dust-gathering ornament were not questionable.

As time passed, I sensed that my talks with my brother began to feel like a time-wasting exercise. His energy level toward moving forward appeared to be dwindling. Several of my attempts to keep our communication going were futile. Upon reflection, I recalled one of our lengthy conversations in which Phil gave me some advice, and he suggested that it would be at my peril if ignored it. He warned me, "You must erase from your thoughts the idea of having well-wishers in Saint Lucia, because every man is for himself. The assumption of genuine friendship no longer exists. Don't be gullible and believe whatever the Saint Lucians say because they tell you yes, to avoid the trouble of explaining their reasons for saying no. In effect, in their language, yes means no, and have no sympathy towards others; don't feel sorry for anyone else's plight." I remember thinking, *wow, chilling words*.

My previous dealings with a businessperson in Saint Lucia, Freddie, had been worthwhile, and at that time, Phil was the only Saint Lucian with whom I was seriously engaging. Having reflected, I realised his attitude had changed quickly to a degree I would never have imagined. He stopped contacting me or returning my calls—our communication was no more. I ought to have been much more attentive and less unsuspecting. My brother's conduct was a reflection of his previous advice to me. I gave him credit for being the first example of his meaning. Indeed, he fitted into the category of those he warned me against. Phil's advice was a plan.

Even with all my efforts at that point seeming pointless, the thought of giving up did not enter my mind. I telephoned my brother once more to express my concern about our disconnection and his reply was shocking:

"You know you have no money, and you are talking about business."

This statement hit my nerve. I was appalled. It contradicted all of our conversations. I was bemused and saddened while trying to figure out why Phil had been so cruel.

Joe's declaration, "You have to have money when you're buying a house in England," a few years earlier, reverberated in my head. That was a classic example of déjà vu.

While I lamented Phil's remarks, Rose was astounded by her favourite brother-in-law's mean-spirited comment—we could not find a reason for this sudden change. Therefore, we inferred that since we had an unlimited budget for the cordiality we extended to him during his stay in England, not forgetting his young family in Saint Lucia, we ought to have been broke!

Phil's Acidic Pill

Amid this episode, Rose was preparing to embark on a solo trip to Saint Lucia. I informed Phil that Upon her arrival, she would begin advertising the sale for our most recently purchased property. I wasn't surprised when he didn't question why I was selling. Instead, in an instant, he asked:

"What is your asking price?"

Once again, my favourite brother surprised me when he said he was interested in buying the property. He offered to pick Rose up at the airport and discuss the matter further. He was excited about cracking an incredible deal. However, he was in no position to know that although I was disappointed, I would not be making such a rash decision on such a vital matter due to my brother's inconsideration.

Furthermore, he seemed to have forgotten that I was a Saint Lucian when he referenced it in his earlier advice. Phil restored communication with me without further interruptions because he was eager to purchase the land at what he thought was a bargain price. He wasn't able to know that I was evaluating the market. I was trying to assess the extent of demand for land since we last purchased it. Phil's actions drove me to take a stance contrary to my principle, thus impacting my lifelong closeness with him. I advised Rose to inform him of our decision to cancel the sale.

Phil had transformed my business aspirations into a game, and I was willing to accommodate him. I intended my action to prove to Phil that I could serve him a dose of his own medicine, a yes for a no. Phil knew I was a man of my word who had never played such games. So, he did all the preliminary work toward buying the land, including the legal aspect, waiting only to complete the transaction with Rose. When she informed him of the cancellation, unsurprisingly, my brother expressed disbelief at my delivering this acidic pill. He was furious. My silent message to my brother was, sorry, buddy, we are not ready yet. We've got enough to keep us going. As I write, I do not know the cause of Phil's changed position towards me.

Stephen N Rosemond

The Intelligence Deficiency Syndrome

Phil's advice regarding attitudes in Saint Lucia was no fiction. Regrettably, the physical improvement of the island did not reflect the thinking and behaviour of a section of the population; instead, I saw *intelligence deficiency syndrome*. Even though there were more job opportunities than when I immigrated to England, specific community segments differed in their attitudes. The lack of determination to work through a transformative process was common. Embracing the fantasy of reaching the top with minimal effort was routine. A new attitude of take-and-take exhibited a lack of gratitude.

Caribbean folks with whom I once mingled discussed these topics in social gatherings. My compatriots spoke of the imbalance of goodwill between our people living in the Caribbean and those in the UK. When those in the UK visited the Caribbean, they gave generously to family and friends there. When our people from the Caribbean visited the UK, they also received lavishly from those in the UK. While we in England did not expect anything tangible in return, we expected memories to extend beyond the holiday periods. By evaluating the depth of my connection with Phil, I concluded that his performance in diluting his sincerity was magical.

The fracturing of what I once considered an unshakeable bond between my favourite brother and me was upsetting. I pressured myself by presuming that Phil's actions were meant, not intending to cause harm, but rather to awaken me. Nevertheless, I was thankful that the Divine Spirit drove him to reveal himself as another within my circle for the wrong reasons. Now that Phil had taught me the ultimate lesson, I had genuine cause to relegate my trusted brother to the back burner.

CHAPTER THIRTEEN

His Statement Was No Bluster

The part-time ventures I managed successfully alongside my career did not stop me from focusing on my profession and maintaining a clean employment record. The saying *nothing lasts forever* seemed relevant in our firm because the company was transparent about its intentions—it was no secret that change *was* coming. Those initial transformations began with the modernization of stations and operational equipment as well as a comprehensive retraining programme for all personnel from the operating department.

Despite those advancements, we continued with the established business culture, which had been fossilised over many years, with employees describing the work as secure, no matter what. The common expression in the workplace was, "You would have to commit murder for your job to be in jeopardy." Working conditions were relaxed, so disregarding health and safety issues was common and adhering to work rosters was unimportant. The staff smoked cigarettes and drank alcohol while on duty. Gambling among colleagues was routine. When I worked at a particular location,

I would participate in dartboard contests, for which we placed bets to win chocolates and cans of soft drinks. This activity was entertaining, and I won a fair share of chocolates.

On Wednesday, 18th November 1987, at 17.00 hrs, my colleague—and good friend—Aiden and I reported for duty as reserve staff members at Kings Cross station. Being reserved meant management could call upon us to work at any other site during our shifts. We had been there for about two hours, having fun playing darts, when the manager telephoned me to pick up a job at a nearby terminal station.

Without any hesitation or delay, I made my way as instructed. Upon arrival, with my rucksack still on my back and heading to the manager's office to take up duty, the following announcement came through the public address system.

"Customers are advised that trains are not stopping at Kings Cross station because of an incident at the station."

I didn't pay much attention because there was nothing unusual about this announcement. However, there was a second and a third in quick succession, each with increasing urgency. Finally, the operations department specified details of what would become one of the worst episodes in the company's history:

"Customers are advised that all services are suspended at Kings Cross Station because of a fire. Customers are advised to seek alternative routes to complete their journey. No train services are operating from Kings Cross Station. Kings Cross Station is closed."

Now, this announcement was unusual because of the use of the word "fire". The company's policy was to refrain from using this word to avoid panic among commuters; instead, they used the code "Inspector Sands" to alert staff of smoke or fire anywhere on the premises. The company's overt use of language in their announcements was unorthodox. This change of protocol was an indication of a severe situation unfolding.

Even though I received bits of information from the public as they travelled through my work area, I never imagined the magnitude of the situation—it was nothing short of a disaster. The inferno that engulfed one of London's busiest interchange train stations on that fateful day claimed the lives of 31 commuters.

The blaze started when a lit match fell through a wooden escalator and below into the machine room. Apart from being the escalator's main engine room, service technicians occasionally stored their equipment and engine lubricants. The gusty wind blowing from the approaching trains in the tunnels contributed to the intensity of the fire.

Rose knew I was scheduled to work at Kings Cross. My wife was distraught as she watched the unfolding events on the evening news bulletins on television, hoping I would call—I had not informed her of my transfer to a different station. I tried to contact Rose multiple times, to no avail. The phone lines were disrupted, and seemed to be constantly engaged. Eventually, her telephone rang for a fraction of a second before she picked up—her breath of relief echoed in my ear. I reassured her of my safety.

Having had no chance at that time to contact my colleagues with whom I had earlier participated in board games at the station, I telephoned my closest friend the following day immediately after waking up from a restless night's sleep. Aiden stated how lucky I was to have been called out for a job.

"You're a blessed man, Steve," he said. "You were probably at Euston Square when all hell broke loose. We just started feeling the heat before smoke billowed into the booking hall. In no time, the whole area was engulfed."

"Was any member of staff hurt?" I asked.

"No. I don't think so. But man, I don't know how the hell we got out." Our conversation continued for about 30 minutes.

Aiden could not have known that his statement about my blessings was no bluster. Did I escape another fire? My home in St Lucia was meant to become an inferno some years earlier from my sister's discovery of a voodoo frog we were told was set up for that outcome. Of course, there is no comparison, but that was the memory that resurfaced. It terrified me when I thought the smouldering at Kings Cross had likely started as I waited to board a train out of the station while I was still on the premises. Instead, my Guardian Angel intervened and pulled me away from the scene of the catastrophe.

Aiden and other members of staff at that station escaped but were left traumatised. Several of them took time off to recoup from witnessing the chaos and passengers being overcome during the deadly event. Aiden subsequently attended counselling sessions for post-traumatic stress disorder, which, sadly, contributed to the onset of his marital problems.

The commission of inquiry that the government subsequently set up required the staff to testify during the prolonged investigation, thus adding to their distress. This incident speeded up the transformation of the company's operating procedures.

Stephen N Rosemond

The Power to Make Things Happen

Before the commission released its report on the fire in October 1988, the organisation had started sweeping changes. It was no surprise when the prohibition of smoking throughout the Underground transport network was promptly imposed. The company introduced a zero-tolerance policy on drugs and alcohol. It incorporated random drug and alcohol testing of staff into the health, safety and security measures—the impact on operations of the entire underground transport system was transformed.

I was unwavering about the direction I intended my profession to head; however, I was conscious of the possible challenges the changing work conditions would present. In sparing no effort to dismiss the uncertainties and maintain confidence in my ability to map out my future, I turned to my usual source of inspiration, appealing to the Holy Spirit through prayer. Too often, we mistakenly decipher circumstances as risks, instantly conjuring fear instead of calmness. Such a reaction boils down to defeatism. I would argue that luck is needed to make headway in life while agreeing that it plays a part. The onus is on us to harness the *good* rather than cling to the fear of what we may interpret as the *bad* element of luck. The bottom line is there can be no advancement without risk.

Sometimes, opportunities present themselves in an obscured way, but we hastily cast them aside without the slightest consideration. Therefore, it is reasonable to conclude that one would need to adopt a positive mindset and vital components such as resourcefulness, initiative, and resilience to realise and explore the promising prospects that derive from change. In essence, we have the power to make things happen.

The Need for Reflection

I would not define the lack of trust, confidence, and poor timing as a misfortune. Neither would I use the expression, *oh, I am so unlucky,* as an excuse for defeat. Progressively, it became clear that I needed to enhance my willpower to turn negative perceptions into affirmative results. I stumbled many times during my journey. Sometimes, I was sad and disappointed, but I never pitied myself.

Many occasions upon which I faltered were the exact instances I became re-energised. These episodes presented the need for reflection—examining my actions and the chance to discover my strengths and weaknesses. I accepted such moments as a chance to improve. For example, the stumble from my association with Phil triggered all my energies toward my profession. In addition,

I saw this as the right time to focus on an equally important topic that was very dear to my heart. It was a wish I was intent on bringing to fruition.

My Reunion With Jenny

There was seldom a family occasion when I did not think about my first daughter, Jenny. I longed for the day she would come over for a holiday, so I decided to introduce the topic one morning at the breakfast table. I was ecstatic when, without a second thought, Rose and the kids welcomed my idea. Rose knew nothing about Jenny's mum but predicted Lynn would never be as excited to part with her 15-year-old daughter. How could I not agree with her logical point?

Lynn had emigrated to the United States, and Rose knew I restored communication with her after Jenny had joined her in recent years. In my brief conversations with Lynn, I touched on my wish for our daughter to join my family for a holiday; her answer was an emphatic no. Given that I had brought my family into the discussion and assured her they were enthusiastic about having their sister and stepdaughter during the school break, she paid more attention but still rejected the idea. Frankly, I did not expect instant approval, so I wasn't disheartened.

My persistence paid off when Lynn finally agreed. The thought of introducing my eldest daughter to her younger siblings and Rose brought immense joy to my heart. Charlie and Tasha wasted no time starting the countdown of the days to the arrival of their big sister. They planned their holiday itinerary—all the events they wanted to attend with Jenny. Rose and I purchased the airfare, and the baby girl I had left in Saint Lucia fifteen years earlier was finally on her way to London from New York—this would be my reunion with Jenny. We all welcomed her with open arms. The instinctive embrace the kids shared was one of togetherness; there was no need for any introduction—my meeting with Jenny for the first time since we parted after her birth was moving. Witnessing my three children singing, dancing, having meals together, and sharing was fantastic. Rose and I packed in as many activities as possible to ensure a successful holiday. Sadly, the time came when emotions set in; the five-week break was over. Jenny was on her way to rejoin her mum in the United States. The summer holiday ended, Charlie and Tasha returned to school, and I redirected my full attention to my profession.

Stephen N Rosemond

One Five-letter Word on My Mind

Margaret Thatcher, the first female British Prime Minister, was elected in 1979 and remained in power throughout the 1980s. Her economic policy reforms gripped the UK during her reign. It would only be a matter of time before the guillotine would reach our human resources. Those national economic changes and our organisation's rapid rehabilitation programme after the Kings Cross fire report accelerated the dramatic changes in the company. My long-awaited desired position of Relief Clerk, for which I had become qualified, disappeared. Naturally, I was disappointed as this situation brought back the memories of my school days when those in authority snatched away my access to higher education; only on this occasion, I knew that it wasn't personal. The company absorbed the existing Relief Clerks who weren't eligible for retirement into other senior positions in various departments.

I knew losing this opportunity to move up to a higher rank wasn't the end of the world. However, having to face the uncertainty in my employment was unsettling. The most impactful outcome was the certainty of a considerable income reduction. The change from receiving hourly pay to a fixed income meant the loss of my pay enhancements. This transformation would disrupt my financial plans. The fact was, I had two clear choices: join the evolving team or carry on in what was sure to become a dead-end job.

The easiest route, of course, was the latter; do nothing. The question I faced was, how do I begin the former in an environment where the competition for positions was steeper? The changes were swift; there was no turning back. While I am not averse to organisational changes, I understand that moving into the unknown can cause anxiety and scepticism. The fear of change hinders growth no matter how discreet the dissemination of such news is. Moreover, we must realise that with change comes winners and losers. I paid close attention to what was happening around me, never losing sight of the positions advertised in our internal publications. I came up with one five-letter word—*adapt*. Adapting to change was the simple solution to my predicament.

An Absurd Policy

A comprehensive programme for retraining the workforce throughout the operating department had begun. Most of my colleagues were worried about their future but showed signs of being trapped in their comfort zone, I too, was anxious. I knew of the personal challenges that lay ahead.

I tried to remain optimistic in a work environment that appeared to be becoming unstable. I refused to submit to negative thoughts about derailing dreams and aspirations.

I was confident that one aspect of the reforms that would be to my advantage was the removal of the existing conditions for promotion and transfer. I view a promotion system based on service length within any organisation as impeding efficiency. In my department, I knew of supervisory and other personnel who demonstrated a lack of aptitude for their positions, notably in decision-making. I was relieved when the company introduced a merit system to replace what I saw as an outdated promotion framework. This change was my moment, but first, I needed to position myself in the line of progress and then wait patiently.

Rejecting the Picket Line

In refocusing on regular work, I drew up my professional development plan and, in mid-1994, applied for a spot on the in-house "Train the Trainer" training programme. This step forward would be the first if my application was accepted and my interview went well. The selection process through Human Resources was favourable; they issued me a starting date for the course.

My colleagues were disappointed to see I had altered my position from a sceptical approach to supporting a company plan they believed was detrimental to our livelihoods. They expected that I would have been the first to join the picket line if the trade unions had decided to call for protest action against the changes. Still, the union leaders had no choice even though they didn't embrace the company plan, so who was I to protest?

The UK's unemployment figures exceeded 3 million during this period, and I didn't want to become a statistic. The government's economic reforms affected many other public service sector employees. Therefore, I wriggled my way into the system and became a certified coach after I completed the course.

I placed one foot in the doorway and intended to maintain this posture until I shut the door behind me. The high pass rate among my trainees energised me and confirmed my competency in assisting potential recruits in achieving their goals. However, my utmost satisfaction came from my students' appreciation in the thank-you cards they sent after passing the course and obtaining their desired positions.

My philosophy about a profession is to ensure that the job specifications and description reflect our ability. I believe one should be suitably qualified when seeking a specific job (unless otherwise stipulated in the advertisement), as it was when I applied for the coach's position. I can't entirely agree that it is wise to seek a supervisory role, knowing that you do not possess the required qualifications or skills. While it is true that one may have background knowledge from work experience, I also believe being proactive in developing your capability through certification for the chosen position adds tremendous weight to your repertoire.

While I acknowledged preferential treatment and prejudices are inescapable, hearing the familiar cries of, "I didn't get the job because I'm black!" troubled me. As our children developed, we always encouraged them to avoid using excuses and attaching blame for their drawbacks. Instead, we wanted them to strive towards achieving their goals, know their limitations, and always focus on favourable outcomes.

Becoming a certified coach and wrapping up several successful trainees in my portfolio meant further strides in my journey. I later submitted my application for placement on a National Examination Board for Supervisory Management (NEBSM) training course at the University of Westminster, which was employer-sponsored. The company later invited me to an interview, and on March 7th, 1995, I received confirmation of my place on the course. I started the training on

April 7th and completed it in December 1995. In February 1996, I received my NEBSM Certificate. I was ready to move on to the next level of becoming a station supervisor.

Blatant Injustice

One long-standing practice that remained in place during the company's modernization programme was the adjustment of shift patterns that benefitted the staff at the local level. The station supervisors, and to a lesser extent the managers, participated in the practice of their teams working outside the official roster. In May of 1996, I learned that sticking with tradition does not mean immunity from the charge of negligence.

Jim, one of my co-workers, and I started our shift at 05.00 hrs, which was to end at 13.00 hrs. We finished our duty at the unofficial time of 12.00 hrs. The saying was we all get a *cut out of the job*. Ten minutes after we left the premises, the control room operator called out for Jim and me via the company's public address system. The supervisors knew Jim and I had left the station because we were required to sign off duty in their office and his presence.

Upon reporting for our early morning shift the following day, the duty supervisor informed Jim and me that the Station Manager had recorded us missing from duty as we had not responded to that call; thus, we would be penalised. Missing from duty was a serious charge that constituted neglecting our responsibility, so I was concerned. The manager summoned us to his office later that morning.

My duty manager, Roger, of Afro-Caribbean descent, penalised me for the offence. He registered a misconduct case and docked my pay; my previously unblemished record was tainted.

I began to wonder why I allowed this to happen even though there was nothing unusual about my behaviour. Nevertheless, I accepted that the long-standing convention was not company policy. I should have been more careful because of my new status as a coach. I acknowledged I ought to have set a better example to my trainees and other team members who looked up to me. Like everyone else who worked at the stations, I chose to take such chances; therefore, I accepted the consequences. Furthermore, I was conscious of the need to avoid jeopardizing my pending promotion. I remained humble and defied the temptation of disputing my manager's decision.

The conversation continued over the next few days but increasingly became puzzling because the situation wasn't as straightforward as I had hoped. My team and everyone who had heard of my predicament judged the ruling troubling as Roger didn't exert the same penalty on my Caucasian colleague and co-defendant, Jim.

The simple question I asked my manager was, "Why did he punish me alone for an alleged offence that my co-worker and I were both charged with?"

The event transpired on the same day at the exact location in the presence of the same supervisor after we had performed the same duty. Yet, the manager treated me less favourably than my white counterpart. To inflame the situation, Jake, one of my station supervisors, and Donald, from a lower grade, both Caucasian, were charged with the same offence within three weeks of my case, and they had received nothing more than an oral warning.

I failed to see how my issue was anything else but direct discrimination. I had never been in any disputes before. I was left to wonder whether I was a target for unknown reasons. Worst of all, the psychological impact of feeling inconsequential crawled within me; it was distressing—the appearance of injustice couldn't be more apparent. Despite the possible repercussions on my future, my inner self drove me to challenge a decision that bore the mark of racial bias.

I sent a written request for a meeting with Larry, my Group Station Manager and Roger's boss, to state my grievance. I was disheartened when my plea to Larry to reconsider this biased ruling was futile. My next option was to pursue the matter through my trade union, hoping for an amicable closure. My trade union representative, Ian, agreed to meet with Larry, Roger, and me. Once again, the Group Manager remained stubborn; therefore, from where I stood, the matter remained unresolved even though both managers considered it a closed case. Larry was renowned for his insensitivity towards non-whites, and in my opinion, he lived up to his reputation by throwing his total weight behind Roger's verdict. But Roger was also an Afro-Caribbean man! So, was Larry using Roger to do his dirty work? My brain was overflowing with suspicions.

Following some sleepless nights, the urge to take the matter further based on principle was compelling. I informed my managers of my intention, to which their response was:

"Stephen, you must accept that you went against the company's policy. It is your right to take the matter further if you wish, but our responsibility is to ensure you follow the rules."

I knew with certainty that I would find encouragement in my Bible. I needed to overcome any enemies conspiring against me. Psalm 7 was my chosen prayer: *O Lord my God in thee do I put my trust...The Lord shall judge the people....God judgeth the righteous, and God is angry with the wicked....*

Testing My Capacity

Taking a manager or employer to an industrial tribunal was rare, at least in our firm. My co-workers were astonished by the courage I displayed in my pursuit of fairness. However, while they supported my moral stance and offered much patting on the back and offers to attend as a witness, it remained to be seen whether the support would translate to witnesses at the tribunal hearing. However, my trade union representative had a different opinion. He was concerned about the sensitivity of my case.

"Come on, Stephen. It would be best to take the knock on the chin, go easy, and pretend it never happened."

He suggested that my decision to pursue the case through a tribunal would damage my chances for promotion and disrupt this long-standing working practice. In Ian's opinion, I would shift the spotlight to this well-established custom. I was incensed by Ian's approach as I considered his response tactless.

The talk of my decision spread throughout the department and led to a unanimous view that I was pursuing a case that would threaten my livelihood; I would become a target of victimization. Of course, I had already seen myself as a victim of injustice in this situation. But what precedent would I be setting if I did nothing? I regarded no action as being more damaging to others like me. Considering the idea of just walking away was outside of my thinking.

Amid my pursuit of justice, I received a telephone call in mid-August 1996 from Doreen, Larry's secretary, that was most interesting. Doreen informed me of the company's offer of a supervisory position at a West London location, which was one of many I had nominated on my promotion documents for the supervisor's post. I was jubilant about the prospect of progressing during my trouble. My immediate thought upon receiving this morale-boosting news was—vindication. The location presented many challenges, but my selection was strategic; I needed a starting point.

Challenges and Opportunities

The position the company offered me was at a place widely recognised for being incident prone. Among the positive thoughts that hovered in my mind was one negative: *was it possible that my manager had cunningly arranged my transfer to a location known for its operational problems?* This terminus was one where the train operators changed over duties. The potential challenges that I would be taking on were: defective technical and operations equipment, common episodes of signal and other track equipment failures, assaults on commuters, and suicide cases—among the many above-ground stations, this spot appeared to be the favourite for those who chose to jump in the path of oncoming trains.

To many, this was not the ideal starting point for their management career—my thinking was different. I saw an opportunity to underscore my ability to work in a challenging environment. I saw unlimited scope to learn and develop the required skills that would enable me to become a proficient station supervisor and an outstanding duty manager in the medium term. I saw nothing other than a turning point in my career.

I accepted the chance with pleasure to move away from the manager against whom I had raised a serious grievance. However, alongside all the advantages was one situation I dreaded. While I wanted to be a hands-on station supervisor, dealing with mutilated human remains on the tracks was one I would gladly remove from my responsibilities if I had a choice. Once I signed the paperwork and received a starting date, there was no turning back. Larry congratulated me at our parting meeting. He wished me well, but we knew we would see each other again at the tribunal hearing.

My Sigh of Relief

On Sunday, 15th September 1996, I started my new job, never losing sight of the tasks ahead. My new managers welcomed me, and I appreciated being in their group. Among my prayers, Psalm 47 was the one I turned to for inspiration to establish a good working relationship with my new team. The nature of my work determined the certainty of a short period within which I would be appraised.

During my third week into my new post, on 4th October 1996, I started my evening shift at 17.00 hrs. Soon after the rush hour was over, at about 19.30 hrs, a train approached the station with its whistle blaring. I recognized this was a call for assistance by the driver, so I made my way to the platform. The driver informed me that a male passenger was behaving threateningly on board. He had told the Line Controller and alerted the Transport Police before approaching the station. The police telephoned me and suggested I hold the train without opening the doors.

Meanwhile, the Line Controller, having overall command of operations, used his unlimited authority to instruct me to get the train moving. This command was in direct conflict with the police's request, and I calmly explained to the controller that the police would be present at any moment.

A service delay exceeding three minutes on the network is considered excessive because of the cumulative impact on the overall operations. I kept hoping that the police would arrive during the expected time. As I leisurely walked toward the red signal I had positioned ahead of the train on the platform to override the automatic signalling system, I breathed a sigh of relief when the police appeared. I immediately sprinted towards the police, directing them to the relevant carriage where the offender was. They took away the culprit, and we resolved the matter without conflict. Soon after, my manager arrived on the scene and questioned what the controller thought was my delay in following his instructions.

Even though the Line Controller commented about my slow walking, he and my manager accepted my subsequent report favourably. I had managed this operation within four minutes. I made every effort to be diligent in my profession without forgetting my pending case at the tribunal.

Judgement Day

Never before had I been inside a courtroom. Therefore, I sought assistance from an independent lawyer to help prepare for this daunting encounter; I needed representation. Upon presenting my case folder, which included my questions to the defence, to him, and reading through my report, the lawyer looked impressed with my presentation.

"Mr Rosemond, why have you come to see me?" he asked.

I was puzzled by this question because it had been about fifteen minutes into our conversation; I answered with a question.

"Why do you ask this quest...?" the lawyer interrupted before I completed my answer with a question.

"You have laid out your case superbly with all the evidence pointing to your advantage. You can present it to the tribunal without my help. You don't need a lawyer to represent you."

I felt a sudden rush of optimism.

One of the pieces of advice the lawyer gave me that was uppermost in my mind was that I provide a copy of my case folder to the tribunal clerk and a second copy to the defence team before the tribunal officer called the case. Passing a copy of my case file to my opponent sounded like a strange idea.

"Why should I do this?" I asked. "Wouldn't I be compromising a possible win?"

"Well, Mr Rosemond, this is the court procedure," he replied.

Although I knew nothing about the process, I remained doubtful about this instruction. The tribunal set my race discrimination case for hearing in June 1997. As the time approached, my anxiety rose, even though I was confident about my preparedness. This moment was another that necessitated the presentation of my special petition to my spiritual guide—Psalm 35 was my choice: *Plead my cause, oh Lord, with them that strive with me. Fight against them, that fight against me*—my judgement day had arrived.

As advised, I handed over copies of my entire folder on the day of the hearing. Did my lawyer forget to impart a crucial piece of information? Did he forget to include *except your questions* when he spoke about passing on my case file? Or should I have used my initiative when presenting the folder to the defendant's team? These were the questions that played out in my mind.

On the other hand, why was I being so harsh on myself? Because let's face it, I followed my lawyer's advice as he told me. The defendant's team was well-prepared with my list of questions. My case was clear-cut; nevertheless, the verdict swung against me strictly based on not having any witnesses.

The promises of three co-workers to testify on my behalf remained promises. I had no regrets and bore no ill will. The presiding adjudicator described my action and presentation as, "commendable and courageous." Larry and his team offered a *no-hard-feelings* handshake when the hearing ended. They congratulated me for my bravery and the professional way I presented my case. Achieving a moral victory was equally rewarding to me as an overall success. I proved I would not buckle under pressure even though I stood alone. I took a position for a cause that I knew was just.

With my tribunal case over, I was thankful that the ramification many had predicted never came. There was no more distraction to divert my attention away from the crucial task of managing my station and I re-established a stable routine. I tried never to deviate from my duties and refrained from all working practices that were not official company policy. I recorded every new assignment as material I would use to demonstrate my abilities in future competency-based interviews. Having spent six months in this position, I decided the time was right for me to apply for a transfer to a higher-level location with more activities: commuter traffic and increased personnel. The reward for the added workload would be a decent rise in my income.

My application was approved, and the company offered me a central London station.

Insubordination

This interchange station connecting three lines in the heart of London presented its own unique conditions. Overseeing this work environment was testing; the probability of attending to daily incidents was significant. Therefore, two station supervisors were required to be on duty from 7.00 - 23.00 hrs. One supervisor covered the night shift from 23.00 - 7.00 hrs. The night duty was no more relaxed because the considerable number of contracted workers and engineering staff on duty during that time kept them on their toes throughout the shift.

I remember Adrian, my long-time buddy who was happy to be firmly grounded in his office administration position, commenting,

"Wow, Steve, I suspect you enjoy stressful work." My answer was no different from what I had given on previous occasions; it was simple.

"Well, Adrian, I seek opportunities and get to grips with the attached conditions," I replied.

During the second week at my new central London location, my colleague Alex, and I started our shift at 7.00 hrs. I was the mobile duty leader, while Alex took charge of the station operation control room. A radio call came from the operations room no more than two hours into my duty.

"Calling station supervisor Rosemond. Will station supervisor Rosemond make his way to Platform 4?"

"Message received," I responded.

In the meantime, I continued radio communication with Alex, who informed me of the information passed on to him by the Line Controller—someone had pulled the emergency stop handle on the train. I reached platform 4 to meet the train operator, who confirmed that a customer had collapsed on the train. Hence, he left the doors open. I made my way to the carriage, where a middle-aged-looking female customer lay on the floor. The motionless customer was being attended to by a gentleman who identified himself as a doctor. The doctor informed me that it was his opinion that the customer had suffered from a stroke and should only be handled by paramedics. I immediately asked Alex to call an ambulance.

Throughout the event, I maintained radio contact with my colleague in the operation room, who relayed the seriousness of the situation to the Line Controller—the clock was ticking; Line Controllers do not favour delayed trains on the system. The platform telephone started to ring, and eventually, a team member took the call and radioed me; it was the Line Controller on the other end.

"Station supervisor Rosemond, you have a passenger who has taken ill on board this train. Can you assist in moving the passenger to the platform while you await the ambulance? We need to get the train moving."

I knew this was a testing request that I couldn't perform. But would my response be wrongly declared as insubordination by my superiors? Such an assertion on their part would be incorrect.

"I'm sorry, sir. I did relay the information to my operation room colleague. *'Mr customer name,'* identified as a medical doctor, is with the casualty. He has advised that only the paramedics should move her because she has likely suffered a stroke."

With an exasperating tone, the Line Controller continued:

"Well, can you assist the doctor in moving the sick lady? We have to get the trains moving."

"Sorry, sir. I don't believe the doctor would contradict himself and remove the sick person. Besides, he's the only doctor on the scene. He alone would be unable to lift the patient, and I am not qualified to move a suspected stroke victim."

The controller wasn't happy about the delay in the service. However, he accepted we had no choice but to wait until the paramedics arrived.

It was the height of the rush hour, which meant the medical professionals would be navigating vehicular traffic congestion in central London and commuter traffic at the station—delay in the service was inevitable.

While I managed the incident with my team, over 100 feet below ground, redirecting customers, my counterpart implemented station control and managed communications. At last! The ambulance arrived, the medical staff took over, and they transported the patient to the hospital. After collecting the relevant information, including the doctor's details for my report, I wrapped up the case. Overall, the incident lasted about fifteen minutes. Going against the Line Controller's advice twice in less than a year was an experience I did not celebrate.

I Turned the Tables

My medium-to-long-term ambition to rise to a senior position, the Group Station Manager level, remained. My plan was realistic, but I didn't believe it would be easily achievable. I would first have to advance to a Duty Station Manager grade. The promotional opportunities continued to surface in our in-house journal while the organisational changes continued at full pace. For the first time, the company extended its recruitment drive to the various universities for the Senior Manager's rank; the concept of head-hunting became customary practice. The stiff competition that lay ahead never deterred me from pursuing my goal. Now that I had positioned myself on the tall ladder's first step, it was out of the question that I would look backwards. The time was right to refer to my professional development programme again.

The post of Duty Station Manager was my focus. In 1997, with Rose's support, I submitted my application to East London's Newham College for an evening spot on the vocational training course for Management Studies. The college accepted my application, and I started in September 1997. I remember getting home from work mid-afternoon in the peak of winter with little time to relax before heading to evening study. I was exhausted and lacked the energy to attend the lessons. The outside temperature was freezing with above-average snowfall, a perfect reason to head for an early night's rest—my family was having none of it; they would not tolerate me missing one study session.

"Come on it's time to start preparing for college," they yelled as I lay on the sofa.

"Hmm, I'm not up to it today. I'm exhausted," I grumbled.

"No-no, you're going to college," Rose and the kids asserted.

Holding onto my arms, Rose pulled me off the sofa while Charlie and Tasha tickled me and demanded that I organize myself to exit the front door in time for college. In June 1998, I completed the course and gained a Business Management Diploma. I am forever grateful to my family for their wisdom in driving me out of our home for an excellent reason.

Now that I had earned my qualification and wrapped up two years of supervisory experience, I was confident my career path was moving along the right track. I wasted no time submitting my application for the Duty Station Manager post immediately after discovering the advertised vacancy. The human resources department endorsed my application, and I underwent a rigorous assessment.

To my delight, I was awarded the new post in April 1999. Was I prepared for this enormous challenge? Such a huge responsibility? Yes, I had no doubt. Being accountable for hundreds of thousands of commuters travelling within my area was exciting. Never had I served in a position of such authority. I became the manager of members of my team who were previously my supervisors, most of whom were senior to me in terms of service. My primary duty as a manager was to build and sustain an effective team through mutual trust, confidence, and support. I was ready to roll up my sleeves.

My role as a Duty Manager involved overall control of four stations, among the busiest in the heart of London. I managed a team of up to 140 staff and ensured the implementation of safety and security regulations. One of my most daunting responsibilities was overseeing engineering works and signal failures, which brought me and my staff into near contact with live rails, with a minimum of 630 volts DC—there was no room for error.

Contempt for Colour

As a Duty Manager, consistently achieving the organisation's objectives without some degree of compromising operations took considerable effort—making the right decisions in the interest of the business while simultaneously meeting customers' expectations was a delicate undertaking that required a unique ability. Most crucially, being a manager from a minority background meant doubling my effort to get the correct balance. Even with unfailing optimism, I needed to be ready to repel the negative overtones that would doubtlessly follow. Such connotations came from a cross-section: the people I served and those with whom I served—some within the organisation sought to undermine my position as a duty manager. Thankfully, my extensive experience in public service enabled me to build my resilience to the prejudiced attitudes I encountered. Some of the biases that I came up against included a co-manager of Asian descent, Roy, who incessantly contradicted all the ideas I put forward during formal or informal management meetings and discussions. While it was his prerogative to do so, his attitude showed a degree of contempt, implying my contributions were unimportant. I brought the matter to Robert, our manager, who had noticed Roy's scornful attitude. I politely requested that Robert urgently address my concern and put a stop to this behaviour. I also told him my intention to manage the situation personally if it continued. During one of our meetings, Roy presented the opportunity for me to remind him of our equal status. As I expected, he did not appreciate my rebuttal and wouldn't acknowledge his discourtesy; Robert intervened in the ensuing debate, resulting in Roy apologizing. From then onward, he changed his attitude, and we became buddies.

Another time, a Caucasian male customer who wished to complain to a senior manager approached a member of my team. The employee directed the customer to my office. Then came a banging on my door: "Knock-knock…knock."

"Come in," I answered. The customer walked in.

Stunned, he immediately made a U-turn upon seeing me and shouted,

"Oh no, another f****ng black monkey!" slamming the door as he walked out.

My spontaneous reaction was to ignore the comment, which I found more amusing than offending. The customer didn't even give me a chance to address his complaint.

In the summer of 1999, I was excited to be the sole Duty Manager during one of the grandest charity music events, Party in the Park, held at London's Hyde Park and in aid of the Prince's Trust. This sensational summer gathering attracted up to 100,000 revellers from home and abroad. The artists lined up to perform were world-renowned. It was a privilege to be in charge for the first time during that spectacular event, drawing enormous crowds through the station I controlled. During the event, a London Metropolitan Police Inspector walked into my station and I saw the portrait of a flustered man in his unblinking gaze. Despite my distinguishable appearance in full uniform, including a name badge and job title, he sidestepped me and approached my subordinate, a white Station Supervisor. After the pair walked to the Supervisor's office, I waited for approximately ninety seconds, then went over to join the conversation. I was amazed to hear the

Inspector's comments about our management of commuter traffic to the supervisor.

"Excuse me, sir, for interrupting," I said. "I am the Duty Manager, and this is my Station Supervisor. It seems I am being left out of this serious discussion about my station. So, can I ask what exactly the problem is?"

"Well, Mr Rosemond," the Inspector responded, "I explained to your Station Supervisor that we are experiencing severe congestion at the street level. I am simply asking that you control the number of commuters exiting your station."

"Inspector," I replied, "we have protocols for managing such events, including extending the trains' waiting time on the platforms to avoid overcrowding at the station." I continued, "As you can see on our monitors, we have two escalators moving upward and one going down, which is in accordance with our safety policies."

"But can't you reverse one of the up escalators to get more people on the trains more quickly?" the Inspector asked.

After I had explained our safety and security system to the Police Inspector, he wasn't satisfied. His suggestion for us to redirect the customers leaving the station to ease pedestrian traffic on the roads was ludicrous.

"Sir, excuse me, you may not have noticed, but this station has three exits; the reason for this is to avoid congestion on our end. Where do you suggest we redirect our customers to?" I asked.

I was courteous by allowing him to air his haphazard views, albeit with a display of arrogance.

I reminded the police of my role on the premises; I told him his suggestions were inappropriate, unworkable, and entirely inconsistent with our security requirements. I considered my time in this discussion wasteful, so I needed to be firm in terminating this exchange.

"Inspector," I replied, "you are clearly seeking to undermine my position as the Duty Manager. Please take over if you believe you are better qualified to perform my role." I gave him clear choices after pointing out his work boundaries. I asked that he vacate the Station Supervisor's office or take over my role as Duty Manager. The officer looked stunned.

"Come on, Mr Rosemond," he said, "it doesn't have to boil down to this. I'm simply asking that you slow down the crowds leaving your station, that's all."

"Sir," I replied, "your request is a recipe for disaster on our premises. I can no longer carry on this conversation as the supervisor and I need to attend to matters outside. I'm sorry, we must leave now."

The Police Inspector walked away glum-faced without uttering another word. I reminded the Station Supervisor about the need to have his manager involved in such safety-critical discussions. I recorded the incident in the station's logbook and sent a report to my Senior Manager. I received a silver award and a performance-related bonus for my overall performance in managing the Party in the Park crowds that day.

Unpleasant experiences of being undermined did not dampen my energy or hinder the effective execution of my work. However, my immediate thoughts after such events were my beautiful children, who looked up to me; they thought the world of me. They were so proud that their dad had this high-profile position. Yet, strangers who knew nothing about me chose to be cocky and discriminatory towards me.

It was unmistakable that such behaviour by the offenders was tantamount to contempt for colour. My Bible remained my source of solace, which I found from my consistent reading of Psalm 47: *O clap your hands all ye people….For the shield of the earth belong unto God: He is greatly exalted.*

Nevertheless, I left those emotions at work and never took them home. I didn't discuss those issues with my family because I needed to protect them from psychological harm. These were all challenges that came with the managerial package. It was heartening that the advantages by far outweighed the aggravation. Above all, my team's appreciation of my performance at the helm of this grand festival boosted my confidence.

How Could I Disagree?

My first opportunity to manage the memorable activity, Party in the Park, in the UK capital left a lasting impression on me, but now, a once-in-a-thousand-year event was rapidly approaching. My work territory of four stations was in the heart of London's entertainment zone; my team's performance had to be flawless to ensure a problem-free operation for the greatest of all—the Millennium Celebration.

Two hundred and seventy-two stations form the Greater London Rapid Transit system. These stations are divided into groups, which vary in the number of stations per group. The planning and organising for the super event by each group in Central London required meticulous coordination among every team. Immediately after the Party in the Park event, individual team meetings became a combined group gathering where the respective team managers met weekly. One dimension was added to ensure consistency between every team—a Lead Manager had to be selected by each group for representation in group meetings and the eventual control of the event at their various locations. How would I know that my management of the Party in the park some months earlier was the prelude to the elevated position to lead the New Millennium Celebrations?

At one of our corporate meetings, Adrien, my previous manager, while I worked as a supervisor at neighbouring stations, challenged my suggestion for an added incentive for our team members working twelve-hour shifts for this special event. I thought my contribution to the discussion was valid because of the anticipated significant strain that was sure to keep our staff on their toes throughout the night shift. This incentive would also ensure all our team remained at their stations during their short breaks. As we exchanged ideas, Adrien stated:

"Stephen, I don't think providing the staff with snacks and beverages is a good idea."

"Why do you disagree?" I asked.

"Have you thought about the cost to the business? We're talking about hundreds of staff!" Adrien replied.

"You're right, Adrien. The staff numbers are high, but don't you believe we should acknowledge our members' efforts under the circumstances? They aren't obliged to take up the overtime duties necessary to guarantee a safe and secure operation. Instead, they could be celebrating with their families. Let's provide these treats as a gesture of appreciation. Furthermore," I continued, "we'll be seeking flexibility from our team for their meal break—how many do we allow to sign off at different times when so many start duty simultaneously?"

Adrien was unsatisfied with my explanation and repeated, "Stephen, we don't have a snacks budget, but we could allow our staff members to bring their food."

"That, too, is reasonable," I responded. "But we mustn't forget that our staff will be working extended shifts, and we shouldn't dismiss that some will likely leave the premises to seek a meal. How do we encourage them to stay on the station in case of emergency during their breaks? It's incumbent on us to promote good teamwork without compromising safety and security."

I later discussed the matter with Robert, my manager, and he understood my logic. Once we had established the conditions, we allocated a budget for our group to provide sandwiches, tea, and coffee.

Alas! The moment was upon us, and the crowds poured into our stations. My position as head of operations in my group was another milestone in my managerial career. At about 1.00 a.m. on the millennium morning, as I patrolled my station among the thousands of revellers, I received a station radio message from the Station Operations Room:

"Calling Station Manager Rosemond. Can you please make your way to the control room? There's a call from Duty Manager Adrien. "I made my way to answer the telephone.

"Hi Steve, this is Adrien," he said. "Look, Steve, my guys have been working their butts off here, and we can do with some stuff on our group. Any chance of surplus snacks in your group?"

"Oh, so sorry to hear that, Adrien. Unfortunately, we only have one tea and coffee machine. I truly regret not being able to assist, but doing so will leave us short."

While I was satisfied that Duty Station Manager Adrien unintentionally acknowledged my foresight, I regretted not having sufficient treats to spare his team. The overall performance of my team, including the station supervisors and my co-managers, was impeccable. At our end-of-event meeting, Robert extended many compliments for another well-managed public event.

"I am honoured, Robert, but let's not forget, my team did the work. We would have all failed without their exemplary performance," I stated.

"Come on, Steve, there you go again. It's time that you start accepting your credit. Without proper *leadership*, the team would've failed," Robert replied.

How could I disagree with my manager's assertion?

The pay structure for my positions as Duty Manager was linked to performance, making it the highest income I had ever earned in my working life. My new status brought a much-enhanced standard of living far removed from our earlier days. We enjoyed the blessing of small luxuries like upgrading the family vehicle and going on family outings. In addition, we could afford Charlie and Tasha's first experience of travelling together to the USA without their parents where they spent their summer holiday with family.

Symptoms of Matrimonial Exhaustion

Travelling to Saint Lucia always generated excitement; I enjoyed the comfort and the sense of belonging whenever I visited. Every trip brought me closer to actualising my aspiration of repatriation someday. One of my life ambitions was to give back to our tiny island. I dreamt of the day I would return and become a regular income source for some of my fellow Saint Lucians; yes, owning a business.

During one of my visits, my schoolmates jogged my memory about a pledge I had made. Thomas reminded me that I spoke of retiring at the age of forty. Well, I could only guess at the time of this pledge that I was going through the process of brain de-cluttering; it was 1998, and I had surpassed that age. Considering the drawbacks I had encountered, I was pleased with the strides we had made. Rose and I were confident that our children were happy; I was satisfied our life was heading in the right direction. We had covered a long distance to reach a position where we needed only to continue with our love and support and maintain our comfort level. I would not regard the relationship between Rose and I as unique even though everyone thought we were a perfect match. Like most couples, we faced our highs and lows.

My wife was soon to embark on her second break for 14 days in Saint Lucia with her best pal, Tina. She would make this journey within one year of attending her grandmother's funeral on the island. I hoped this ladies' time-out would rejuvenate her. Admittedly, I was already missing my wife just at the thought of being without her for that time. On her part, I observed combined excitement and anxiety as her departure approached; my presumption was homesickness was setting in.

Nevertheless, Rose and her Saint Lucian friend, Tina, whom she first met at their workplace, were on their way to enjoying their Caribbean holiday. Remarkably, their personalities were miles apart, but the fondness they shared was incredible. Tina was an extrovert who enjoyed partying. I could only imagine that she was the life and soul of every party she attended and loved the attention. She was never short on conversation. Rose was in every way the opposite. They shared a country of origin, their place of work, birth date, and marital status. There was nothing else that I saw that they had in common. Their holiday ended, and the kids and I were thrilled to have Rose back.

As time passed, I observed Rose shifting away from her natural disposition. She seemed to have the desire for a new lease on life. Her change of attitude was visible; she was becoming more self-assured, and I endorsed her boosted confidence until our discussions gradually moved from constructive to opinionated. Most peculiar, though, was that our lows appeared to be surpassing our highs. *Was it peer pressure working?* I wondered. I was unable to pinpoint the precise cause of her mood swings; I dismissed these as symptoms of matrimonial exhaustion, which we would subsequently manage amicably. However strange it may sound, I thought, Tina's marriage was hitting the buffers, so was Rose feeling left out?

Less than one year following her return from Saint Lucia, Rose talked again about a third break back to the island. I was dumbfounded because I saw no justification for another holiday. Her suggestion begged the question, what had suddenly changed? What stimulating discovery did Rose make during her last visit? Were her experiences so encouraging that they required fast-forwarding such a decision? I was ready to listen to her new schemes and opinions, provided there were no diversions. I would not be entertaining any strategies or thoughts I knew would not be practical or feasible. I took a firm stance and declined Rose's call for another holiday. This occasion was one of the few cases where my position was uncompromising.

Uncomfortable Listening

I know of the urges that derive from a holiday, but I also know that such desires can often be nothing other than fantasies. Sadly, in Rose's case, it was no illusion. There was no limit to her referencing her new acquaintances in Saint Lucia during our conversations. I was familiar with some of the names she talked about, one of whom was a weathercaster, the brother of my old schoolmate. In jest, I stated that I knew of his family, so she had spared me from introducing her upon our future travel to the island. I expected some reaction from Rose; there was none.

I was conscious of Rose's continuous dislike for the English lifestyle, but the weather was her greatest loathing. It was convenient that we shared the aspiration to return to our island for good. Despite her fervent desire, I did not view, plan, nor expect such sentiment to materialize into an overnight dream come true. While we still longed for eventual repatriation, there was never any cast-iron agreement regarding the timing. We were not ready to make such a dramatic move. In any case, While Rose favoured a hastier exit, my approach had always been methodical.

Our many past dialogues, experiences, sacrifices and shared goals did not stop my wife from drifting away from our plans. She underscored this change by suddenly questioning the need to continue our investment-linked policy I had initiated some years earlier. This event caused my first flicker of doubt about the strength of our connection. I sensed a crack forming in our relationship but didn't consider our differences irreconcilable; I saw no threat.

The chats between Rose and I were always fun, enjoyable, and full of laughter. However, my refusal to accept her demand this time for her was uncomfortable listening. I noticed a build-up of anxiety when I expressed my opinion about her new perspective. Conversations with my wife started becoming more restricted because I was concerned about inciting annoyance. I chose to adopt a new strategy by giving full attention to other topics that did not include Saint Lucia. While I continued to hold my breath about my different approach, I alone could not guarantee the avoidance of any other disputes.

Rose's Declaration

The discomfort I spotted in Rose during our exchanges brought suspicions and concerns. While not intending to exacerbate a tense situation, we needed to resolve whatever it was that continued to be troubling her. My instincts kept pointing to an issue my wife desperately needed to let out, but I didn't know what it was. At home, Rose stood on the stairs leading to the upper floor from the hallway while I remained on the bottom landing as we spoke. In a gloomy tone and staring sideways, the person I chose to be my wife, who was indeed my life, finally broke her silence.

"I don't think I can stay here much longer,"

I thought I hadn't heard her correctly. I stood numb for about five seconds with my mouth open and hands stretched out. I asked, "What did you say? What do you mean? What are you talking about?"

After pausing for about thirty seconds, Rose's explanation was incomprehensible; it was senseless. She continued.

"I've decided to return to Saint Lucia because I no longer wish to stay in England. We've sacrificed enough, and it's time for a different approach."

I wasn't sure how to react; I was startled. Rose's declaration was unthinkable, mind-blowing, and unacceptable to me. Such an attitude could derail everything we had discussed. Most importantly, our children were still in college and progressing exceptionally. I was aware of the consequences for the children of broken families. Such hardships were not what I wished our children to endure.

Rose's revelation was sensational. It came across like a sledgehammer to my face. Her facial expression turned to a mixture of conscience-stricken and relief.

CHAPTER FOURTEEN

Corridor of Insanity

Unquestionably, we all will face setbacks in our lifetime. However, we become aware of issues facing our neighbours, which we never predict will land on our doorstep, because we try to position ourselves so that such complications bypass us. Knowing that my wife and I were two individuals with distinct values wasn't mystifying. But while facing our divisions, it was critical to remain alert to stifle the wishes of the unrighteous on every side.

Rose and I had always enjoyed a harmonious relationship, so without hesitation, I will admit that I became increasingly worried about the changing home atmosphere. While my intuition led me to believe our circumstance was under control, my wife revived the contentious holiday topic, to which I objected once more.

Rose failed to see any rationale in my opposition, which she described as unreasonable. In retrospect, I had fulfilled whatever she desired without any resistance. "No" was not a word I had previously used emphatically concerning Rose's demands. Therefore, my unbending stance on this occasion meant I was backing away from my practice. I wondered whether I had inadvertently given rise to this intransigence out of love by agreeing to conscientiously initiate all business or critical decisions in the home rather than insisting on joint initiatives, jumping in on every occasion to offer support. Should I have allowed Rose to make her own decisions, irrespective of the results? We had proven that teamwork was a vital part of our relationship. I'd always provided whatever my wife requested, whether such a request was a need or a want, and I'd sung her praises at every opportunity because I saw her as the perfect wife. A one-way apology became normal; even though deep within I knew there were occasions when I didn't have to accept responsibility.

I began to feel that I no longer knew what to expect from my wife, despite us sharing our lives for the past 19 years. Rose's desire for another break gave me the impression that she was expressing her view about the state of our marriage. Was she cunningly conveying that her life needed rejuvenation? I wondered. Well, deep within me, I pitied my wife. I cherished Rose; I appreciated her and was concerned she was misguided. Uppermost in my mind was the welfare of my children and wife.

Safeguarding Our Bond

I never shied away from owning my faults, nor did I waver in sharing my successes. I welcomed Rose's objections to my ideas and suggestions as opportunities to re-examine and make amends where necessary. It demonstrated my willingness to offer each other support in resolving differences. This method would form the basis for strengthening and sustaining a solid partnership. In contrast, Rose interpreted my oppositions as unaffectionate and critical, while I considered them open and honest expressions of unconditional love. I therefore saw her behaviour mirroring that of increasingly irritable spouses.

Amid my expression of love was the element of harmony. I valued our relationship, so I yielded to the power of love and sacrificed in the interest of peace. There may be various opinions about my approach toward Rose. Some readers may agree that I may have been too generous. Others may hold the contrary view that I restricted my spouse's role or undermined her ability to take responsibility. Irrespective of the various notions, I will acknowledge that my method was not the best. Nevertheless, I was committed to safeguarding our bond. In addition, while I described the extent of my sentiments towards my wife as extravagant love, the thought that I was sowing the seeds of a false sense of security never escaped my mind.

I became worried that our marriage was on the wrong course, so I would make whatever adjustments possible to get our relationship back on track; I knew our keeping a healthy alliance would be disappointing to those who bore us ill wishes.

Rose and I agreed to avoid disagreements in public or in our children's presence. We decided to spend more time out together as a family. We varied our recreational activities with a mix of what the average household did; ten-pin bowling was our favourite. We went to the movies and theme parks, and our dinner outings and general social activities were more frequent.

I appreciated the respite that followed, but an unexpected detour in my journey would mark the beginning of a new phase. It was the prelude to our evolving relationship.

The Passing of George

In January 1999, Rose and I received a sad telephone call from Leo, a friend who had been introduced to us by Rose's elderly uncle, George. Leo informed us that George had suddenly passed away.

I first met George soon after Rose and I moved to London in 1979 and before he became a widower. Uncle George, who had lived in England since the 1950s and had no offspring, was God-fearing, quiet and reserved. We lived in the same borough of London, approximately three miles apart. We appreciated George's closeness, and he valued ours, too. Among his few associates, his highest esteem went to his niece, Rose. Apart from being a father figure, one more basis for his high regard stemmed from his insatiable appetite for her cooking.

George's favourite dish was fish, but he hated preparing it himself. On Saturdays, Rose always included fish in our meals; whether it was herring fillets for breakfast, deliciously cooked with garlic, peppers, and a mixture of fresh herbs, paired with Caribbean hard dough bread and cocoa tea, or fresh tuna with vegetables for dinner. We ensured the delivery of Uncle George's fish meal, for which he was always grateful.

His best-loved pastime was baking, so he never failed to keep our share of the mouth-watering homemade fruitcakes he regularly baked. We shared Christmas gifts, but he displayed his utmost gratitude and trust when he disclosed his most confidential business. He further showed appreciation by appointing Rose one of four estate administrators and by including her in his beneficiaries list.

The sad fact is, in our Saint Lucian society, whether or not there are justifiable reasons, it is often inevitable that after the passing of a loved one, much rivalry among the relatives arises over the deceased's possessions—George's case was no exception. His estate was complex and needed legal intervention. Having played our role in managing and settling his affairs, we wanted no part in the anticipated dispute among the family members and others who presented themselves as his loved ones after George's passing. Rose and I retreated peacefully from the fray that followed.

It became a Reality

It would be dishonourable to overlook Rose's deceased uncle's monetary gift, which, as predicted, resulted in an unthinkable backlash and resentment from relatives. Nevertheless, I continued with my usual attention to work, and essential family matters. Rose returned to her moot desire for the Saint Lucia holiday. Since she had received George's gift, she insisted that my use of finance to justify an objection was no longer valid. She was now seeking to return to Saint Lucia for an extended and unspecified period. Regrettably,

I could no longer persuade my wife to relinquish her urge. Therefore, my alternatives were to either stay away from all participation in her decision, or give half-hearted support with the hope that she would change her mind. My life commitment to marrying Rose was one I intended to uphold.

I envisioned a destabilizing situation after much self-reflection. Knowing of my wife's firm determination to travel, irrespective of my opinion or our lack of preparedness, I thought we should discuss the matter more broadly—why not make the visit more meaningful? Why not explore the possibilities of running a small business there? Rose agreed to talk over the issue, so we started a dialogue.

During our previous visits to Saint Lucia, we discovered numerous gaps in how the business community conducted trade on the island, particularly in the retail sector. We got the impression that all the island retailers procured their inventory from a single supplier because of the woefully inadequate commodity choices and poor quality product.

In addition, patrons had no purchase guarantee. The ambience was claustrophobic. The term merchandising was unheard of, and, most important of all, customer service was non-existent. We saw the island operating on a false economy. Rose's supervisory experience in retail prompted us to examine such a possibility. We began by brainstorming for potential business ideas we would model on UK standards. What had been a concept was fast shifting toward becoming a reality.

I suggested to Rose, "Why not plug the gap and offer a distinctive experience to Saint Lucian shoppers? How would you feel about owning a variety store in Saint Lucia?" After much deliberation, Rose agreed to go along with the idea. The plan would include Rose running her retail store in the Caribbean while I stayed in England. I would continue in my employment until early retirement. I projected that I would return to join her in 2011. I would manage the kids, ensuring they completed their college education and preparing them for entrance to university. The children and I would visit Saint Lucia during holidays from work and study in the interim.

We figured out the business would begin sometime during the last three months of 2000, allowing us a minimum of eighteen months of further planning and organising and begin trading for Christmas. In the meantime, Rose consulted with one of her closest cousins, Manuel, with whom she grew up on the island. Manuel had become a prominent businessperson with much influence and was well-positioned to make recommendations.

One of his much-appreciated inputs was to offer rental space from one of his commercial properties at a concessionary rate. In early 2000, I travelled to Saint Lucia while on holiday from work to oversee the legal aspect of setting up the business. I was to secure the registration and licenses and meet with the relevant stakeholders, including registered customs brokers, who would help. It was also an opportunity to meet with Rose's cousin; my journey was a success.

After my return to England, we set the ball rolling on the other crucial part of the adventure. It was time to obtain the inventory, including shop fittings, equipment, and any necessities to facilitate the project; my past experiences in the trade served me well. We directed all our purchases to the freight-forwarding company whose services I had employed in the past, including storage and packaging.

Meanwhile, Charlie and Tasha continued to make us proud as they excelled in their studies. Our bold and chatty teenage son was approaching the end of his final year in college. His impressive final results exceeded the requirement to secure a place at any university best suited for his intended profession. However, he had planned to take a break from schooling to broaden his work experience before returning to study. While at college, he volunteered to be a radio announcer at an East London hospital following a stint at a nearby community radio station. His chosen degree path was radio broadcasting.

Tasha's end-of-term assessment came through with an impeccable score of straight As. Rose and I were perfectly content with our children's excellent achievements. The kids' progress reports invalidated my brothers' "making our kids foolish" claim years ago because of our nurturing style. Tasha's tutors recognised her eligibility to apply to two highly acclaimed universities in England. Because of her exemplary academic performance, they recommended the University of Oxford, with the University of York as the second choice for her chosen linguistics programme, so she applied.

I remember Rose and I raced out of bed one night upon hearing a sudden burst of crying from Tasha's room. We had no time to imagine what was wrong but knew she needed us. Tasha was sitting at the edge of her bed with a stack of books spread out as she sobbed. With my arms around her, I asked:

"What's wrong, Tash? What's wrong?" She continued sobbing. I was sad to see the overpowering emotions of our baby daughter, yet confident that whatever the problem was, her mum and I would rectify it. As a dad, if I could not end my children's stresses, I would do whatever was necessary to curtail them. Rose asked:

"But why are you crying so much? What's the problem, Tash?"

With tears streaming down her face, she spoke, "Everyone expects me to go to Oxford."

"Who is everyone, Tash?" Rose asked. Unsurprisingly, Rose and I were at the top of her list. Tasha replied:

"You, Daddy, my teachers, and the principal."

We were sad but relieved because our daughter's concern was easily solvable. Rose and I reassured Tasha that everyone guided her according to her abilities.

"Tash," I said, "we are all so proud of you. You did great in your exams because you were determined to succeed. You did it because you could, showing you have what it takes to do well," I continued. "Your tutors recommend Oxford because they know you are capable."

"But Daddy, you all expect me to go there, and I don't want to let you and Mummy down. I'm very nervous," Tasha replied.

"No, Darling," Rose answered. "Only you can choose what you think is best for you. Only you can decide which university you wish to attend. You're doing this for yourself, so you won't disappoint anyone." The three of us continued our discussion until our daughter was about to fall asleep.

We woke up the following day to reflect on what had happened the previous night. Tasha decided that she would attend the interviews at both institutions if invited. Subsequently, Oxford, followed by York, acknowledged our daughter's brilliance by asking her for an interview.

I accompanied Tasha to her first interview. We applied a de-stressing technique as we drove the fifty-seven miles to Oxford—we sang, laughed, and joked for most of the journey. We also prayed and vowed to accept any result as a blessing from God. Tasha's written and oral assessment was exhaustive. When it all ended, I saw her radiant smile as she walked out of the assessment room. She had reached the required standard in the oral exams; her written evaluation was marginally below the qualifying threshold. The family was content to celebrate the overall results as God's will.

With only days to spare for her second meeting at the University of York, Tasha was upbeat; the thought of non-fulfilment never crossed her mind. She and I were looking forward to starting our 7 a.m. journey by train, and once again, we prayed for spiritual guidance. At the end of our trip, the anticipative look on Tasha's face said it all; she was ready for her assessment. After I waited for approximately 3 hours, Tasha walked through the exit. The comprehensive evaluation was over. My daughter's jump in the air with arms spread out was indicative of a winner. We hugged each other and merrily made our way to the train station in time for our scheduled journey back to London. Rose and Charlie weren't surprised by the news of success when we arrived home. Once again, we acknowledged the work of our spiritual guide—it was all according to his will.

The year 2000 was proving to be the most eventful for the family—it was an emotional year, too. The time was approaching for Rose to leave the UK to begin her new business life in Saint Lucia. Our son's decision to defer his studies fitted into our plans. After further thorough family discussions, Charlie was excited that working in a new environment alongside established broadcasters in Saint Lucia would allow him to gain hands-on experience developing his career. At this moment, Rose, the children, and I had completed the plans, and it was time to execute them.

Charlie began applying to the leading radio stations in Saint Lucia. We were amazed when he received an immediate response from a popular Caribbean-based radio station asking him to attend an interview in January 2001.

In the meantime, I requested that the freight forwarders ship our 40ft metal container to Saint Lucia during the last week of September. It was a 10-day voyage ahead of Rose's scheduled trip in October. Rose would arrive in time to receive the cargo from the customs brokerage firm

I had chosen during my earlier visit. Our young man, Charlie, would join his mother in time for Christmas immediately after completing college in December of 2000.

Having done our due diligence and carefully organized the practical and legal aspects of the venture, the groundwork had gone as intended and we agreed that our business idea would become a reality on November 1st, 2000.

Our First Bumper Christmas

The thought of guarding against complacency was uppermost in my mind. The success or failure of this monumental assignment would rest on Rose's ability to manage her business. Although she was confident and embraced the project with great enthusiasm, I knew it was a huge responsibility for her. I would provide long-distance support, reverting to my previous buying agent's role without compromising my profession; she would employ two customer care assistants. Having Charlie support his mum during the busy Christmas trading period was most convenient.

We were determined to take on a different business approach in an environment where it was customary for shoppers to jump over boxes in store aisles. Rose and I agreed on the most notable and unheard-of pricing strategy: promote a sale during Christmas. The feedback from Rose was that our competitors dismissed our idea with scepticism, but our customers were delighted. According to Rose, the branch manager of a long-established company that owned several shops throughout the island walked into her store.

"What's that I'm hearing? A grand sale at Christmas?" he derided.

Rose approached him, introduced herself, and quietly replied, "Yes, we're having a sale. Would you like some assistance?"

"Ahhh, you're the owner of this new business?" he replied. "But businesses don't cut prices at Christmas!" he declared.

"Of course, but we're a new business, so we can apply new ideas," Rose replied.

She stated that after the customer scanned through the many unique items on display, he exited the store with what she described as a mixed reaction of admiration and confusion; he loved what he saw but wondered about our game plan.

We had created a retail outlet stocked with household and gift items, body care, and the widest variety of greeting cards. Ninety per cent of our inventory was unrivalled on the island, so we had no direct competitors. We had introduced a British retail concept with the motto: "The Store Where Quality Matters," and we lived up to it.

As the season peaked, Rose realised the need to recruit additional staff for the increasingly hectic period, so she employed three family members as temporary sales assistants. She also extended business opening and closing hours, which was new to shoppers. Our bravery in adopting a fresh marketing strategy, breaking with the established local practices, paid off with our first bumper Christmas. The rewards significantly exceeded our expectations. Instantly, we became known island-wide, and we had set a new trend.

Now that the season was over, it was time to work towards normalising our new family setup. Charlie attended his interview, and the radio station granted him a renewable, three-month contract. I appreciated his keen interest in being alongside his mum in managing the business whenever he was off duty.

A Test of Fortitude

Running your own business may sound simple to those without knowledge of the essentials. Everyone knows that without finance, there can be no enterprises. In my case, without grit, there would be no startup. It required immeasurable mental, emotional, spiritual and physical stamina.

In a small society where overcoming envy can be an ongoing phenomenon, knowing and managing the threats to our well-being is imperative. Our responsibility is to remove any chance of competitors and the wider community revelling in our misfortune. Therefore, one of the ways to overcome difficulties is to avoid all distractions; Rose needed to keep her eyes fixed on the target. Any contrary action would jeopardise our efforts and the sacrifices we had endured. It was a real test of fortitude.

Rose's Memorabilia

It is indisputable that trust is integral to the success of any relationship, just as maintaining confidence is a mutual obligation. I was clear about my role, and I was unwavering. Our agreement to head in the direction of doing business in Saint Lucia under pre-defined terms was a move that would decisively test our support and loyalty to each other. I would not deny that the thought of my wife being no less than four thousand miles away across the Atlantic for a considerable period was sufficient reason for goosebumps springing up over my body. Allowing Rose the opportunity to take the lead in this project was the ultimate means by which she would, in time, demonstrate her ability to rise to the challenge.

As time progressed, my days were getting longer; however, Rose never allowed me to wait for results. She kept me updated on the day-to-day operations, primarily through email and the occasional telephone call, while I provided the support she requested.

It was no surprise that Rose had conveniently forgotten to disclose some critical information to me, bearing in mind the numerous times we had communicated. Inevitably, there are not too many incidents one can conceal on a 238-square-mile island. Within twelve months of her arrival in Saint Lucia, people who cared about us, including relatives and a life-long friend, were concerned by Rose's behaviour. They needed to pluck up the courage before sharing their worries—I understood their reluctance to inform me of my wife's indiscretions.

The reports I received were not heartwarming. They were dangerously unsettling. My natural tendency was to seek an explanation from Rose about the information, but first, I had to answer my own questions. Rose's supposed introversion was consistent for a significant part of our marriage; could such an attribute have just melted away? How did she wear a disguised disposition for so long? Would Rose expect me to believe any explanation or excuse for her deeds? I had grossly underestimated my wife. I was second-guessing myself.

Did Rose intentionally leave a *clue* for me to discover, or was it a colossal blunder on her part to have forgotten to take away her memorabilia?

The revelations prompted me to reflect on the setbacks Rose and I had been experiencing since her return from her previous holiday. I recalled Rose's strange behaviour when she dawdled about my request to view the holiday snaps she had collected from the chemist, giving excuses to view them later. Although I wondered at the time why I couldn't see them sooner, I dismissed it. Now that this thunderbolt hit me, I realised I was heading into a storm I had never imagined encountering in my life. Without a pause, I set off on a *fishing expedition,* looking for clues, anything that would confirm my suspicions at the time of my dismissal of the pictures from the chemist. But would I be able to manage the supposed evidence I was looking for? I was willing to test myself.

My final search of our archived documents in the cellar was where the proof lay. Rose's lewd holiday beach snaps taken on a bright sunny day in Saint Lucia and other pictures from her first trip were staring me in the face. I needed no more proof—Rose had been having an affair since her first visit with the meteorologist she had talked about in the past.

All in the Name of Love

The jolt I received from this discovery shook me profoundly; nothing I had experienced before was comparable. It was a destructive, gut-wrenching punch that raised my anxiety to anguish. I suddenly discovered that I had allowed my highest trust in Rose to cloud my judgment.

Consequently, it dawned on me that I had lowered my guard and inadvertently reneged on my commitment to my Creator. I felt that I was facing dual battles of emotion and what I judged as spiritual warfare. I had to face up to the act of contrition. This moment, the jarring and saddest of my life, was when I had no answers to my question.

Why and how did I not continue to make time to give thanks and praise to my God? I had enjoyed the protection of the Eternal Spirit throughout my existence. I possessed the evidence of untold blessings, yet I had allowed myself to slide into the category of those who turned to God only in their desperate time of need. No matter how I tried, I lost all capability to reason. I needed first to accept the moment for absolution and then turn to my single formidable shield—my prayers. I gained solace from the knowledge that I serve a forgiving God. He would accept me through his grace and mercy because he knew of my precarious situation; it was a crushing challenge.

I reached out to our general practitioner, who prescribed me anti-insomnia medication because I wasn't getting enough sleep. The feeling of helplessness was consuming me. Therefore, I embraced the stupid notion of seeking comfort from alcohol. My anxiety elevated to a level that would be consequential to my livelihood. I was spending more time out of work than at work, thus causing my employment position to look ever more untenable. My doctor enhanced my medication and prescribed anti-depressants.

While I struggled to get through my worsening condition, my employer spared no effort in their support. However, they had no alternative other than to review my employment contract. My manager, Robert, was superb; he was highly empathetic and did whatever was within his power to help me through this traumatic period. He arranged a series of counselling sessions through the company's medical department. He also granted me extended paid medical leave and visited me weekly.

It became evident that my poor mental health required long-term intervention. Consequently, the unwavering support I received from my firm was not sustainable. The results from an independent medical report for an overall assessment were incompatible with my terms of employment. Thus, it became necessary for the management to reconsider my position. I could not be employed to carry out my duties in an all-safety-critical environment. The inevitable happened; my career ended on medical grounds, and my job in England was no more.

Having gotten the new status of being unemployed brought me no consolation. I wished the fake comforter, alcohol, was real so that my problems would disappear. My mind was racing in overdrive as I imagined the unimaginable. The mental impact was harsh. I was battling against the thought of an alarming future, a sense of hopelessness with my world spiralling downward.

I kept asking myself why I was a co-sponsor of a plan that brought on such despair, potentially bringing about our demise. I wished away all the lingering thoughts about the consequences of my actions—the dismantling of my small family. Our health and well-being were all in jeopardy. My feelings were nothing short of desolation, and all of this was in the name of love. I was staring through the corridors of insanity.

I maintained communication with Rose, whose tone was guilt-ridden throughout this turbulence. Even amid such disarray, our conversations seldom ended without her request for personal and business wants. And, yes, I continued to fulfil her demands. But why, I hear you ask? My simple answer is that I don't know, but I do know that I deemed my decision to cooperate with Rose ludicrous.

Did I expect Rose to reflect and get back to focusing on our family and the task at hand? Well, there may have been no logic in my thinking—I trusted her to reconsider, if only for the love of our children.

An Invalid Claim

The depth of my emotions engendered thoughts about facing a gloomy outlook. I saw no more reasons to carry on as a tug-of-war raged inside me. The echoing voices deep within cheered me on,

"To hell with her. Let her go, Stephen, you've been through enough. Life isn't worth living anymore."

The second pleaded, "Come on man, pull yourself together. That's not who you are. There is so much more to live for."

A third, "Come on, Stephen. What about the kids?"

My perpetual concern for our children was the deciding factor that pulled me away from the edge of the precipice. Submitting to suicide, an ungodly temptation, would mean doubling the affliction upon my innocent kids; they were not answerable, and my sole responsibility at that time was to protect them. Charlie was on the island at the time and was aware of the developing situation—his mother had told him, and he remained neutral. Tasha was suspicious that a severe problem was unfolding—but I never discussed the matter with her. Instead, I continuously reminded her to focus on her studies. I needed to find my way out of this predicament, but first, I had to acknowledge my role.

My chosen path would enrage Satan as I rejected his lures. I had nothing more to do with the bottles of alcohol that I stored in my cocktail cabinet. I turned to serve Lucifer with his most hated repellent—prayers. But first, I drew my strength from the words one of my tutors had imparted during a personal conversation when I attended the University of Westminster.

"Stephen," Mr Mahoney advised, "never say you can't. Whenever you are faced with a difficulty, you should think about a previous situation that you thought was beyond you, but you managed to conquer."

I turned to my King James Bible, and Psalm 46 became my daily recitation:

God is our refuge and strength...Therefore, we will not fear...He maketh wars to cease unto the end of the earth...The Lord of hosts is with us. I also gained inspiration from reading John 10:10: *The thief cometh not, but for to steal, and to kill, and to destroy. I am come that they might have life and that they may have it more abundantly.*

Such experience further reminded me that there would be no fulfilment in my life without my divine guide, just as I am convinced that karmic debt is a notion we must all consider when mapping our destiny. I prayed to the Lord, asking for forgiveness and healing from this disease of despair. However, there was one condition I had to fulfil if I was serious about seeking God's pardon, I had to be able to forgive. The teaching from the Bible, Ephesians 4:31-32, was pertinent to my cause:

Let all bitterness, and wrath, and anger, and clamour, and evil speaking, be put away from you, with all malice: And be ye kind one to another, tender-hearted, forgiving one another, even as God for Christ's sake hath forgiven you.

I had no easy answer, but I was adamant about pulling away from changing an appalling situation into a full-blown disaster. I first had to gather my mental strength, find my true self, and continue my journey in a new direction.

Back in Saint Lucia, twenty-year-old Charlie relished his new-found celebrity status as a radio announcer, prompting his employers to offer him an extension of three months in the post. This opportunity would mean six months with his mum if he chose. Charlie accepted the offer. I was pleased that while our son was savouring his recognition, he remained committed to completing his education. Immediately after his stint at the radio station, Charley returned to England in time to prepare for his studies at the University of Bedfordshire, where he would remain for the next three years, and he chose to reside in the nearby town.

My Total Anguish

Tasha was preparing for her new learning adventure in Yorkshire. We had established that she would live at the University Halls of Residence during the first year of her course and then continue her studies at the prestigious Sorbonne University in Paris. At that moment, I saw a one-way signal pointing to my future. Before informing Rose and the children of my intention, I reevaluated a plan I was single-mindedly going to execute. I had never decided without Rose's input; in this instance,

I felt obliged to break with my tradition. It was out of courtesy, but leaving no doubt in her mind that I was not seeking, or needed, consensus, I notified her I would be selling our home and returning to Saint Lucia.

Discussing the matter with our son and daughter was agonizing, especially for Tasha—the tears streamed down my face and hers as we hugged while I reassured her. I had informed Rose's brother Cheddy, about what had transpired between Rose and me. He expressed dismay and was broken-hearted by the events.

Rose and Cheddy had often exchanged visits between London and Manchester, and he adored our children. Indeed, Rose and I had viewed him as the apparent guardian of our Charlie and Tasha in the event of unforeseen circumstances. Cheddy was grateful to have kept in contact with me throughout my ordeal. Most importantly, I told him of my intentions. Without reservation, he agreed to my request to have Tasha at his home in Manchester, about 58 miles from York, during her study breaks. From the moment I contemplated selling our home, there was one crucial matter I was compelled to fix before listing the property with a real estate agent.

Stephen N Rosemond

The Good Bastard

Did I mention that our London address was nothing like Back Street? Undeniably, Chrissy and Tariq did an excellent job reminding me of Saint Lucia, where nothing was off-limits. My neighbour had grown her paper distribution business to one truckload, five times a week. Her front garden space was not sufficient to store the increased deliveries, so she used the pavement, leaving room for only one-way pedestrian traffic. I witnessed several residents and passers-by grumbling about what had become unsightly, but no one spoke plainly. Worst of all, I couldn't believe that our local authority was unaware of the transformation of our neighbourhood into a commercial area! This condition continued for approximately seven years; it would hinder the sale of our property, and I had no qualms about eliminating that deterrent—I took to writing again.

In my letter to the local council, I pointed out the hazards of such a condition.

I wrote: "Can you imagine the result of a spiteful individual throwing a lighted cigarette or even a match into these bundles of newspapers? Sir, it is with grave concern that I plead. Please attend to this dangerous business to avoid a tragedy." I added, "Please note, should I not receive your response within seven days from the date on this letter, regretfully, I shall have no option but to bring the matter to the media's attention."

Within two days of delivering my letter, I received a response from the health and safety department thanking me for my genuine concerns. They also wrote to Chrissy and Tariq, instructing them to cease operation within seven days.

Thankfully, the authorities did not reveal the complainant's identity to my neighbours. Once the newspapers disappeared and normalcy was restored, Tariq angrily told me how cruel humans can be. *Was he talking about himself?* I thought.

"Steve, you won't believe it," Tariq said. "Chrissy has been doing her business here for so long, troubling no one. Now, some son of a bi*ch bastard reported us to the council."

"Oh no!" I replied. "Wow, Tariq, some people are heartless."

While I uttered those words to Tariq, my inner thoughts were, *You're talking to the bastard; only this one is good.* I was relieved and deeply grateful that the matter had not turned out like the pigeons. I was ready to place our property on the market. Still, to avoid raising suspicions and uncovering my identity as the villain Tariq referred to, I opted against attaching a "For Sale" board.

The real estate agent agreed on a clause that permitted me sufficient time to exit the property upon the sale. Fast-forwarding my exit from the

UK was an event I undertook with a heavy heart—the time to quit had arrived.

Within weeks, I had sold our home, employed the services of the freight forwarding company for the packaging and shipment of our belongings, and in a state of total anguish, I was heading off to Saint Lucia. This agonising lesson is the basis for my assertion that extravagant love does not guarantee respect or reciprocation.

God is Good

I tried to suppress the awful feelings, but the flashbacks were vivid. I struggled even to imagine that my return to Saint Lucia to be with the woman who was supposed to be my wife would be comfortable, yet I wanted to believe there would be something left to salvage from our marriage. Throughout my twenty-three years in England, I hung on to my vision for our repatriation to our country. Regrettably, the changed circumstances weakened my position, precipitating the untimely, involuntary, and painful return. What I knew for sure was that this leg of my long journey had ended. Sitting on the plane awaiting take-off seemed like an everlasting hold-up, triggering a flood of memories of old and recent times that overloaded my brain. I drew comfort from one such recollection that brought a smile: Tariq's anger towards the bastard he never knew, even though he was staring him in the eye.

Mama Ray was happy to have me back closer to her, but she expressed deep sadness about how it had occurred.

"Poor jab Stephen," she said, "Ou ca feh moi la-pen. Par worry. Bondieux cai bennie-ou ish-moi." (So sorry, Stephen, I feel sorry for you. Don't worry. God will bless you, my child.)

"Par worry Mama, soo-play, par key-tay moi feah-ou la-pen," I replied. "Moi cai alright. Bondieux ca condwee. Bondieux bon," I responded. (Don't worry, Mama, please, don't feel sad for me. I'll be all right. God is in control. God is good.)

I have remained eternally thankful to my creator, Lord and Saviour, for the qualities he instilled in me. He gave me the necessary tools to ensure my safe navigation through turbulent times. He allowed me the foresight and vision to set up the foundation on the Caribbean Island, where my journey would continue. He rewarded me for the sacrifices I had endured for years. He gave me the wisdom to cultivate the knowledge I had acquired in the line of investment on the island, which yielded handsome dividends. He guided me along my journey, overcoming each obstacle thrown in my path. He allowed me the fortitude to maintain peace and stability while I steered through this exhausting trek. He gave me the understanding to reason, rejecting the temptation of the forces of destruction. He gave me the courage to make decisions that secured my family's well-being and my return to my native land despite the timing.

This arduous journey is testimony to the significance of sustaining faith in God's power. I am thankful for the blessings from the Eternal Father for allowing me a second chance to rediscover myself. My chosen paths reaffirmed my steadfastness in confronting, for better or worse, the complexities that seemed inescapable. My determination to tap into the positive energies within me has thus far remained unaltered. With this certitude, I attest that while it is paramount, prayer alone will not cut it. By 2002, I had completed a 360-degree cycle; it was time for me to begin a new life back on the island from where my journey as a *Third-Worlder* had begun twenty-three years prior.

MY SPECIAL PRAYER

Dear Lord, you are my God; you are my creator.
You are my Refuge and my Redeemer.
It is in you, Lord, that I place my trust. It is to you I give my soul.
Forgive me for the sins that I have committed against you.
My life is in your hands, dear Lord.
Take me, Lord, and make me as you will.
In the blood of Jesus, I pray.
Amen
****

END

www.ingramcontent.com/pod-product-compliance
Lightning Source LLC
Chambersburg PA
CBHW072145070526
44585CB00015B/1005